James Croft lives quietly with his dog in the Kent countryside, never happier than when cutting logs in the woods with his chainsaw. Yet this maverick was educated at the Royal Naval College, Dartmouth, and for 40 years, inspired by his love of an extraordinary woman, lived a very lively life as a scrap dealer and a maker of things snapped up by the antique trade. He saw his creations sold as the genuine article in fancy auction rooms, and displayed as '100% authentic' in hotels, restaurants and art galleries all over the world. Life was never dull after he 'swallowed the anchor'!

*To Niv & Liz (don't put
your literary knickers on! ...)

with best wishes

from*

# SWALLOWING THE ANCHOR:

## THE STORY OF A
## DISREPUTABLE MIDSHIPMAN

*down & out . disreputable

mike Irving.*

# James Croft

---

# SWALLOWING THE ANCHOR:

# THE STORY OF A
# DISREPUTABLE MIDSHIPMAN

AUSTIN & MACAULEY

A CIP catalogue record for this title is available from the British Library.

**ISBN 978 1 905609 88 8**

www.austinmacauley.com

First Published (2009)
Austin & Macauley Publishers Ltd.
25 Canada Square
Canary Wharf
London
E14 5LB

Printed & Bound in Great Britain

# DEDICATION

To Jean, who changed my life.

## ACKNOWLEDGEMENTS

Many thanks to John Goldsmith, my only too brief
business partner, who encouraged me to write this story
and also to Peter Shaw for all the advice on writing
matters of which I understood so little. Finally, my
heartfelt appreciation for all the time given me by my
sister Ann, who has helped me throughout this
endeavour.

Not far along the road from where I was standing that May day in 1956, waiting for a Fratton Park to Upnor trolley bus, were the run-down stands of Portsmouth United Football club. I had been brought up to regard football as a sport predominantly played by the lower classes, with men wearing things called shin-pads, egged on by crude shouts and the noise of rattles. My idea certainly wasn't for heading towards that kind of life – but just where I was heading, I was not sure! First thing was to get the hell out of Portsmouth!

Behind me a high brick wall hid the grim buildings of the Naval Gunnery School, HMS *Excellent*. A little way along, an arched entranceway surmounted by a gilded Admiralty crown, gave access to the bleak establishment beyond. A naval rating, wearing a wide white belt and shining black leather gaiters above his boots, stood on sentry-duty watch by a barrier which was hinged to the wall of the small red-brick guardhouse. Across the acres of parade ground stood the main buildings, with their stone floors, iron radiators and brown paint – I knew them only too well – loathsome, gaunt and foreboding – because only the day before, my life had been a part of all that. Then, I had been a naval officer. Now, I was 'out', a civilian, probably looking somewhat incongruous at a bus stop in that working-class district of a dockyard town, dressed in narrow-bottomed cavalry twill trousers, suede shoes, white shirt and cravat, together with a lovat-coloured sports jacket with a single vent, tailored by Messrs. Gieves of Bond Street, the cost of which was to be paid off at the rate of £1 per month. I was probably trying to look suave, like some archetypal young toff who knew a bit about the world and was on his way up in life. In reality I was a little frightened, anxiously wanting to get to the railway station and away, because I knew that my life had descended into a mess. My few personal possessions were in the new-looking officer's grip on the pavement beside me. I had arranged for my tin trunk to be sent on by P.L.A. It was all over, and I knew I was facing uncertainty.

The street was nearly empty except for three or four people waiting at the opposite bus stop and several men in caps on old upright, gearless bicycles, stolidly pedalling towards the Upnor Road. Each was slung with his obviously army surplus haversack and one of these had the top of a thermos sticking out. They must have been clocked-off early from some shift or other, well before the hooters went. Just for a moment it occurred to me they might be lucky; their lives might have some purpose. The only vehicles I could see approaching were a trolley-bus, going the wrong way for me, and a small brown Morris van, rattling over a patch of cobbles, with the wording 'Kelk and Son, Plumbing and Electricals', written on its side. The scene and smell was one of the dirt and drabness of lingering post-war poverty.

It might be just too easy to blame my father for the reason I was at the bus stop and the mess I had got myself into and for just about everything... but I do. It's the genes; they seep down from generation to generation, it's inescapable and you have to accept it. But because of these genes, one of the very few things I do have to thank him for is being able to extricate myself whenever things are looking a little tricky.

My father was a strangely secretive man, never telling anyone much about his past. His parents, who once again, he never spoke about, had given him the two Christian names of Arthur and Adolphus. This last, rather unusual name, I only found out about many years after I had first become interested in people's initials and had asked what the second 'A' stood for, only to be told it stood for Allison. At what stage, and why, he ditched his real name of Adolphus, will forever remain an unanswered question. What little I did know was that he had been educated at the well-known Public

School of Haileybury, during the Great War – which presumably meant his parents had been of a certain class and comfortably off. At the school, he had become a Classics scholar and excelled at sports, before going on to enter the Royal Military Academy, Sandhurst.

His name headed a list in a column of *The Times*, dated 9th. August 1921, under the heading 'Civil Service Commissioners', stating that he had been successful in gaining entry for 'service in the Cavalry, Foot Guards or the Infantry', achieving top marks of all the young gentlemen who had sat the examinations two months earlier. His marks were 10,448 compared to the last to gain admission, who had scored a mere 5,824.

After he had died, wanting to find out more about his past, I rang the Records department at the Royal Military Academy. A very helpful archivist found the year of his entry, and then there was a pause. Unusual, I was told, he had simply been *'struck off the strength'* the following year. No reason or explanation is given and what this term implied still remains a mystery. I have often pondered just what 'struck off the strength' meant because at the time he would have been deemed to be serving under the King's Rules and Army Regulations and if he had been guilty of some serious misdemeanour he would almost certainly have faced a Court Martial or been simply dismissed with ignominy. This would have appeared in the records held at Sandhurst; however, no reasons are given for his return to civilian life.

Only on very rare occasions did he mention the past. The one thing I *do* remember is being told that during his time at Sandhurst it was compulsory to practice pig-sticking, just in case your regiment found itself serving in India! What he did from the year he left the Military Academy up to the start of the Second World War, when I first became aware of him as my father, was never mentioned, even by my mother, who must have known. Only much later did I become aware of veiled family rumours that first of all he had gone to America, where he had been a house-painter in Los Angeles, and later on had been employed as a chauffeur to someone in the early film industry. He had tried to patent some idea for cine-projection involving the use of prisms, which came to nothing and then became involved in murky dealings along the Mexican-American border, after which the Californian State Authorities finally arrested him and he was deported through the infamous Ellis Island in 1922. I guess that must have been the date, because when his Californian State chauffeur's badge turned up in his effects many years later, that was the date it bore. It was little wonder perhaps thereafter, whenever America was mentioned, he took on a look of sneering contempt. How he made a living in the thirties remains a mystery to this day.

In the appropriate column of my birth certificate, dated 25th May 1935, it is noted that he was '*of independent means*', living at an address on the edge of Hampstead. By all accounts, he was now beginning to be called *Gant*: no longer Arthur, certainly not Adolphus, not even Allison. To some apparently, he was known simply as The Gant. To this day no one has ever been able to explain the reason as to why, or how, this new name came about. All I know is that Gant is the name of an upmarket American clothing company, with whom by a strange coincidence I did business many years later!

I do thank God that there were some rather more mollifying genes to be had at the crucial time of my parents' coupling and in this respect I was lucky, because in contrast, my mother came from a mildly successful Portsmouth family of traditional naval stock. Her father achieved the rank of Captain and commanded the Royal Yacht *Victoria and Albert*, on which he was accompanied from time to time by my grandmother on crossings to the Isle of Wight, when Queen Victoria went to her beloved Osborne. So, the gene aspect didn't look too bad for me now. For a start there was my grandfather, who I only knew from a sepia photograph of a splendidly bearded naval officer holding a sword. Then there were my mother's two brothers, both naval officers, who she told me had commanded minesweepers in the North Sea. One, I later found out, became the Secretary for Surrey County Cricket Club (although at the time it worried me in my youthful ignorance to think this uncle had sunk so low as to take on a lady's job, stabbing at a typewriter.) The other became one of the directors of a large mowing machine manufacturer not far from Guildford. Rather grander, and shadowy, were two more uncles, both admirals: one lived at No2 Church Row, Hampstead, London N.W.3 (a very upmarket address by any standards), who was my godfather and the sender of a ten shilling note every Christmas. How on earth my father had come to make connection with such a stately man as this (I only ever saw him once...) I do not know. Perhaps it was in the palmy pre-war days at a party after some Hampstead Cricket Club match – that would make some sense... anyway, I have always assumed it to have been a careful and possibly useful choice of godparent! Then there was a great uncle: another admiral, who lived in Folkestone and who in the early thirties was Engineer-in-Chief, Pacific and East Indies station. He once told me he had shot pigeons from the bridge of the battleship he was serving on at the time, which seemed a tremendously exciting thing to have done. The Engineer Rear-Admiral was in some way related to my mother's side and knowing what I know now, both of these retired naval officers lived on meagre pensions, just sufficient for them to enjoy genteel and orderly lives and to be able to settle up each month for their gin, bitters and soda siphons delivered by the wine merchant.

So, with these kinds of stalwart antecedents in mind (and perhaps my own dreams of one day aspiring to have a soda siphon!) it was hardly any surprise to learn that it was to be my destiny to be next in this naval line. As it was to turn out, this only too soon came to an abrupt end when I did something called *swallowing the anchor*. This is an old naval expression generally applied, with some disdain by those of a certain rank, to a fellow officer who leaves the service early... *'Damn bad thing you know – young so-and-so, he's swallowed the anchor'*. Perhaps shades of my father were hovering, I was a chip off the old block with those genes – little Jimmy, on whom so many hopes were pinned, never fancying a service life and a retirement of pink gins, perhaps croquet and naval blazer with a badge on it – no, I think I had been irrevocably cast in the mould of my father, Gant.

By the furthest stretch of my imagination I could not have dreamt that not long after that awful period called adolescence, when I was a grown-up midshipman, I would have helped the beautiful Fiona Campbell-Walter, Europe's most famous model of the day, across the gangplank of the cruiser *Sheffield*, one dark evening in the docks in Greenock, or been ordered to entertain Princess Alexandra on board that same warship, when she was berthed in New York. By then I had seen half the world and a lot had happened.

I certainly would not have guessed that not long after this, I would end up with a criminal record, fall for a married woman, own a second-hand Dormobile and a mongrel dog called Jarvis – a creature I could still cry over – and be living a harum-scarum life of irresponsibility, travelling the length and breadth of England, trying to make money dealing in junk, as well as living the double life of a libertine, between a near derelict two-roomed basement off Gloucester Terrace on the edge of Camden Town, costing £4.10 a week, and a Regency house overlooking the Channel. In London, my room was so damp that sometimes my bed steamed when I turned on the electric fire and I invariably went to sleep listening to the noise of trucks being shunted back and forth to the St. Pancras goods yards.

Neither would I ever have imagined that there would be idyllic times spent in a small peasant farmhouse, bought with the fruits of my success, in the hills on the southernmost tip of Spain, where I could lie at night, and through the open bedroom door, see out across the Straits to where the lights of Tangier glinted through the darkness eight miles away and hear the throb of diesels coming from the fishing boats out at sea, while lying, bathed in languorous satisfaction, very close to the woman who had so wonderfully let me seduce her at the start of my adventure, and who is the reason for my telling this story.

It must be as they say, 'you make your own luck', and there can be no explanation as to why fate favours some with bizarre events throughout life, whereas to others it dictates a year-on-year pattern of accepted normality. To me life always seemed to lead to some of the most disorderly and unlikely twists and turns. There can be few clean-handed innocents – well, almost – who have woken on a Sunday morning to find themselves and what they were doing at the time, suddenly splashed across the banner headlines of a national paper, nor for that matter who have had the compliment paid to them by having artworks which they had simply dreamed up, appear on the front cover of *House & Garden*, more than once, or seen them exhibited in, admittedly rather lesser, American museums, as time went on. It was only through those infamous family genes that I was lucky enough to inherit a fertile imagination and a touch of deviousness which enabled me, together with a bunch of the most unlikely people, to conceive and make artefacts that have gone on to decorate thousands of American and European homes, restaurants and hotels, some of which continue to turn up as 'fakes'. It is certainly highly gratifying to know that my efforts in this respect, gave both a great deal of business, profit and pleasure, to an entire generation of dealers – some honest, some not so honest – also everyday collectors, who were interested in pop art and the acquisition of artefacts of a bygone era.

**********

The story really begins when I first began to be able to remember events of my life in sequence.

We were living in a seedy ground-floor flat, just off the Finchley Road, the Blitz had started and people talked of German bombers called Dorniers, being over Cricklewood. I am only guessing now, but if there ever had been any palmy days, when I imagine my father might have been something of a Hampstead lounge lizard, if I was to believe his description on my birth certificate as being 'a man of independent means', those days were well and truly over, judging by Flat B, 56 Aberdare Gardens.

For some reason, best known to the War Office, he never received call-up papers, which must rate as somewhat surprising bearing in mind the level at which he had passed into the Royal Military Academy. Instead, taking us with him, he went to Somerset, where he drove a tipper lorry, somehow contracted to the U.S. government, collecting and delivering shingle, helping to build aerodromes for Dakotas. And so, London and the early days of the blitz were left behind and life began again in a village not far from Taunton. My father was rarely in evidence. Sometimes he would arrive in the dead of night on a motorcycle called a Panther and he might or might not still be there in the morning. If he was I was sure to get a sixpence and sometimes something exciting like an aluminium mess tin, then he was gone again.

Our house was rented from a coal merchant, it had a yard beside it on one side and on the other a small forecourt which had a petrol pump with a large glass top on it and letters saying Cleveland, because the business had once doubled as a garage. There were never any carpets and in this new home, not even lino on the kitchen floor, it was just bricks and it was cold except when a tall black, paraffin-smelling stove, called a Valor was lit, which cast patterned shadows onto the ceiling. The upstairs was an expanse of dark stained floorboards and at night a world of small Prices' nightlights, which threw more shadows onto the big sheets of stuff we had to put over the windows for the blackout, so the German planes couldn't see you. Apart from something my mother called an airing cupboard and the beds, I remember only two bits of furniture; one was a kind of square armchair, very scuffed, with a big hole burnt in one of the arms, presumably where someone had fallen asleep and left a cigarette burning, the other was a table which had two wide flaps which folded down and a big drawer underneath, on top of which stood a big wooden gramophone, with a handle and the picture of a small dog on the inside of its lid. There was something special about the airing cupboard because I knew at the back there was a cardboard box, tied up with string which had blobs of red sealing wax on the knots. My mother said it had something called an heirloom inside which had been given to my grandparents by Queen Victoria when they had been on the Royal Yacht. One day, she told me she would show it to me, but meanwhile I was never to try to get it out. A few years later, when the box had been hidden away once more in a different airing cupboard, I was going to find out the significance of the secret of its hiding place.

Out at the back was a small garden where my mother tried to grow lettuces and radishes in a patch of earth near the outside lavatory, and a rusted corrugated iron fence prevented anyone from getting into the village allotments which came right up to the coal merchant's property.

**Preparing for war**

Suddenly, without warning, my father's visits stopped because I was told he had gone away to Wales to drive a caterpillar tractor excavating coal for the war effort. Goodbye Old Haileyburian!

But that was not before, somehow, inexplicably, he arranged for me to become a boarder at what I now understand to have been an extremely exclusive preparatory school which had been relocated to Somerset for the duration of the war, to be housed in part of the mansion situated on the great estate of Earnshill. The school even had its own cadet corps, complete with children-sized 1914-18 army uniforms. By now I had become ashamed of the petrol pump outside the house and I realised that we were rather poor, certainly in comparison to most of the boys at my new school, who had such grand names as Bonham-Carter, Hart-Dyke, Wooley-Dodd and Murray-Hudson and whose parents came over in motor cars, every now and again, to see them. Perhaps this was the first time some forebear's gene, alien to my father's, subconsciously told me that one day it wouldn't be a bad idea to try to make some money! Meanwhile the staff, and in particular the headmaster, who was always scratching his bottom because he had been wounded there in the first war, strove not only to give me a very good education but helped stimulate my small boy's imagination by allowing such freedom in and around the magnificent 17th century country house, which housed the school. And it was the result of this stimulation that was going to play a huge part in my life a little later on.

We were told never to be a cad, to behave properly, never to be vulgar, which meant not talking about lavatories or 'having babies' and always to live up to the school's motto, which was *'Erectus non Elatus'*. I somehow don't think you'd get one like that today! We were told this translated roughly as 'upright and not swanky'. I leave you to think about it! As to not being a cad and being completely honest at all times, sadly I have to admit that I did not achieve good marks in this department as time went by. I suppose that was the 'erectus' bit which passed me by. As to being vulgar, that was a huge temptation as well as being exciting and it got me into serious trouble for the first time.

One night after 'lights out', in the middle dorm, I was overheard talking to the boy in the next bed, who was telling me about something he had seen during the holidays. He had been in a cave down by the beach near Lyme Regis and he had seen two grown-ups taking off their clothes, until they had nothing on and then they had started what looked like hitting against each other when one of them bent over and the other stood behind. I listened, riveted with excitement. Last thing, he said, they made a kind of howling noise and then both lay down, it seemed like one was on top of the other. Then he had run away. '*Who's talking?*' asked an unbroken voice. It was Franks, the dormitory prefect who was twelve. From the tone of our whispers he had guessed something was the upright and honesty bit of the school motto, I replied as best I could. After a pause Franks replied that he thought we were both very vulgar and we would be reported in the morning, at which I think I began to cry.

As the crocodile of small boys filed towards the panelled dining room, I was drawn aside by the headmaster, who after a nervous scratch of his bottom, said that if I ever talked about things like that again I would be expelled. '*Croft,*' he'd said, '*you are a disgrace to the school.*' It was just as well that I didn't get expelled, as if I had, I daresay I would never have gone on to the Royal Naval College at the age of thirteen to become a naval officer and all that was to follow would never have happened. The thought of being expelled was the low point, not only of that term, but of all the terms following, until finally I was made head boy and I knew I was safe. I *was* going to carry on the family tradition!

Before this, however, a lot of things were going to happen. The war came to an end and just before my last term another family move took place. My father was 'doing something' in London, where we were to join him for a few days before going to live down in Folkestone with the naval uncle who was a Rear Admiral. My father would join us later. Although by now worrying thoughts of having to pass my entrance exams and having to sit before the Admiralty Board were very much on my mind, the thought of going back to London seemed very exciting. At the same time I found it hard to believe that life in the country was about to end, especially as my friend Mr. Mountstevans, the village grocer, always seemed pleased to encourage my visits to watch him weighing out rations on his huge brass scales, when I could also ask questions about the serried rows of little drawers whose contents sounded so alien to me, and also look at the rows of tea and coffee tins along the shelves, each with its big gold number on the front. Sometimes he even let me help load up the wicker baskets of the delivery bicycles.

There were not going to be any more visits to the dairy on the edge of the village where the kindly owner's wife sometimes let me ladle out the warm, creamy milk, with a long-handled dipper, into the big brass-bound churn which went onto the milk cart for its morning rounds. I always seemed to make her laugh, with all the questions I asked and she was always telling me that I certainly had the gift of the gab. She wasn't the last!

I wasn't going to hear the hiss, and then experience the smell of burning hoof, as I watched the blacksmith bend to hammer on the red-hot horseshoe, with the horse's leg held firmly against his leather apron, nor was I going to see another of my special friends in the garage where they charged up accumulators, which it was explained to me, made wirelesses work and where there were special glass jars with acid in and had what they called 'terminals' on them. No more seemingly endless summer days of running through the long grass of hay meadows, chasing butterflies; no more clank of the harvesting machines or watching ladies from the Land Army standing up the stooks of corn behind them.

It would be more than 20 years before it dawned on me just how important my childhood perambulations round the village had been, keeping an inquisitive eye open, wandering and rummaging.

More than anything I was going to miss those expeditions looking for 'junk'! Junk has a special place of its own in the story.

I have often wondered if all small boys are fascinated by junk. Junk to me had an allure of its own – often found in strange, forbidden places, sparking the imagination as to its origin, how old it was, why it had been finally discarded and who it had belonged to –

were they now dead? When had an old acetylene bicycle lamp with a brass top last been used? Who'd thrown away a bone-handled knife with the blade worn almost to nothing? Who had used the old treadle sewing machine, or last put a coin in the rusty cigarette dispenser on its twisted stand…? There was still a 6d piece stuck in the chute. How had all this ended up behind the old shed by the village allotments…? Perhaps boys like Hart-Dyke, from a more effete and cultured background would not have been so interested in the possibility that they might discover all these discarded bits and pieces I found so intriguing. To me however, whatever the fascination, it was deep-rooted. It seemed to awaken an awareness as to the worth of just 'things' and money and possessions, of wastefulness and the value which someone might attach to something which they regarded as simply junk, or scrap. It occurred to me that it must all have some real value that could be realised in actual money terms, because I had seen things like an old candlestick or copper saucepan in Watercress Jo's pram. Watercress Jo was a tramp who came through the village each summer. All his possessions, together with a few bundles of watercress he'd collected from the ditches down on the levels and hoped to sell, were in the dilapidated old pram he pushed. The wheels were very small and he went from house to house along the main street trying to sell his cress but most people were wary and once he had his fly-buttons undone and everyone saw something pink – but he couldn't help it – and he trundled out of the village with the odd thing he had been able to pick up if it had been dustbin day. Such items as a candlestick were surely of no use to him, which made me think he sold them.

*********

It was summer and by now things were beginning to change. The first small thoughts of seriousness had begun to creep into my thinking. Thoughts about what it meant going into the Navy and responsibility, even about sex. By comparison to these liberated times in which the young grow up, none of us knew much about this subject in the 1940s and riveted in my mind there remains the memory of one last encounter with two of the village boys who said if I joined them, one of them would tell me 'something really bad' – something about every boy's hero in those days, Dick Barton, Special Agent. So, crouching down behind the wall of the vicarage kitchen garden, after a look round to see if all was clear, my friend the urchin began to slowly recite a poem.

*Down in the valley*

*Where the green grass grows,*

*There is a lady without any clothes.*

*Along comes Dick Barton, top hat and stick,*

*Down with his trousers and out with his dick,*

Then, speeding up a bit, he continued,

*But he put it in a bit too far,*

*And out came a baby in a racing car.*

This was the ultimate in shocking vulgarity, but needless to say I was gripped by the thought.

He then went on to tell me he knew someone who had rubbed his willy and made white stuff come out. This, I was sure he was making up, but he did have a very knowing look when he said it! After this, I wasn't long in catching up with things myself!

\*\*\*\*\*\*\*\*\*\*

A wave of excitement swept over me when I found myself standing in the midst of all the tumultuous bustle and smell of steam on arrival at Waterloo. From every direction came the noise of engines and the shout of porters with their barrows and the rumble of carts piled high with luggage, all to a background din of closing carriage doors, of whistles and the throb of city life outside the station. An open-sided taxi with a horn the driver squeezed in emergency took us to 48 Parliament Hill, a rather gaunt and gloomy-looking building, four or five storeys high, built in dark red brick. Here my father had rented a furnished flat on the third floor. In the half-dark we climbed up stone stairs with heavy embossed brown paper on the walls, the iron banisters painted an unwelcoming dark green until, on a landing we stood outside number 14. I looked around, the inside of the place smelled musty and above the door where you came in, there was a peculiar metal box, which it was explained to me was a gas meter, into which my mother had to put a shilling before she could make our tea. I knew by now that my mother was used to trying to put a brave face on things, but I instinctively knew that she didn't like the place any more than I did and I think it was that night that I had a nightmare about being expelled and never getting into the Navy because it had been found out that I had broken a window of an old storage shed belonging to the coal merchant, which stood behind the petrol pump. And worse than that, once inside, I had stolen some electrical parts still wrapped in oiled paper, in small boxes, which I then tried to sell to my friend at the garage where they did the accumulators! Now that I know a little more about myself and what tempts me, it could well have been true... maybe it was! Either way, it was the noise of the early Hampstead traffic which reassuringly told me I hadn't been expelled and my father, for once, was in the next room. And I was still on course for my glittering naval career!

I certainly didn't like it there. My father, in his trilby hat from Locks, came quite often and the only good part was being taken to Hampstead Cricket Club where there were some squash courts and he could show me off playing against grown-ups – as I was beginning to show talent, on account of my prep. school being one of the very few to have a court – and squash, after all, was a game for gentlemen! I must say it did make me feel good and rather important. Careful, I thought, I must not forget the *'Erectus non Elatus'* bit of the school motto.

On Sundays my father would take me along when he went to visit the naval uncle, Brian Babb, who was always reverently mentioned because he owned his own flat and lived not a mile away the other side of the Finchley Road. Sunday was the day people called in and had a drink. Here it smelled of cats, and after entering from a dingy, tiled hall with its stained-glass door, the inside of the flat was equally dingy with just one window giving onto a small garden on a lower level. It did however have a thick carpet, which impressed me, and what seemed like a lot of furniture, such as leather armchairs, none of which had cigarette burns on them and small tables scattered with magazines, a big sideboard made of some dark wood, some pictures and along one wall there were a number of randomly-spaced nautical prints. I felt awkward there, just listening to them all talking; my tall, thin uncle who chain-smoked and coughed a lot, and his irritating wife called Joan who seemed a bit bossy. If my father happened to be out of the room she constantly referred to Gant, or even worse, 'the Gant', who'd done this or that. At first I had no idea who she was talking about but eventually I realised that this was what they used to call my father all the time. It all seemed very odd. Was this the way a naval officer's family ended up, I wondered, living in a dingy flat, not much better than ours, without so much as a brass telescope standing on a mahogany table in a room filled with models of ships like the *Victory* and shelves lined with leather-bound books? It must have made a deep impression, all this and the fact that the two of them lived in the permanent smell of cats and kept either asking just how I was getting on, rather condescendingly, and what I thought about going to Dartmouth or for ever talking about this person called Gant.

One Sunday, we were joined by my father's brother, Uncle Richard, who I knew had done something in the past which had meant he was forced to leave the army after he'd followed his elder brother into Sandhurst. Something he'd done in India meant he had been cashiered, my mother told me, but nobody ever talked about it and that, as well, has remained a family secret. But what I had discovered, or so I thought, was that maybe the tall coughing uncle was, in fact, rich after all, because, at the end of the small garden beside a bin, in which they burnt the rubbish, I found the remains of cheque book after cheque book, in a tin waste-paper basket, waiting to be burnt. The remains were the stubs of course, things I knew nothing whatever about, but what excited me was the fact that all had very large amounts carefully written onto them – such as twelve pounds eighteen shillings and sixpence, in fact almost any sum up to something like forty or fifty pounds and that meant you could become rich if you were a naval officer, which was a great relief! Of course, then, I didn't really understand how money worked. And another thing I discovered was that the irritating aunt seemed to dominate my father and was involved in some sort of business venture with him, buying old woollen clothing, such as socks and worn-out jerseys, which they then sold to be re-made into cardigans and skirts and things, all of which were in very short supply in the years after the war. Had I but known it, this was a strange and scary portent of things to come! One Sunday, I'd heard one enquire of the other as to whether 'they'd had a good week', I think it was in some place I'd never heard of called Willesden, 'and what the weight had been, also had the dealer (whoever he was), given them a good price'. Did this really mean that they went around, from door to door, not much better than rag-and-bone people, asking if anyone had any old socks and pullovers to sell? I was ashamed at the thought and I was glad that no-one from my school lived nearby, in this part of London, who might have said he had seen someone called Mr Croft, like a boy was called at school, who spoke in a very decent accent asking for old jerseys in the house next door! I don't know how long this venture lasted but the word 'dealer' kept cropping up whenever my father and this aunt happened to be together and I wondered what part in all of this the man called *a* 'dealer' might play … it didn't sound a very good way of getting money to feed a family to me. I would have been much happier if I had been able to say my father was on the Stock Exchange or did things connected with the cargoes of merchant ships. But alas he wasn't, and I was just left wondering what life and earning money was all about.

It was not very long before this brief stay in London with those Sunday visits, came to an end, and one morning I found myself in my best long grey trousers at Charing Cross, bound for Folkestone. I had been informed that my father would be staying on in London and meanwhile we were going to live with yet another uncle, this time the one who was Rear Admiral, in some way connected on my mother's side.

The Rear Admiral was old and his wife had fairly recently died and it appeared that my father had come to some arrangement whereby my poor mother would in effect look after his needs, cook and housekeep and we would all live in our allotted rooms upstairs and in the kitchen – the one exception being that on Sundays we would all eat in the dining room – and we always had to come in by the back door, never going into the lounge where the Admiral used to sit listening to his wireless.

In exchange for my mother's efforts, we had a roof over our heads and later I discovered that what remained of his estate would be passed to us. If I had known at the time, I would have been incredibly excited but for the moment I knew I should have to behave with some decorum, unlike the village life I had enjoyed so much. The house looked alien and disturbingly impressive to me, standing in a short cul-de-sac, lined with privet hedges, it stood at the end, sharing the perimeters with four other broad-fronted residences of some considerable 1920's quality, all of which made for an off-putting air of gentility. It was little wonder, that certainly at first, I found it irksomely unappealing, but I did get used to it, as I had to, because it was to become my home for the next seven years. The only time I could relax and mess about on the big lawn behind the house, was when the old man went out, donning his long, dark overcoat and black homburg hat, before setting off for the Conservative Club, walking briskly, swinging his stick with its brass ferule clacking the pavement as he went. You always hoped this was about to happen whenever you heard the noise of flushing coming from the old man's cloakroom, under the stairs – a lavatory we could only use in emergencies – where, by the small corner basin, the old man kept his downstairs bottle of patent hair restorative, by the name of 'Barker's Patent Liniment', and a real tortoiseshell comb. Funny what you remember!

\*\*\*\*\*\*\*\*\*\*

Now, my last term, this time as head boy, loomed with the promise of a watch from my father if I was successful in getting into the Royal Naval College. At weekends he would come down by train from London, always in the same old trilby, coming into the kitchen, where he would always pat my mother on her behind, which I thought a bit odd. Bottoms were vulgar and stirred thoughts of sex. And talking of bottoms, at the start of that last term, a new South African divinity teacher arrived who was also to be the rugger coach. I can't speak for the boys, but I found it a bit odd that he was always to be found hanging about the changing room, before and after games. On one occasion, after a match catching me alone, he took me aside, saying, *'Good game Croft. Splendid try, that second one of yours. Just one or two things about your tackling: come up to my room, after the match tea, I've got a couple of photographs I'd like to show you of how the Springboks do it.'* So, feeling flattered, but just a trifle uneasy, I took up the offer… *'It's with the shoulder… go down low, see how it's done? I'll show you.'* It was just a bit strange how after each demonstration we both somehow seemed to end up on his bed and there was a bit of jerking, which I didn't like at all. I could hardly tell him that I didn't want any more instruction and said 'thank you sir' and hurriedly went downstairs feeling confused. I never told anyone about my so-called 'lesson' as I saw no reason why I should – after all he was a master, doing his best to teach me how to tackle better! I found out years later that he didn't last a second term.

I am pleased to say that the incident did not stop me from passing my entry exams, nor did it stop me from making a sufficiently good impression on the Selection Board of admirals and psychiatrists etc. who clearly thought, misguidedly, that I would make a good naval officer, because I finally did become one of only

21 successful applicants, out of a total of over one thousand who had originally applied to gain entry to the Royal Naval College.

I got my watch for Christmas.

On 28th December 1947 a brown, official envelope with the Admiralty crest on it, arrived stating that my commission was to commence as from 15th January. There followed various instructions, one of which was to report to Paddington main line Station where compartments eleven and twelve had been reserved for officer cadets, on the 13.15 express to Exeter. A travel warrant was attached to the letter – 3rd. class, via Exeter to Kingswear. I held my breath as I looked at the last line – 'you will be met by an escorting officer on arrival' it stated tersely. All the boyhood aspirations were suddenly turning to reality!

Before all this however, the most pressing of the instructions was to visit Gieves & Co. of Bond Street, Military Tailors & Outfitters by Royal Appointment, on 17th December to be measured for my uniforms. Accordingly, my father with the beady Auntie Joan in tow, met me at Charing Cross and together we took a taxi, stopping at Lillywhites on the way, so that I could buy a new squash racquet. Up along Piccadilly and turning into Bond Street, the cab finally came to a halt outside the illustrious premises of Messrs. Gieves & Co., Military Tailors & Outfitters by Royal Appointment. Here I was deposited, in my grey suit, very much relieved that my father said he wouldn't be coming in with me – especially as he was wearing his well-fingered old trilby – assuring me that the staff inside would be quite accustomed to seeing naval cadets, like myself, coming in for their first uniforms, mention of which made me feel most important. The taxi moved off and my father gave me a final wave as I watched him disappear into the late morning traffic, with me wondering what he was still doing up in London and just why he wasn't down in Folkestone any more.

Feeling proud – well wouldn't any child of that age – at having arrived at this stage, on the threshold of my naval career, I walked confidently into this staid world of officers' outfitting, with its dark mahogany counters piled with bolts of cloth, swatches of materials and display stands draped with impressive-looking uniforms and large glass cabinets arranged with an assortment of swords, hats and caps, some with gold braid, some without, along with tall patent leather boots and velvet-lined boxes holding rows of medals, together with all the other varied accoutrements of life in the Services.

I remember well, now with much amusement, being called 'sir', – or 'sor', as they pronounced it – with every other breath, by a fawning member of the Gieves' staff whose job it was to measure me. After all, 'sor' was going to be a customer of the firm for many years to come, but little would the tailor's assistant with his tape have guessed that he had been taking the inside leg measurement of a youngster who was more of an independently minded Somersetshire tyke with a broad imagination, rather than a young gentleman whose destiny was to become an officer of the so-called Senior Service.

Little wonder that the IRA made an attempt to blow the place up some years later, the business being looked upon as having been an iconic institution of the Officer Class for the past one hundred and fifty years. As it happens they had no luck, other than persuading Gieves that their days of predominance in that particular trade were over, forcing them to move into the more modern world, joining up with Hawkes of Savile Row.

The following week I had to go to London again, this time feeling distinctly grown up, as Gieves had phoned to say my uniforms were ready for a last fitting.

'*Now 'sor',*' said my man with the tape, '*I trust everything is shipshape,*' as I emerged from behind the fitting booth curtain, wearing my doeskin uniform for the very first time. '*Very nice indeed 'sor,*' he said looking me up and down with his professional eye. 'Just the cap size now, shoes and collar sizes and within a day or two everything will be on its way along with all the other items young 'sor' will be needing. It will be all packed into your sea-trunk and sent down to the address we have – in Folkestone, isn't it?'

The black tin trunk duly arrived at the Admiral's house a few days later. It looked important. On the lid, *J.R.N. CROFT*, right in the middle, in letters of sloping script about four inches high. The old Admiral watched as it was brought down the front path and said that he had once had one, but it had long since gone, battered and scratched after all his own sea-going days. Now, up to my room, helped by my mother, my every fibre of urgency throbbing with each lift of the stairs, barely able to restrain myself with anticipation as to its contents which I knew would contain things like shirts with stiff collars, leather gloves, my shoes and, I was told, a *'gentleman's housewife'* – pronounced *'hussif'* – in which there would be everything for making running repairs to socks and jerseys together with needles and two cards of black and white cotton, small skeins of wool and, lastly, a small pair of Admiralty scissors. And sure enough, there were shirts with holes for cufflinks, stiff collars – studs not provided – and horn buttons on the 'No.1' doeskin trousers, for the braces – officers never wore belts – these were like heavy webbing and had the admiralty mark on them. Last of all, saved up so that I could put it on, was my No.1 reefer jacket with its white flashes on the lapels. I could barely contain my excitement: and all this for free because I had been one of the lucky 21 selected from the original 1,280 who had taken the exams in October... I say that without swanking, always remembering the *'Erectus non Elatus'* motto of the school, but looking at the shiny tin trunk and its contents, I did feel justifiably proud. All of this was mine! I put the doeskin reefer on; took one of the caps with its gold filigree, officers' badge, on the front and went to look in my mother's wardrobe mirror. I was an officer! My mother smiled and just said: 'that really suits you, Jimmy.'

This was the siren call of the sea, the Service; the continuation of my family's tradition, my country's naval heritage, with its once illustrious fleets and the officers who commanded it. I was already listening in my imagination to the strains of a Royal Marine Band, which my uncle had told me used to play stirring tunes on the quarterdeck of one of the great battleships he had served on, whenever she was at anchor.

Little did I know that before I left the college and first went to sea, that those great naval days were already gone, never to return. There would be no anchoring off Kowloon on the China Station, no East Indies Fleet, no Mediterranean Squadron, no more the romance of distant seas and strange ports of call while *Britannia* ruled the waves. Slowly there was to be an insidious closing down of a system which had outgrown its times, giving way to desk jobs, with reliance on automated data and bright new technocrats justifying themselves, as the new breed of officers came up from the lower deck or entered the Service from some red-brick technical college, or at best, one of the new universities… but now was not the time for misgivings, not for even imagining any other future as I stood on the lino floor in my bedroom, wanting to tell the entire world what it was like being an officer at the age of 13.

My father was still 'up in town', in the Admiral's words, so he did not see me the day I left home dressed in my uniform and cap, going out through the back door to stand proudly by the coal bins to have my photograph taken. My mother's old and trusted box Brownie duly did the job, with the sliding metallic click of the shutter being flipped over as the snap was taken. At the front of the house, before getting into the taxi for the station, the old Admiral looked me up and down standing by the front door in his customary Homburg and, smiling, wished me the best luck in the world. I was off to Dartmouth.

My grip, just like a holdall, (supplied by Messrs Gieves of Bond Street of course), canvas with leather trim and my initials large on one side, which I held purposely outward, gave the final touch of importance to the journey and I was hoping everyone would notice me. Crossing the station entrance outside Charing Cross, on my way to the underground I received my first salute from a naval rating. I remember going red with embarrassment, thinking how absurd it was for this man, no doubt tough and experienced from the recent war, to have to salute some small, pink-skinned officer cadet. Failure to salute an officer in uniform was an offence and the man knew it. Little wonder that many a disgruntled seaman referred to their young officers as '*pigs*'! Either way, it was a great moment.

And more little 'pigs' there were on platform No 6 at Paddington, excessively proud and animated, waiting to board the express to Exeter. I am sure I was not the only one to feel his confidence slowly ebbing away once the journey's end neared and in the growing gloom of dusk, the engine steamed past Paignton and on towards its final destination of Kingswear. It was here, on the gas-lit station, on a January evening in 1948, that a group of young boys, little more than children, made their way down the wet slope of the quay, to board the primitive, old ferry, whose grinding chains were to pull them to the Dartmouth side of the river Dart, to begin a new kind of life. A dark-blue bus, with the large letters RN on its side, awaited them along with an unsmiling lieutenant standing by its open door.

The Navy driver coaxed the bus through its gear-changes, taking them up the steep incline towards the college. The officer sat looking straight ahead as if quite oblivious of his very silent young charges on the wooden seats behind him. On rounding a last curve, the imposing buildings of HMS *Britannia* came into view and we were there – the R.N.C.

\*\*\*\*\*\*\*\*\*

My abiding memories of the years spent at Dartmouth are those of feeling an eagerness to succeed in the competitive and challenging surroundings in which I found myself and an overriding feeling of impatience. Early on, I used to feel privileged to be in the company of boys with names such as Rooke, Rivet-Carnac and Hornblower, (there were many others too, whose names I cannot recall.) Most people think of Hornblower as the fictional character dreamt up by C. S. Forrester, but check the history books and you will find there were illustrious admirals, who bore each of the names which I mention and remember well from my Dartmouth days. These cadets were their descendants, who were themselves carrying on in their footsteps. Later, I came to the conclusion that their presence at the college had marked the end of an era and that the traditions of renowned naval families was fast fading out.

This was an era of freezing cold baths each morning, never walking, but running at the double, everywhere, to the mess for meals and from lecture room to lecture room. Of having to be meticulously turned out, particularly for the day's first drill and inspection on the parade ground, after breakfast, before marching in to lectures to the strains of the Marine band. Days ended with your having to lie to attention in your bed the moment you heard the pipe heralding the arrival of the 'rounds inspection party', daring not to move as the officers passed the rows of iron bunks, looking to left and right. You just hoped no irregularity would be spotted in the way you had laid out kit on the flap of your sea chest, if it was, you were in trouble.

It was a highly disciplined life, governed by the mindset of a naval hierarchy that had barely changed since the early 19th century, so far as the treatment of young officers was concerned. Now it was 1948, and still boys aged a mere thirteen, like me, were being taken into the Service and subjected to, what today would be regarded as an unjustifiably harsh, and even sometimes brutal, regime.

Just how harsh can be judged by the fact that for smirking during a lecture, I was given what was called a 'No. 11' (even punishments were numbered!) This meant that rather than going up to the playing fields or squash courts that afternoon, I had to change into my games clothes and instead, report to the Physical Training Instructor's office at the gym, hand him my No. 11 chit (small piece of official paper on which my name was written, together with which punishment I was to receive). I seem to remember that there was also a No.13, which was just a longer No. 11, presumably to be administered even more nastily! I was shown not the least pity by the P.T.I, who handed me a 303. rifle and took me outside onto the path, and there in full view of all the other cadets on their way to athletic enjoyment, made me bend my knees, holding the rifle above my head, and told me to 'frog march' until ordered to stop. It was not fun. Inevitably it wasn't long before I sagged to my knees and with tears of desperation beginning to ooze out, I was given an encouraging light kick and ordered to keep going. And on it went, until I never wanted to hear the dreaded words 'No. 11' again! Luckily, I didn't.

For more serious infringements, such as arriving late in the mess, or being caught not running or being badly dressed – or worse still, guess what – failing to salute an officer, you were given 'cuts', (a beating) to be administered either by a Cadet Captain (college equivalent of a prefect) or your 'House Officer', generally a man in his late twenties who took his life in the Service very seriously. Either way, I can assure you they meant business. I got cuts just once and you certainly knew you had been beaten! Good stuff – I'm sure Their Lordships thought it helped build your character the way they wanted!

The worst, which I feel I must mention, was to be given 'Official Cuts' – I recall only one instance during my four years at the R.N.C. that this happened. A boy called Sears, broke bounds to see a girl. He was caught. Then followed the official procedure of the Captain of the college having to inform the Admiralty of his decision, so that they in turn could inform the boy's parents who could then either withdraw their son from the Service or allow the punishment to proceed. Needless to say, it went ahead. Sears was marched to the gym, under escort, where the entire complement of *Britannia's* officers paraded in ceremonial uniform, complete with swords, to witness the poor seventeen-year-old being tied to a vaulting horse, after which the Captain read the appropriate paragraph from King's Regulations and Admiralty Instructions… *"to suffer cuts for the aforementioned offence, this day, the 17th day of October 1950…"* Happy days they were, those, being 'licked into shape'!!!

Just what kind of 'shape' this was to be I was beginning to wonder. I was reading the works of the French philosophers

Rousseau and Voltaire at the time, and by now, being 16 years old this led to a rash of over-imaginative ideas about liberty and freedom and how life *should* be lived, with the result I began to be plagued by seeds of doubt as to whether I was really committed to the naval way of life.

Times were changing, a new breed of cadets were entering from State schools. The Government had finally abolished the entry system for 13-year-olds (poor Messrs. Gieves!) There were rumours that the Fleet was to be reduced and that many naval officers would wind up not going to sea, but sitting behind a desk, in places like Rosyth or Bath: it didn't exactly sound like the kind of Navy I had been brought up to expect. Added to which, being captain of the squash team I enjoyed an insight into life outside the confines of the Service, visiting the more liberal-thinking public schools and some of the select squash clubs which hosted matches against the R.N.C., along with the occasional challenge to play on private courts owned by rich individuals, who lived in style in country houses. Squash, in those days, was something of an elite sport and particularly on a visit to one of these houses, it was a stimulating way for me to broaden my perspective of what the outside world of 'civvy street' was all about and see for myself just what success could bring. I was hardly likely to experience anything like that, living in the old Admiral's house, an existence with virtually no social life whatever; except that is, when one or two friends of my mother's occasionally slipped in through the back door for a chat and for whom she kept a bottle of British sherry at the back of the china cupboard. It struck me that being a successful businessman was far more exciting than having to face year after year of exams, struggling for promotion on paltry pay. But sadly the die was cast and so it was that at the end of 1951 I sat the passing out exams, failing in mechanics, but luckily being given such high marks in French that I achieved the necessary level to make it to the next stage... going to sea, in the Training Cruiser, HMS *Devonshire*.

*********

If, as a little boy, one had aspirations to become a sailor – as I had done – then '*Going to sea*' was surely the culmination of all ones hopes and boyhood dreams. The time had come, college was over, excitement and new experiences lay ahead. The nagging doubts I was having about the future during the last few terms at Dartmouth temporarily retreated. Now, just two terms on board the old three-funnelled cruiser, HMS *Devonshire*, whose rusty old Babcock & Wilcox boilers had until only recently derived their power from coal, separated me from the time I was to become a midshipman.

Now stripped of her guns to expose vast areas of wooden deck ideal for training purposes, she stood high in the water, her bows blunt, her funnels upright. She was in every way a symbol of a dying past.

The ship was berthed in the naval dockyard Plymouth. Fuelled and provisioned ready for a three-month cruise, waiting to take on board another unsuspecting batch of cadets, some of whom now included numbers from each of the Dominions. Toughies from the Antipodes, Pakistanis who endlessly blew their noses in the showers, nostril by nostril, Indians and Canadians, together with other hapless fellows who were hoping for a life at sea, along with a spattering of '*special entry*' boys who came direct from State schools under the new Labour government scheme.

Each term on board was referred to as a '*cruise*' – to be either in the Mediterranean, West Indies or Scandinavian waters and it was my luck to have the West Indies as my first. I was greatly excited at the thought of this but sad to say, the word 'cruise', I very soon discovered, was a misnomer of the cruellest kind. Today it is suggestive of pleasure, idleness and time on one's hands. However, this period of seagoing schooling was going to be more akin to spending time in some floating remand home smelling of fuel oil, in a grey metallic world of asbestos-sheathed pre-war cabling, pipes and air ducts, and being overseen by tough, unpleasant petty officer instructors who in turn were commanded by seemingly equally unpleasant officers who, to any layman, would have been taken as being unnecessarily and relentlessly vicious, doubtless with the intention of imbuing you with the *'right stuff'* – seeing if you could *'take it under pressure'* and to *'sort out the men from the boys,'* by the standards of the Navy in the 1950s.

HMS *Devonshire* was most certainly not about to go 'cruising'*;* of pleasure and idle time there was to be an absolute minimum. In fairness, towards the end when the awful test of 'taking it under pressure,' was over, I did discover that most of my tormentors had been quite decent men whose apparent beastliness masked, in the majority of cases, an understanding and simple man.

It is no exaggeration to say that the challenge facing our everyday life on board *Devonshire* was physically and mentally daunting. You were driven to the point of exhaustion from the moment you heard the dreaded tannoy – which meant you had to spill from the warm cocoon of your hammock, hurriedly dress, ready for your first inspection, before scrubbing decks for half an hour, no matter what the weather, all before your breakfast at 7:30 – and so on until finally, the moment of longed-for relief arrived and you could ease yourself, exhausted, into the warm sheath of your hammock. And even then, when all you wanted was sleep, you might be woken for a 'night watch' at some ungodly hour, which meant standing bleary-eyed, trying not to fall asleep again, at some imaginary 'action station!' Some cruise!

It was however, intriguing to see the ocean growing calmer, day by day, its waters finally turning to clear azure blue-green, under the semi-tropical skies as the ship headed south. I saw my first flying fish, flitting from swell to swell as the ship steamed further into the warmth of the Caribbean. Excitement ran high on the first sight of land. It was Beef Island – a *real* tropical island, smallest of the Virgins.

Now Beef Island is a tourist paradise for yachtsmen and well-heeled American sun-seekers. In the fifties it was barely inhabited, home only to just a few fishermen, a small dot on the charts with nothing to be seen from seaward, except an endless palm-fringed beach, stretching in both directions, where, in some places, the palms ran right down to the water's edge.

It was here, just outside the reef, that *Devonshire* was to remain at anchor for a whole week – thank God for *some* relief! – so that the cadets could paint ship and become acclimatised to the heat, particularly the awful temperatures generated inside the hull. Daily, before resuming any afternoon's instructions, we were ordered, rather than allowed, to row ashore to this deserted paradise, to swim in the small coral inlets and the shallows just inside the reef, before going back on board once more to face the full rigour of afternoon drills, to be followed by evening instruction classes. It was relentless.

As some consolation, a steady offshore breeze kept the temperatures to bearable levels both throughout instruction periods on deck during the day and also in the sticky heat below decks at night, should you not have been fortunate enough to find one of the few places where you could sling your hammock topsides. Nights spent sleeping in an almost perfect heat, under the canopy of limitless stars in a tropical sky, were special and helped feed my imagination, thinking of the inevitability of what lay ahead and whether or not, at some time in the future, I might do something else in life. I wondered...

For another eight excruciatingly long weeks, *Devonshire* sailed further down the Antilles while I and all the other cadets had to endure seamanship class after seamanship class and drill after drill in the baking sun, all the time being moulded into officer material, with never a single moment for self-expression, or so the Board of Admiralty hoped.

These were the days before the islands became spoilt by development and the exploitation of the tour companies and cheap air travel. I liked nothing better than to look out at the passing islands, fringed by mile after mile of white beaches, seeing little other than the occasional small fishing boat just offshore, which made me think how wonderful it would be, to be able to enjoy the kind of life my imagination told me that might be waiting to be had on those romantically named places we steamed past, such as Martinique, St. Lucia and Guadaloupe. It certainly was not the kind of life that I was living, shackled to King's Regulations and Admiralty Instructions, having to practice taking starsights, just as the evening zephyrs wafted in off the Caribbean and it was possible, if the ship was close enough to land, to hear the faint incessant drumbeat of steel drum music, coming from what I imagined was a kind of paradise… a far more dangerous siren call than that of a Royal Marine band playing during parades at the Royal Naval College!

Although it makes me smile now, it was during those first days in the tropics that I dreamt of being able to live like Hemingway, of beachcombing and encounters with dusky, alluring Creoles. So perhaps it was just as well that the only place we were allowed ashore was little uninhabited Beef Isalnd – otherwise I feel I might have been tempted to make a run for it! It was very hard for me to think of stark reality and how my home, for what it was, and destiny, lay in drab old England, leaden-skyed, just post-war and far, far removed from these exotic possibilities which all stimulated my thoughts of freedom and independence. Life was merely titillating with me, tantalizing and arousing the impossible desires and thoughts of an adolescent, beckoning with what could have been a fatal allure towards the challenge of an unknown future. Reality of course was life in the floating steel hull of the *Devonshire*, one of H.M. ships, sailing under King's Regulations and Admiralty Instructions, subjecting me to the narrow minds of men with tunnel vision, who thought only of the years of service in front of them.

On board, as weeks became months, reality was a constant and desperate effort to end every single day without getting into trouble – to have a 'clean sheet' – before, after what seemed like an eternity of sweat and the smell of fuel oil and the hum of the ships' generators, the vessel at long last headed north once more for the Atlantic, Plymouth Sound and home.

By now I was slowly becoming mindful that the die was in fact cast and that I did *not* intend to remain in the Navy for good. Slowly I began to take less and less interest in all aspects of instruction and although I undertook all my duties with seriousness, I knew they were eventually going to lead me nowhere. My befuddled adolescent mind was consumed with incomprehensible feelings and ideas; all of which were hopelessly impractical, but ones I could not dismiss. Half my brain was crammed with details of anchor drills, wire hawser strengths, engine room pressure gauges and the theory of submarine warfare, while the other half was lost to my headstrong inclination to leave the Navy and what I might do, should an opportunity occur.

It would have been ludicrous to expect a 13-year-old to sign an agreement as to how many years he intended to stay in the service; it was however accepted as a fact that you would remain an officer until the day of your final retirement. Even Their Lordships, whose coffers held your meagre allowances, would still have a financial hold over you until you died. Now that I was almost eighteen I could not come to terms with this thought. I wanted independence. But at the same time I was sensible enough to know there was nothing I could look forward to by way of an alternative career. I felt I would be perfectly capable of adapting should the chance of another profession come along. As things stood, it was hardly likely to. I couldn't look to my father for any help in this respect, I knew, with him penniless and all the odd things he was up to. He wasn't going to accede to what I knew he'd think of as stupid ideas of an irresponsible juvenile – that's the way he'd put it – and he would put everything in my way to stop me resigning, which was the final option. Anyway, he certainly wasn't going to have access to the kind of money needed to support me whilst I might try to qualify for some other job, and so my boats would have been burnt.

Once swung into my hammock, through all those last nights spent in the tropics I lay thinking of what I might end up doing, should I take the plunge. It was going to be bad enough telling everyone I knew, that I had left the Service – eyebrows were sure to be raised – let alone not knowing how I would make a living, but the worst of all would be having to tell my father. Better perhaps to hang on for a year or two, I thought, before taking a final, fatal step into what was referred to as 'civvy street'. In a dream I could just hear those disapproving voices... *'My word! What a damn bad show, young Jimmy leaving the Service.'* Then I heard the dreaded call of the quartermaster piping *'rise and shine'* and I was back in reality.

\*\*\*\*\*\*\*\*\*

   I couldn't turn my back soon enough on the menacing grey hulk of the *Devonshire*, once more securely moored in her berth, surrounded by the cluttered dockyard and I did my best to blot out the thought that it was only going to be four weeks later I was going to have to face life on board once again. The express from Plymouth rattled me back into my old world and the tiresome existence backstairs in the kitchen and small lino-covered bedroom in the old Admiral's house: the events of the past three months might well have been nothing more than a chimera.

It was early on during this leave that the episode of the heirloom occurred.

My mother's heirloom, as she called it, I knew was the silver tea-set which had been presented to her mother by Queen Victoria on the occasion of one of her visits to the Royal Yacht, which grandfather Babb had commanded. I knew it was her one treasured possession and since moving to Folkestone was now hidden away in the back of the upstairs airing cupboard, behind the Admiral's sheets and my shirts and other bits of laundry. It was in two old, stained, brown cardboard boxes at the very back. I knew full well it was there and from time to time I would slide one of the boxes out and look at it. It gave me the sense that through these, I was connected to great events back in the 1800s and whatever was inside was terribly valuable.

One morning I went to get a fresh shirt out and I happened to notice to my astonishment that the boxes were no longer there. Instinct told me immediately something serious must have happened and I went down to the kitchen to ask my mother the reason for their disappearance.

She was cleaning the Admiral's breakfast plates and without lifting her head from the draining board, she said in a sad and resigned voice, that no, they weren't there any more, because she had had to sell them on account of something that had happened in connection with what my father was doing in town. I knew very well that she must have felt terrible and sad, that last link with her parents and a happy childhood, probably ending up in some pawnbrokers and I felt disgusted that someone as capable and worldly-wise as my father had fallen back on something like this, forcing her to sell it. To make matters worse, when I next had a look at my Post Office Savings book my mother had always kept out of temptation's way in one of her drawers, I saw all the little sums that had been put in over the past few years, which had last amounted to £11.3s.6d, had been withdrawn, just leaving a balance of 1s.6d, so that the account would not be deemed closed for good! There could only be one answer to this – my father! This strained relations with him even further and whenever I looked at him after this I felt almost as if I was estranged, thinking how he couldn't have stooped much lower!

On the brighter side, I was now allowed to make the occasional telephone call from the dining room where the phone stood on a corner bracket, and as I had started shaving regularly, I didn't have to ask the Admiral if I could use his bathroom with the huge copper geyser and the spent matches under the pilot light. It was accepted that I had grown up! And so it was time for girls and trying to show off in the town by getting into pubs and getting slightly drunk on vintage cider and Double Diamond and always wearing a cravat and swearing a lot using the word *'bloody'*, hoping you'd be overheard. At the tennis club, where I was now having lessons, I would wear my blazer with hoped-for panache with its naval crown embroidered on the pocket and the words Squash 1950.51.52 underneath. I seem to remember one or two small excitements and the touching of suspender belts on the banks of the Hythe canal and even an orgasm-provoking experience of feeling a nipple, before a hand brushed me away and left me damp in my grey flannels. Once I managed to overcome my embarrassment in a rather seedy little tobacconists down by the harbour when I asked for a magazine I had been surreptitiously told about, called *Caress* which had short stories in it about men and women almost having sex. It described in lurid detail what went on with men and women almost up to the point when they actually 'put it in and did it'. To my utter shame my mother found it under my pillow one day but she just smiled. I don't recall knowing anyone of my age who had 'done it' then – a few talked as though they wanted you to think they had and went on about French letters and how there was a book called *Ideal Marriage*, which they said was amazing. And to make these kind of matters even more interesting, in the house opposite, where another retired naval officer lived, not as senior as the Admiral, a strikingly beautiful girl called Sonia had come to live, rather like us, as her parents had been killed somewhere abroad. Eagerly one day she agreed to play strip poker in the garage when everyone was out and the old Admiral asleep. Things had just got interesting when the door opened and there he was, the Admiral, standing in his homburg, distinctly unamused and saying something about filth. That was the end of that! At least he didn't tell my father. That would have been the last straw.

I had only been home about a week when, without any explanation, my father arrived on a Tuesday afternoon and stayed. It transpired he had now suddenly become an accountant – yet another string to his bow apparently – and was going to work in the Folkestone offices of a small holiday camp which was a few miles down the coast. Each morning, always in his trilby, he would go to the garage and take out my mother's bicycle with its basket on the front – his and my mother's sole means of transport – and pedal slowly away using the three-speed he had had fitted, down the wide avenue and on into town where the offices were close to the Junction railway station. I never went up that way because I dreaded seeing him in those bicycle clips, which he sometimes forgot to take off, and more likely than not, wearing his Old Haileyburian tie, or even worse, his blazer which could be seen a mile off with its cream, dun and purple striping. Talk about embarrassment. Although I liked her a lot for all she did, I also felt a pang or two of shame whenever I met my mother in the town, out shopping, on the bicycle, because my father had caught the No.107 bus from the end of the road for a change. I think I only knew one boy whose family had a car, as it was, but seeing my parents on a bike was too much and on days when this happened I thought it better going back to sea, rather than having to endure incidents like this, even if I had become disillusioned with naval life.

My mother still had no fridge in our kitchen. The larder was still filled with the same things: the Kilner jars of home-made chutneys and jams made from gooseberries that grew in the Admiral's garden. The lavatory just inside the back door was still unpainted, although the distemper was powdering off here and there and the old iron cistern was getting rusty again.

\*\*\*\*\*\*\*\*\*\*

The twenty something days of leave sped by and almost before I knew it, I was facing the prospect of a depressing journey back to Plymouth, where the *Devonshire* lay waiting. These next three months were to be the last I would spend as a cadet, thank God. After that, well, who knows, at least I would be a midshipman.

All I knew about the second cruise was that it was to be in Scandinavian waters, first port of call Kristiansand, before going further north towards the Arctic Circle and the Lofoten islands. It was customary for the cadets to be allowed some time ashore in the friendly Norwegian ports and in Kristiansand, the town looked on the yearly arrival of the *Devonshire* as something of a social event, involving sports competitions against the town's college and any of the Norwegian naval ships which were in port at the time, together with visits to the town and nearby fjords, all of which culminated with a dance before sailing north again.

This time however, there were rumours that instead of going to the chilly waters of the Lofoten Islands, *Devonshire* was to spend two weeks at anchor in Bantry Bay, in southern Ireland, where the cadets were to put ashore each day to perfect their drill in readiness to be part of the naval contingent lining Parliament Square for the coming Coronation of Princess Elizabeth. I wasn't too sure about the Bantry Bay bit, having already learnt how excruciatingly boring endless drilling can be, but going to London to take part in such a great pageant as the Coronation did sound exciting – as did the idea of being allowed ashore in Kristiansand and the dance especially. The latter conjured up thoughts of Nordic blondes and free-love and a myriad of other imagined excitements which could happen if you were allowed ashore.

As it turned out, I was not to be disappointed. There was a dance, there was a girl.

On the day after the dance, the cadets were allowed one free afternoon ashore before preparing the ship for sea. I remember taking the girl's hand as we walked along the rocky edge of the fjord and I felt her fingers tighten in response. There was a strong smell of kelp left along the shoreline after a low tide and we undressed each other, trembling with sensual anticipation. I recall thinking how her small breasts barely protruded at all as she lay back and smiled, taking my hand and positioning it on her velvet smoothness. Only the gulls and terns, wheeling overhead, watched my first attempt at the act of love. It was hardly a romantic night spent beneath silk sheets, drifting in and out of sleep between lovemaking, but nevertheless it set in motion an irresistible urge to enjoy similar pleasures, whenever and wherever the chance might occur. A libido too strong for my own good had been set in motion! Thank you girl, the girl who watched as *Devonshire* slipped her ropes and slid away towards the open sea. I was one of the cable party in the ship's bows and I saw her on the jetty, but discipline meant I couldn't wave and hoped that she understood and didn't think me heartless.

Back at sea, the stressful routine never let up. Bantry Bay came and went. My indelible impression of the little of Ireland which I had seen, was of it being a melancholy place, strangely deserted judging by the scattering of lifeless village cottages close to the strip of land which had bizarrely become our drilling ground. The odd bark of a dog coming from an empty street and the far away chug of an old Fordson tractor, were the sole clues that the place was inhabited at all. Ten days and it was time to put to sea once more – the old routine was waiting, with those dispiriting cold night watches, the smell of diesel and the noise of dynamos, and always under the constant gaze of the instructors. Through the Bristol Channel, past The Lizard and Start Point, which marked the entrance to Dartmouth harbour, and finally to H.M. Dockyard Portsmouth, for one last final run of exercises in readiness for Coronation Day. After that, buses up to London to the Horse Guards barracks, where we were billeted for the night, before a 6a.m. march to Parliament Square, in order to take up positions for the long wait until the stands were filled and the procession started… standing, standing, motionless, eyes to the front, hour followed by hour, rifles shining, wet with drizzle, until finally, the one command you were waiting to hear… *"Atten–shun. Royal Salute. Present Arms."* And then the tumultuous roar as the Royal Carriage passed, and one's part in the spectacular event was done.

The final weeks of the 'cruise' were spent in a feeling of anti-climax, practicing navigation off the Cornish coast before returning to Plymouth for the last time and final exams. As a matter of pride, although my heart was no longer in it, I made an effort to pass. In fact, I did quite well.

\*\*\*\*\*\*\*\*\*

An Admiralty Fleet Order had gone up on the mess-deck notice board, ordering each cadet to make three choices as to the preferred fleet in which he would like to serve during his midshipman's time. The choices were between the Mediterranean, the Far East, which took in the war zone of Korean waters, and lastly the West Indies. In reality there was only one choice, but I thought it would simply be pushing my luck too far to ask for a return to the magic of the West Indies. Besides which, with the Korean War still on it would be tempting fate not to opt for the possibility of seeing action and at least putting to the test everything I had trained for. I duly submitted my first choice as Far East squadron and as my second, the West Indies, with the last, the Mediterranean. Mountbatten was C-in-C there and had a reputation for making life none too easy for very junior officers, being a severe taskmaster and a stickler for discipline and dress, and that was the last thing I wanted! Far better a duffel coat and the relaxed dress up on the open bridge of a frigate off the North Korean coast, banging away with her 4-inch guns at a Communist train as it emerged from one tunnel and tried to make the next in one piece. Rumour had it this was an amusing, if serious, pastime, if your ship was in the right place at the right time. And you got a medal for it!

The reply signal came in two days later. Everyone was round the notice board. I searched for my name and… I had got the West Indies, in the cruiser HMS *Sheffield*, flagship of the British West Indies fleet! That was the dream posting of course, the one I had not dared asked for! Almost everyone was excited and an end-of-term atmosphere swept through the confines of our living quarters below decks.

Fully aware of the *Devonshire*'s movements and that there was new business to be had now in the way of new midshipmen's uniforms and other sartorial delights, two representatives of the Bond Street emporium of Messrs. Gieves & Co., appeared on the mess-deck. They may as well have been agents acting on behalf of the Admiralty, whose task it was to mould you into 'officer material' by taking you into the comfortable bosom of 'service life'… such as offering susceptible young men – mere boys – such inducements as spanking new uniforms, quite free, which came along with limitless credit, in case you took a fancy to being kitted out in a new suit or fancy sports jacket. A temptation hard to resist! But **I** certainly didn't want to be moulded by anyone: I wanted to be myself! If I had had the common sense to think about it – so very rare at that age – something might have said, *'beware the gene that lurks, you know how your father ended up!'*

Meanwhile, the well-scrubbed men stood beside their small collapsible tables, tailors' tapes slung round the neck, waiting for such easy prey, smiling obsequiously, ready with small notebooks into which each measurement could be jotted down. If you succumbed, as most did, without knowing it, yet one more aspect of your life-to-be in the service was being sealed.

*'Something in the way of a lightweight jacket'*, to go along with your tropical *uniform?'* This followed by more fawning assurances that whatever 'sor' ordered, it would be sent down early in the coming leave. *'We always use the best horn buttons, sor, of course!'*

I left the dockyard a few days after those obsequious tailors' measurings. And that was it. I had been longing for any kind of respite from the authoritarian regime of the past four and a half years and now it had finally arrived.

By now I desperately wanted to cut the ties of home life. I am sure my mother knew this and I think my father sensed this also, as he began showing a distinct antagonism towards me, keen on any occasion to put me down whenever I said the least thing derogatory about the Navy, even the most trivial details. I certainly dared not mention the fact that I was thinking about chucking it in.

*'You've no experience Jimmy, none at all…if you think there is anything better than the Navy… the trouble is with you, with all your introverted ideas. You piss before the water comes'* – that was one of his better ones. Little wonder that whenever we passed each other, outside in the garden for example, where he liked to fiddle among the Admiral's vegetable

patch on his days off, not a word passed between us. On such occasions my pent-up frustration made me naïvely think that one of these days I would show him how wrong he was. Still, it's a great expression that, about pissing!

He still went off each morning on the old bicycle with the wicker shopping basket in the front – nowadays I would simply have thought him marvellously eccentric, but in those days it really shamed and alienated me, and we were beginning to have less and less in common. He simply didn't want to understand what my feelings were.

My official papers from the Admiralty arrived two days before the Gieves boxes containing my new uniforms. The buff envelope, with its anchor crest, included joining instructions and a travel warrant to Portsmouth, where *Sheffield* lay in basin No.6, *'access to H.M. Dockyard via the north gate'*, where I was to report to the officer of the day once aboard.

The taxi driver knew the north gate and on turning onto the dock I saw the *Sheffield*, long and grey and low in the water, her two slightly raked funnels and her big eight-inch guns and the name *Sheffield* in large cast-brass letters on her side, aft, under the quarterdeck. This was *my ship*; and when I crossed the gangplank and was saluted by the quartermaster, I was acutely aware that the moment I stepped onto the ship's deck, it was the high point of my life to date, and at that precise moment, the thought of turning my back on life in the Navy was the furthest thing from my mind – I was 18 and an officer, being saluted onto my first ship!

Nor does it take much imagination to know how I felt the following morning – I didn't care, if by custom, I still had to sleep in a hammock – when the newly arrived midshipmen were gathered together in their new 'gunroom' home, with its few rexine-covered armchairs and buttoned benches and big mahogany mess table, to be briefed by the young sub-lieutenant who was in charge of us, as to what our various duties were to be in the forthcoming NATO exercises, and what we might expect during the ship's flag-showing cruise thereafter in the West Indies.

I listened with rapt attention to every detail. After putting to sea, our passage was to take us through the Dover Straits, north to the Faeroe Islands and the Denmark Straits where we were to rendezvous with vessels of the American 5th Fleet for exercises under wartime conditions for 10 days. The threat from Russia was still very real and it was rumoured that the Allies had laid atomic mines in the Straits. On completion, Greenock, on the Clyde, was to be our last port of call before heading across the Atlantic for the island of Bermuda, which was going to be our home port for the time we were to be stationed in the West Indies. After provisioning with tropical stores we were to rendezvous with the HMS *Gothic* – an Elder & Fyffes passenger vessel, which was to serve as the Royal Yacht while *Britannia*, was being built. We were to act as *Gothic's* escort through the Panama Canal, and on to a position midway in the Pacific where we would be relieved by a ship of the Royal Australian Navy. Having completed escort duty, *Sheffield* was to return to the West Indies, putting into Trinidad, Curaçao, Jamaica and some of the smaller islands of the Antilles, lastly visiting Havana (still under Batista's rule), before returning to Bermuda to make preparations for sailing up the Eastern Seaboard of the United States, to 'show the flag'.

Unquestionably, this promised to be the experience of a lifetime! To be given a chance like this at the age of eighteen, was unbelievable, and it was something I was not about to miss, even though, in my most private thoughts I knew that I was going on this irresistible ride at the expense of the Admiralty, because my independence was more important and that at some time in the not very distant future, I would be 'chucking it all in', as my father would have said!

Still I listened in a state of bewildered excitement as the gunroom sub. went on… *Sheffield* would call at ports on the Gulf of Mexico, Galveston, the port of Houston, New Orleans, coinciding with the Mardi Gras, then Mobile and Pensecola in Florida, where the Navy trained some of its pilots, then on to Norfolk, Virginia, Baltimore and New York… we could hardly take it all in. And more – Boston, Newport, Rhode Island, then across the famous cod-fishing grounds to St. Johns, Newfoundland, ending with a final passage down the St. Lawrence to Montreal. It took a few moments for the magnitude of our voyage to sink in.

Our Captain was to be Keith McNeil Campbell-Walter, to be promoted Commodore for the time we were on station. Above him, C-in-C West Indies, Vice-Admiral J. P. Stevens would be flying his pennant on the *Sheffield*, his flagship.

It was barely conceivable that such prospects of adventure could seem more lavish!

What Marks, the sub-lieutenant in charge of the gunroom, didn't tell us was that Keith McNeil Campbell-Walter was of aristocratic Scottish stock and was arguably the most imposing and handsome man in naval uniform. Well over six foot tall, with a permanently tanned and weather-beaten face, his looks were formidable, in the mould of Kurt Jurgens, the film star, but more refined. Accordingly, he had sired a daughter, Fiona, who had become the most famous international model of the day – unbelievably attractive and certainly every young man's dream, soon to be married to the German industrialist Baron von Thyssen. It was understandable and easy to forgive the very slight narcissistic bearing our Captain sometimes adopted being blessed with such good looks. In no time at all, I discovered he was a man of powerful presence, nevertheless given to adopting the slightest smile of understanding whenever he might be watching any of his midshipmen's attempts to perform their best when under his gaze. His eyes had a look of warmth as if amused by their efforts. If your eyes did meet his – something of a risky thing to do with a ship's Captain – it was just possible I thought, to detect, however small, a bond between the two of you.

So this man was to be our commander, upon whom we were to rely for our well-being and safety, during the many months to come. Ultimately it is up to the Captain of a ship as to whether the lives of his young officers, not forgetting their duties, are to be enjoyable or not. All of us, at some time or another, had been warned that there were some officers who regarded midshipmen to be little more than irksome nuisances in a warship, even after one day on board *Sheffield* I am sure I was not alone in thinking the portents were good. A good atmosphere ran throughout the ship.

For the present, our small comforts rested with the three stewards who served our meals and saw to our needs in the gunroom, laying and clearing the big single table, seeing our midshipmen's bar was tidy and its bottles and glasses stowed correctly for sea. They also swept the Admiralty-pattern gunroom carpet before we emerged for breakfast each morning, and all this made me think that by comparison to what had gone before, this really was turning out to be the life of a young gentleman officer!

Each of us signed for and marked our own bottles for the bar, and it was accepted that as long as you did not report for duty drunk, you could drink as much as your meagre pay would allow. A bottle of gin was 2 shillings, whisky slightly more, sherry and liqueurs worked out at 3d. a nip. What a life! You were positively encouraged to smoke, although if you appeared to be drawing more than 20 packets a week from the NAAFI, something might be said. A couple of us took to smoking a pipe occasionally, Balkan Sobranie being the best tobacco, but in reality I think I hoped it would make me look like a hardened sea-dog and although it really could warm your hands by holding the bowl, if you were on the open bridge, the craze didn't last. The cheapest smoke was 'Blue Line' – cigarettes especially made for the H.M. ships, a shade acrid, but only 4d. a packet, whereas all other brands came in tins, at 8d. a time, the favourites being State Express 555 in yellow tins and Benson & Hedges in red. These were 2d. more than all the other brands like Capstan and Navy Cut which could be had for 6d. Why everyone didn't die of lung cancer I will never know.

The day before we sailed, conscious of being watched by some of the dockyard workers, who obviously hoped that something interesting might be going to happen, I carried out the very first of my officer's tasks by directing the crane when the last of our heavy stores were being loaded. Luckily it went without a hitch.

*'Hands to Harbour Stations'* was piped at 12 noon next morning.

On *Devonshire* it had been the cadets who manned the capstans and heaved on the wires and ropes as the orders were shouted at us through the megaphone from the bridge: *'now slip the for'd spring, slip the breasts'* – orders which we all understood – but this time, as midshipmen, it was we who saw to it that the seamen who had mustered at their allotted positions for putting to sea and carried out this morning's commands. Campbell-Walter stood watching procedures, the navigating officer beside him. Pennants for leaving harbour had been run up on the command from the signals officer, water-tight doors had been closed and slowly, with a shudder every now and again as the engines ran astern, the *Sheffield* turned towards the harbour mouth and with the odd wave from the shore, slipped out past the Nab Tower towards the open sea.

I was lucky enough to be midshipman of the watch – midday to 16:00 – up on the bridge as general dogsbody, taking the odd bearing for the navigating officer or ringing the engine room to give them the cruising revolutions of the ship's propellers which would enable us to make a good 15 knots as we passed the Needles Lighthouse and headed up the Channel. Some time after my watch I found myself on the bridge again as I wanted to see the Kentish coastline, from Dungeness on to past the Goodwin Lightship, to see if I could recognise any landmarks of my disappearing youth.

The radar showed what I took to be a number of fishing boats off Dungeness and through the binoculars I could see the first of the Martello towers past which I'd cycled when I had my first bike with a Sturmey Archer 3-speed. From mid-channel the diminutive buildings above Folkestone harbour were just perceptible through my binoculars. Detached and surreal, seeing my home landmarks slipping by in the distance, accompanied by thoughts of past times, life when I had paid 2 shillings for a ride on the motor boats in the pleasure pool along the road from the harbour. I was able to make out the road leading up from the port to the town shopping centre. Bizarre to think that my father might be pedalling down from his office by the station to the butcher's he favoured as it was a Friday and time to afford a joint. He would be wearing his Haileyburian blazer under his old mac for sure, with his old trilby wedged firmly on. I wondered if anyone I knew was looking out to sea as I sailed past in *Sheffield* ...any girl, anyone from the tennis club... perhaps even the smallest chance the old Admiral might be walking back from his customary daily snooker game at the Masonic Lodge? He would have known it was a cruiser. I hadn't had the opportunity of telling my mother which day we would be going up channel; otherwise I knew she would have made a point of walking up to the cliffs to catch a sight of us. It was strangely unreal to think that just eleven miles to port was my world of adolescence and I was very glad that I had left it behind. I was 'at sea'.

**********

In the ensuing days the weather worsened and our stewards had some difficulty in serving us at mealtimes. The odd soup was spilled and our bottles rattled on the bar and the watch-keepers came in wet and cold. We were expected to encounter winds of storm force 10 once we were up past Scapa Flow. I looked forward to it, as I had no difficulty in keeping my sea-legs by swaying to counteract the roll of the ship each time the rising swell took her over. Earlier on we had seen the Northern Lights, before the cloud came over, infinitely distant up towards the Pole. I imagined we were sailing into a world where the forces of nature ruled supreme and the ship and all the men on her were no more than helpless flotsam, however strong our turbines and whatever course we chose to lessen the powers of the sea we were encountering.

I had been attached to the torpedo and anti-submarine officer for action exercises. At my station I was alone, and just below the bridge was a kind of steel-sided lookout post, open to the elements. Here I was supposed in some inexplicable way to read something called the *'angle of attack'* from a brass instrument fixed on the side of this lookout position, but it was totally clogged with grey paint and apparently had not been in use for some time, so the whole thing was a waste of time as I didn't understand the angle of attack theory anyway. Theoretically, I was supposed to pass down these readings to the officer with his torpedo crew by the tubes, but as the instrument was totally useless, together with the fact that I never discovered if there were people waiting by the torpedo tubes, all I could do was pretend to be busy and look interested, should any of the watch officers on the bridge above me look over to see what I was doing. In truth, not being much interested in service paraphernalia, particularly bits which didn't work and were hopelessly outdated this was a waste of life. I was keener to wonder at the enormous natural forces that were now engulfing us between the troughs and peaks of unimaginably huge waves and the sound of our bows crashing through every surge of rolling water.

The intensity of the bad weather increased. For a further five days we endured the relentless storm, towering crests of dark Arctic waves, like ominous hills rolling towards us under a screaming wind which had touched force 14 on the Beaufort Scale, thrashing each crest to breaking point as *Sheffield* headed into them. Our wooden sea-boats were reduced to splinters on both port and starboard sides and it was dangerous to move on the open deck. We heard that one of the forward turrets of the American light cruiser "Chesapeake" had been buckled to the point where it had been torn from its housing. It was bitterly cold and sleep was barely possible, however tired you were. It was vital that the quartermaster at the wheel kept the ship's heading directly into the oncoming sea; broadside and the ship could have been in serious trouble. As it was, one night during the middle watch, the watch some seamen dread, the ship rolled over more than 40 degrees and all those of us asleep in the chestflat woke and froze. Someone said, '*Christ!*' before we sensed stability return and she rolled back with a groan of metal plates. The responsibility and judgement of Campbell-Walter must have been at their uttermost limits and we were all aware that he had not left the bridge during those five desperate days and nights.

As a life experience, those days in that incredible Arctic storm would never be forgotten. As a purely naval experience it was no more than a 'war game' to make sure Campbell-Walter, our Captain, for whom now we all had the utmost respect, was able to report that his ship had been brought up to fighting readiness, although even she was tired and old. My own thoughts dwelt more on what had gone before in these forbidding waters – of the men and ships that must have suffered appalling fates on the Russian convoys to Murmansk and how death must have come in the loneliest and bleakest conditions imaginable. By contrast, lucky boys were we, our gunroom bar plentifully stocked with Booths and Haig, which had hardly been earned by the latter's wartime standards, certain of our return and knowing we were bound for the West Indies to show our country's flag and to enjoy ourselves. One of our fleet did however join those convoymen. Death came to one of the American pilots who misjudged his approach to the flight deck on one of the American carriers soon after flying operations had been resumed in the better weather off Greenland.

With the sound half blown away by the wind, a bugler sounded the last post from our bridge as we passed the spot where his plane had gone down. It was food for thought; at eighteen you think you are immortal.

Sleeting rain and a medium swell greeted the dawn on completion of the exercises. Signal lamps clattered between the ships, each Captain wishing the other *'God's Speed and Safe Passage'* as their courses diverged, the Americans heading west for the Newfoundland Banks while *Sheffield* headed south for Greenock dockyard, in order to make final preparations for passage to the West Indies.

Dockyards throughout the world look the same. Each time I saw one, it reminded me of the jumbled heaps at the back of the old agricultural repair yard beside the village garage I had last seen ten years before, but now this naval scene was piled high with stores and equipment, all covered with a film of dockyard filth, the air filled with the smell of fuel oil and the clang of metal and the clatter of rivet guns.

We did not stay long. Our smashed sea-boats were craned away and replaced with new ones, freshly painted Admiralty grey with the name *Sheffield* on each of the bows. All hands fell to cleaning ship and carrying out any light repairs that were needed. We had time to enjoy our meals once more, served up by the stewards in our gunroom which wasn't rolling from side to side any more and talking about girls, reading, drinking and playing cards, happy being slightly dissolute for the two days we were in harbour.

The first evening in dock, when I was midshipman of the watch, Fiona Campbell-Walter came to see her father who was waiting on the officers' gangway to meet her. It was somewhat incongruous, this elegant, ravishingly good-looking model, in a sumptuous fur coat, stepping gingerly through the quayside detritus and our Captain in his evening mess-dress with all the gold braid and his weather-beaten face, greeting her as she stepped on board.

There was also a second unexpected arrival in the form of someone who arrived in what looked like a staff car, with a small pennant on the front. Coming up the gangway, he stepped onto the quarterdeck and in the silkiest of Oxford accents, bade me good evening as I saluted him, and asked if someone could bring his trunk aboard and he be shown to the Commodore's cabin. It did not come as a surprise to me when I learnt he was a diplomat of some standing, Sir Roland Gibbs, who had been appointed Governor of Bermuda and he would be sailing with us to take up his new posting.

Just before we sailed however, I nearly found myself in extremely hot water… from time to time being given to a hint of over loquaciousness, I had fallen into an animated conversation with a reporter from the Glasgow Herald who had come down to the dock to see if there was any story to be had regarding the exercises which had taken place with the Americans. *'Well,'* I expansively explained, *'winds gusting Force 14-15 are almost too much for some of our ships to survive, let alone the American ones,'* and *'did he know that a gun turret had been ripped off the U.S. cruiser "Chesapeake"?'* Oh dear! Apparently the following morning when the papers had been delivered to the breakfast table in the officers' wardroom, there was appalled consternation! Who the bloody hell had been shooting his mouth off like this? And this talk of nearly foundering, and the "Chesapeake" put out of action? I kept my head very low for the next few hours, but luckily with all the officers too preoccupied in making final preparations for departure, the incident was not investigated further.

A few nights out, after dinner, as the weather was warmer, several of the midshipmen were on the quarterdeck together with some of the other more senior officers and our Captain, who was sitting on one of the vents, chatting to Sir Roland. All of us had drunk more than was perhaps wise, but it was at times like these that any inhibitions between the midshipmen and the other officers evaporated and someone suggested that I get my one-wheeled cycle from my locker and give a demonstration right there on the quarterdeck, weaving between the various hatch-covers and bollards – which I did, thank goodness to everyone's amusement, including the Governor's. I was, I fear, given to small bouts of exhibitionism and the whole escapade could have been very embarrassing, showing off like that! One may well wonder how a one-wheeled cycle comes to be aboard one of Her Majesty's ships in the middle of the Sargasso Sea… the truth is that it was one of three given to my brother, sister and myself, a legacy of the dark days of the winding up of the cycle company my father had been involved in. I had my suspicions that on the final delivery made by the works lorry there may well have been three items missing.

**********

A calm sea and a gently heaving swell, coupled with clear blue skies and the first sight of flying fish meant that the Bermuda Islands could not be far away.

For a few days *Sheffield* lay berthed in the then almost unused naval yard – by this time there were no ships permanently on station in the West Indies – situated upon one of the string of smaller islands which run out from Hamilton, the capital. Now it was *'all hands to painting ship'*, the atmosphere on board relaxed and happy, only marred by the unhappy incident involving the sub-lieutenant in charge of the gunroom, who was attacked by a shark while swimming in one of the small coral inlets close to the dockyard. The poor chap had half a buttock taken and there was a lot of blood. The incident was reported in the local press, adding by way of soothing the island's visitors that no shark had been seen inside the reef for over ninety years and it was still quite safe to bathe! Our unfortunate young friend had not found it so: twenty-two years old and he would have been 'invalided out' with a paltry pension. The Americans airlifted him to hospital and we never saw him again.

On the last day before leaving, again courtesy of the U.S. Navy, a new sub-lieutenant arrived to see that we behaved ourselves – tall, smooth, immaculately mannered, the product of an old aristocratic line of naval officers, with the wonderful name of C. P. R. Arbuthnot.

Throughout our stay, while the cruiser took on tropical stores – an exciting thought of what lay ahead – one of the midshipmen's duties was to run the officers' launches and also the Commodore's barge with its cast-brass dolphins supporting its cabin roof, through the reefs to the jetty steps in Hamilton. More often than not the officers would be accompanied by lightly-dressed, classy, fragrant-smelling women. One couldn't help but be envious and it was always worth a surreptitious look back into the cabin, if you happened to be at the controls. One of the coxswains said he'd seen one of the lieutenants trying to get a girl's breast out and another said he thought he had actually seen the communications officer '*doing it*' with a girl sitting on his lap and her evening dress was pulled right up. I don't think any of us were slow to learn what drink and ships' parties did for you!

Admiral Stevens, the Station C-in-C duly arrived just before we sailed to take up duty for Royal Escort. He remained a distant figure whilst on board and we only saw him from time to time up on the bridge. Maybe he was past wanting to get the sun – he must have been at least fifty something!

We rendezvoused with the *Gothic* in the Gulf of Mexico. A small private viewing platform under an awning had been constructed above her bridge for the Royal couple and from time to time you could see the Queen and Prince Philip as we steamed abreast of them a few cables distant.

The passage through the canal, with the Royal party clearly visible on their viewing platform just ahead of us as *Gothic* entered the lock first, was another memorable experience, as was the surreal manner in which both vessels appeared to be steaming through the centre of a rainforest, the tall tropical trees running right down to the canal banks. A warship, or any ship for that matter, must be a strange sight viewed from the tropical forested banks, her masts sliding by, a matter of yards away, above the top of the canopy of trees on either side.

Once through the Canal *Gothic* and *Sheffield* took on water in Bilboa. No sight of our new Queen and I can hardly blame her. Our dockside berth offered nothing visually attractive. Everyone was sweating profusely and the smell from the dock was appalling – dirty South-American commerce at its worst: black oil tanks, rusting iron posts of the first oil jetty sticking up to a back-cloth of diesel-discoloured palm fronds. And large birds, looking suspiciously like vultures, perched along every roof edge along the quay, hoping to scavenge for any bit of filth some undisciplined, untidy seaman might throw ashore. Definitely not a place for any traveller to linger, particularly our new Queen. Finally we headed into the offshore breezes of the great Pacific Ocean for our unusually long voyage, certainly in peacetime, of ten and a half thousand miles, there and back, to some position close to Australia where we were to hand over escort duties to the Royal Australian Navy.

Crossing the Atlantic you do see or at least make contact with a few passing cargo vessels, or see some familiar piece of flotsam, either thrown overboard or a piece of dockside rubbish washed out by the tide months before – a broken crate, an oil drum or a rubber tyre. By contrast, in the Pacific, not a single man-made thing is seen from dawn to dusk. The two ships steamed on alone, in nothingness, save for the blue sky and a sea stretching away to infinity.

Then, one day, something strange. I heard the clack of our signalman's lantern coming from the bridge and looking out I saw a small vessel, no longer than 200ft, riding the ocean swell, perhaps two miles ahead. I saw a return signal – this was in code, just a few letters of the phonetic alphabet. At first I thought it might be a small whaler, loitering on its way to the Polynesian whaling grounds, but this, in code… odd. Very definitely not a cargo vessel and making no headway at all, the only vessel we had encountered in our crossing so far, thousands of miles from land. Soon everyone on deck was talking about it and there was speculation as to what the ship was doing there. There seemed a sinister edge to the encounter as we passed and the signal lamp became silent, leaving her still innocently riding the swell.

Word filtered down from the bridge just before she became a speck on the horizon. This ship was the most distant outpost of our chemical weapons development programme at Porton Down, so secret and so dangerous that the only place on earth where she might not become a disaster of unimaginable magnitude if anything went wrong was plumb in the middle of the largest expanse of water on the planet.

Boredom had now set in. Below decks, the heat was insufferable and little work was done. No one seemed to care. On we steamed, until eventually, somewhere in latitude 35° south, we handed over our escort duties to a frigate of the Australian Navy. The crew, and I suspect the officers as well, became restless, thinking of the long passage back across the Pacific before being able once more to step ashore, returning to civilisation and being able to look forward to a break from the torpor of day after day out in the Pacific, and who knows, some new experience or better still, some *'fun'*.

But suddenly, however, a buzz of excitement ran throughout the ship. Word had it that the C-in-C had asked the Captain to alter course and make for the Marquesas Islands, a day's run north-west.

This tiny group of islands, first discovered by Captain Cook, is the most remote in Polynesia. Their details have not been re-charted since the 18th century and so it is Cook's precise details which appear on the Admiralty charts kept in the locker on the bridge. The island our C-in-C had chosen for a brief stop was Nuku Hiva, and had last been visited by a warship in 1934. Ringed by reefs and the huge Pacific breakers, the beaches are only to be reached by carefully handled launches. At first sight the island appeared forbidding, with dark cliffs covered in dense vegetation rising steeply from small curved beaches where the silvery, lapping wavelets run up onto the bleached sand. As for the myth about Polynesia and the beauty of its women, it is no myth; it is undeniably true. There are no comparisons to be made on earth, although there are some travellers who say the Andoman Islands compare in beauty, but those have been traded with for centuries and the women there have been coarsened by coupling with seamen. None but a handful of Europeans had ever landed on, or even sailed by, these small islands of the Marquesas, which must be the closest to anyone's imagined paradise. I was lucky!

The French Navy claimed the Islands in the 19th century, putting ashore several missionaries, one or two of whom were very soon boiled and eaten. This diet must have become disagreeable, as finally God must have won a few more children, and Parisian French began to be taught to the island's population thereafter. Despite the work of the holy fathers, cannibalism had lingered on intermittently for another generation or two and so it was that by the time *Sheffield* arrived off Nuku Hiva, there could well have been a few inhabitants whose grandfathers would have happily eaten one of their neighbouring islanders if relations had gone awry.

*Sheffield* lay at anchor, just outside the reef, in a bay of unsurpassed beauty. On the shore I could see a single tin-roofed building, set back from the beach, flying the tricolour. On landing we learnt that the resident governor was away visiting one of the other islands. A smiling headman said it was an honour to have such a great naval vessel visit the island – the last had called many years ago. If we were to stay, the islanders would entertain us that evening with dancing and singing, he told us in almost perfect French. In reply we said we would be very pleased if that happened. It struck me that this was the stuff of dreams, little wonder that Fletcher Christian fell under the spell of a place such as this! Sadly, *Sheffield* was to weigh anchor at first light, the following morning.

I wandered about by myself, mesmerised by the island's beauty and fell into conversation with one of the inhabitants, speaking in my best Greenwich interpreter's French, unable to resist the temptation of tactfully enquiring about the reputation these idyllic islands had for cannibalism. I remember clearly not knowing the French for cannibalism and saying something like, *'quelqu'un qui mange son voisin.'* (someone who eats his neighbour!) He didn't seem to mind my faltering question in the least, telling me his grandfather, who lived on the neighbouring island of Hiva Oa, had indeed eaten human flesh, many, many years ago. *'C'etait comme ca'* (It was 'the way of things')," he smilingly told me. This was surely the most bizarre moment – there out in the bay lay *Sheffield*, my ticket home to dirty old Portsmouth and the real world. Maybe *his* was the real world I thought.

In gathering dusk festivities began. Everyone, except for the watch-keepers, had gathered on the beach under the palms to witness what turned out to be the most erotic and extraordinary spectacle imaginable. Dance after dance, thirty or forty dusky, beautiful young female islanders sang, while others danced opposite the men to rhythmic, sexual drumming, swaying to the music in their grass skirts, in ever-increasing intensity, nubile breasts exposed and shaking to the drumbeat, the dusky nymphs worked themselves up into a final crescendo of ecstasy, trembling and writhing, ending with a final thrust of coupling with the man opposite. It was nearly too much to bear. If the count had not been exact and the greatest care taken to see that everyone mustered on the beach for our return to the ship, it is indisputable that a number of seamen would have jumped ship and stayed on to savour the limitless delights of this little island where money did not exist and where one's contentment would run in the veins of nature, following in the steps of Fletcher Christian and his men from the Bounty. A place whose only contact with the outside world was the three-monthly visit paid by one of the supply ships running up from Tahiti.

It has since become a haunting memory to believe that I had ever been there and once, a year later, back in London, I walked into an upmarket travel agent near Trafalgar Square, pretending I had been left a large amount of money and now wanted to get to an island in the Marquesas, called Nuku Hiva. Bear in mind it was well before tourism had changed the world. A week later I was sent a possible itinerary, which involved sailing in a passenger cargo vessel from Southampton, through the Panama Canal, disembarking at Balboa and taking the train to Vera Cruz from where another ocean freight line ran a once-monthly service to Pitcairn and Tahiti. Once there, if I contacted their agent Monsieur Yves Delbranges, he would arrange my final passage by schooner to the Marquesas. In all it would take me 14 weeks to make the trip and cost £3,150.

\*\*\*\*\*\*\*\*\*

Our first landfall after this was the Coast of Mexico.

The old port of Vera Cruz was everything I imagined old Spain would have looked like. One long tree-lined Ramblas with decaying, flaky honey-coloured buildings along either side, with all the magically architectural shapes one associates with Spain of the 18th century. Dusty and dirty, the clamour one encounters when the entire populace is trying to make a quick dollar and there is little chance and even the cars seemed barely working. The scenes were wonderful, romantic and marvellously redolent with the whiff of the ancient world of the Conquistadors.

I had no money left at this stage although there had been precious little to spend it on during the past few weeks, but had managed to buy my first camera so that I could capture some of the passing images which our cruise was providing. I did take a few pictures, but then, as usual, I had to sell it to be able to squeeze the maximum excitement out of the next port of call. I was pleased in hindsight to have been broke in Vera Cruz, as it meant I opted out of taking a day's trip to Mexico City with some of the other midshipmen and instead had to accept the fact that I must mooch about the old town by myself, soaking up all the wonderfully seedy atmosphere which was utterly new and fascinating. On the edge of town I came upon a scene which might have come from any one of the great romantic movies of the thirties. Exploring the remains of a ruined hacienda, any signs of whitewash long faded on the plaster walls, the shutters hanging broken from where windows had once been, I came through to an inner courtyard, my nostrils filling with a strong and delicious scent of oranges. Intrigued, I inspected further and through a side archway I found another smaller colonnaded court lined with orange trees and in the middle a pool, the entire surface of which was covered by petals of the fallen blossoms, their smell accentuated by the evaporation of the remaining water. Being broke sometimes does have its advantages!

Now, although I didn't know it, the die was all but cast. I had no idea that within the ensuing five weeks and two ports of call, I would have finally crossed the Rubicon and made my decision to leave the Navy.

It was meeting a girl, needless to say, that made me decide to take the last fatal step. The event occurred in Trinidad.

The island's governor held a reception for the officers of "*Sheffield*", at Government House, in Port-of-Spain, which all the midshipmen had to attend. There, out on the lawn, I took more than a distinct fancy to a nice-looking, somewhat enigmatic, Yugoslavian girl. She lived in Trinidad on account of her father having fled the regime under Tito. Her father owned a freighter, which had originally been registered in Split, but now, after his escape, he was trading along the coasts of North and South America. With his family safely on board his ship, the freighter had put into Port-of-Spain, seeking refuge, and it was there that the family had decided to stay. The vessel was re-registered in Panama and he became wealthy. His story and how the girl from Split had ended up in the tropics appealed to me enormously.

During the ten days the cruiser was berthed in stinking Port-of-Spain, every moment I could spend ashore, I wooed the girl, even learning a few words of Serbo-Croat. We laughed and kissed a lot, walked along endless beaches fringed by palms and lay on the warm sand gazing adoringly into each others eyes, naïvely thinking that true love had come and how excruciating our being apart might be. I told her I never wanted the ship to leave, but leave I must and I promised somehow I would be back. I don't know if she really believed me, but at the time it didn't really seem to matter, as my head was full of romantic notions that somehow I *would* be back, with tantalizing ideas of enjoying some kind of blissful, tropical romance – calypsos, dancing under the stars to the tune of Begin the Beguine, again and again. These kind of dreams seldom come true, but at eighteen one can be forgiven for believing that they might, given the sense of adventure such ideas kindle under the circumstances in which I found myself. Perhaps you can put it down to young Jimmy having caught a touch of jungle fever out there in the tropics *'Stupid asinine infatuations of yours,'* – I feel sure! is what my father would have said!

It was a potently sad and emotional night when the lights of Port-of-Spain finally faded from view and I found myself once more back in reality, midshipman of the watch and shackled once again by Queen's Regulations and Admiralty Instructions. I would get back, somehow, to see this girl again, I told myself, no matter what the circumstances or whatever the consequences. From the bridge I looked back at the ship's wake, glowing with phosphorescence in the dark and I felt all the impotence of being sad and angry at the same time.

I hoped she would write, but for now it was off to America, to *'show the flag'* – what we had come for, and in the meantime I was just going to have to grin and bear it!

\*\*\*\*\*\*\*\*\*\*

Back in the 50s even the mention of America held some special excitement. Few, except the very privileged, had made the transatlantic crossing and similarly only Americans who had seen war duties in Europe, had ever been to England. The cultures were miles apart. Their own roots lay in lonely hardship and endeavour and any visitor who made the long crossing was met with lavish generosity. They knew we had had a hard time during the war, they were proud to have been allies and share something of a common heritage and now that a British ship was coming complete with a real English admiral, they intended to show their appreciation in ways that certainly we midshipmen could barely have comprehended.

What happened was this. A day or two before we were due to arrive in a new port, a notice went up listing all the official functions and welcoming celebrations, including dances and cocktail parties, to which the ship's officers, including the midshipmen, had been

71

invited. Some it was compulsory to attend, unless you happened to be on watch and then came a second list from which you could choose any particular invitation you fancied that had not already been taken up by one or other of us... on offer were invitations to rodeos, country club cocktail parties, private dinners with Mr and Mrs. So-and-So at a ranch, staying overnight, family dinners and dances, oil company barbecues and even seats to watch American football (not appealing!) The list of excitements seemed unending, together with the other activities it was compulsory for all the midshipmen to attend. It very soon became a hard routine to keep up. Just when you might have thought there would be a pause from partying, *Sheffield* would be open to visitors, who would stream on-board by the hundred, asking you just to speak to them 'in such quaint English', or explain how the eight-inch guns worked.

The oiling berth in Galveston, which is the port of Houston, was where I first stepped into America. The mail had come aboard; there was a letter from my mother, but sadly nothing from Trinidad. The heavy smell of fuel oil hung over the place and momentarily it all seemed something of an anticlimax, except the sight of some of the largest and most exciting cars I had ever seen, parked outside the Port Authority building. However, what fate had waiting for me outside the entry gates to the dock was another matter.

Houston is a big-talking powerhouse and headquarters of most big American oil companies and the city and its inhabitants were waiting to welcome us in style – we poor old English boys with our captivating accents, they were going to make the ship's visit one that none of us would forget.

It all began with a 'bash', given by the Association of Texas Cattlemen, held at City Hall. All the officers went in their tropical mess dress and anyone who was anyone was there; big ranch owners, cattlemen large and small, along with Texan oil company men, with their sleek overdressed wives and some with very pretty sun-tanned daughters. A few even carried on wearing their Stetsons late into the evening. The swing music was good and all the dancing

72

well lubricated with drink. Our hosts made sure copious amounts of Bourbon flowed, along with every type of tequila cocktail, rum and beers, and even the odd martini if you were trying to be sophisticated, and all this did not mix well! Nobody seemed on their best behaviour, but it didn't seem to matter. I think the Admiral and his party had foreseen this and left early, leaving the rest of us to see out the bash to its conclusion.

I do remember, just, feeling that due to all the drink, most of us midshipmen and quite a number of the other officers as well, had let down those Texan Belles when it came to the dancing! The band played its last tune some time well after midnight and we all piled into various transport to get us back to Galveston.

Fate was waiting in an all-night diner, where we thought it might be prudent to sober up with coffees before going back on board. There were a few customers still sitting in the booths and from a chromium-plated jukebox the catchy tune of Mexicali Rose was sentimentally oozing out, accompanied by the smell of fat coming from behind the counter. In retrospect it seemed unlikely that my fate was going to be sealed irrevocably by a chance meeting here.

A group of three older men and a girl, the men in tuxedos and the girl in evening dress, who had obviously been to our welcoming party, looked up with exclamations of delight as we made our somewhat noisy and very noticeable entrance in our evening uniform. They rose with further happy cries and lurching with the full effect of many Bourbons and Southern Comforts, joined us at our table to our slight embarrassment. There is always something rather squirm-making when older men shower you with compliments. As they had also just come from City Hall themselves they seemed determined to carry on where they had left off. It all turned into quite some conversation. At one point I admired one of the men's ostentatious black and gold cufflinks, embossed with a miniature oil well – *'In that case Sir, it is my pleasure that you accept them as a souvenir of this evening,'* he said removing them. *'My name is Tom Payne, mine is the Bayshore Oil and Gas Company and these here are my partners. This young lady, my daughter,'* he said stroking back the girl's blonde hair. *'We're all so mighty pleased you young fellas have seen fit to honour us with a visit down here in Houston. We're proud to have you here. Bayshore's in the Commerce Building, right here, downtown and if there's anything we can do for you all, just drop by and let us know – we're proud to have met you!'*

Once back on board I lay awake in my hammock, thinking. I had an audacious idea. I decided that I would go and see this man Thomas Payne. So, as I had no particular duties the following day, on the pretext of having to go and look for something which had been lost at the bash the previous night, I walked along the wharf to the dock entrance, outside of which there was always a line of Chequered Cabs. I had about $30 in my pocket which I thought would be enough to get me into Houston and back.

**If only for fun, A 'poseur' to the last**

The big Chevrolet wallowed along the freeway into the city of Houston and a few minutes later I found myself outside the Commerce Building. Above the glass entrance doors hung the Stars and Stripes and the flag of the Lone Star State. I was aware of a few glances coming my way as I stepped into the air-conditioned atrium, wearing as I was, my crisp tropical whites and officer's short-sleeved shirt and cap, feeling a bit self conscious and by now a little nervous, thinking the man might not even remember having met me. A board on one of the marble columns near the elevators, listed the various corporations whose offices were in the building. 12th. floor, Bayshore Oil & Gas. The Otis lift was smooth and quick. Now I was really nervous, but at the same time quite determined. All I remember is that the suite of offices I stepped into was heavily carpeted, and there I found my man, Thomas Payne, smiling as he got up from a huge desk, now very sober, offering me his firm Texan hand.

It was strange, him calling me 'sir'. *Take a seat sir; it was some party last night; I hope you don't lose those cufflinks.'* He had remembered me! *'So, James, what might I be able to do for you? I do know my daughter would like you to come out to our place for some tennis, but she's away in Charleston today to see her aunt. So now then, tell me what's on your mind.'*

I went straight to the point and asked him if he would be able to get me a job in the oil business, out here, in Texas. This would be in easy reach of Trinidad and the Yugoslav, I was secretly thinking, and not far from any one of those other alluring islands in the Caribbean.

His reply was immediate. He said he would be delighted, suggesting he might first arrange for me, at Bayshore's expense, to go through business school before joining the company. Hearing him say this, I could hardly contain myself; I had obviously impressed him, but then this was the name of my game, like doing something extra well when the Commodore was watching! This was the vital break I needed; to have a job to go to and what a job! This meant I would be able to leave the Service and look forward to a future, which I was going to shape for myself rather than be listed as one of hundreds of young officers struggling for seniority. Eight years as a lieutenant, exams, struggling to become a *'two and a half'* (Lieutenant Commander).

After a few days thinking about the irrevocable step I was about to take, by which time *Sheffield* had sailed, I steeled myself for a confrontation with the officer whose duty it was to watch over the progress of each member of the gunroom during their first seagoing experience and I knew it was not going to be easy explaining that I wanted to resign my commission, to someone whose life was rooted in the Service.

When the time came, the mild-mannered naval officer listened, looking more perplexed than anything else and even slightly embarrassed. He just nodded as I said the final words. He couldn't know what I felt. Was I sure, he asked. I told him I had made my mind up. He seemed genuinely worried that anyone would want to turn their back on such a golden opportunity as being in the Navy and want to go back to civvy street, even if it did mean getting into the oil business. He ended by explaining any submission to leave the Service would have to wait until we got back to England, as any letter of resignation had to go direct to the Admiralty and could not be handled by signal. Somehow I had the impression that he didn't really believe me.

Back in the cramped quarters of the gunroom someone had a record on with a calypso going and I was met by the usual raucous hubbub and laughter which went with the first drinks at the end of yet another easy day, with everyone looking forward to the next port of call. A bit subdued, I sat on one end of the Admiralty leather banquettes and had a momentary thought about the step I had taken and the inevitable talk I'd get from my father. He wouldn't do it in the kitchen, he'd take me into the dining room, like he always did when he gave me a lecture, when the Admiral was asleep, or listening to the wireless in his sitting room. God! *That* was going to be awful.

Inevitably, it did get out that Croft was resigning and a few attitudes did change; some of the other nine mids treating me with a little disdain, some even with downright antagonism. Mostly it was just a shrug of the shoulders. It wasn't as though I was going to let any of them down in any of our joint duties even though I knew I had passed the point of no return. I was still going to behave like an officer. I kept my thoughts to myself and life resumed its normal course.

Our cruising days were turning into weeks. Port followed port. Up around the Gulf of Mexico, New Orleans and again south, unexpectedly, to Belize in British Honduras on account of a deteriorating situation in neighbouring Guatemala, before we had ten days back in Bermuda, re-victualling and sprucing up the ship, ready for the next stage of the cruise. Some nights I took a camp bed to the upper deck, with just a blanket for the first few hours before sunrise. In the warm tropical air I sometimes lay and thought of the consequences of my decision to resign, wondering whether the Commodore had been told, but whenever I was up on the bridge his attitude seemed the same as ever.

With *Sheffield* once more back in dock, one afternoon I found myself midshipman of the watch, when a telling portent of the future took place. I had asked to go along the jetty to check the ship's mooring wires, which took me past some storage sheds beside a small side-dock. To my astonishment, there, gently bobbing in the oily water, I saw what must have been hundreds upon hundreds of old leather cordite cases, which used to be for carrying the propellant up to the heavy guns. Short, fat ones, something like leather buckets, complete with handles, and others, of more slender proportions, which little did I know at the time were much sought after for use as waste-paper baskets and walking stick and umbrella stands and each worth twenty pounds or more in the antique market. All, I could see, were riveted down the seams with large copper studs and appeared most beautifully made and I remember only too well thinking what a waste it was to 'ditch' things like that. I presumed they had been cleared out from one of the sheds, as the Bermuda dockyard was soon to be closed down. I thought no more about it at the time, but only a few years later that sight came back to haunt me, thinking of all the naval detritus which might well have value in a second life.

Before resuming our flag-showing duties further along the eastern seaboard of the United States, *Sheffield* sailed for one last time back into the Caribbean, by way of Cuba and some of the smaller islands, to Barbados. I still had no letter from Trinidad and I was beginning to wonder whether I would ever see my Yugoslav again.

Now, the cruiser lay at anchor off Bridgetown in Barbados. Close by the landing jetty there, the town's Yacht Club is situated, where rum, mixed with fresh limes and treacly sugar-cane juice cost next to nothing, and it was there one evening that two other mids and myself got hopelessly drunk and found ourselves well after midnight, staggering about the beach. The last officers' launch had long since returned to *Sheffield*, leaving all three of us quite oblivious as to the serious trouble we were in. Orders were that all midshipmen had to be on board by 23.45 hours (a quarter to midnight.) Officer-like behaviour the last thing on our minds, we lurched, laughing, drawn with abandonment, towards the noise of pulsating, tinny music coming from a row of corrugated iron shanties which lined the road above that part of the beach. What we expected to find, I have no idea, nor did any of us care, I suspect, we were too far gone! From a voyeur's position, just inside the entrance of one of those shanties – the one which had the word 'Club', scrawled in white paint on a length of plank, over the door – I stood agog with what I saw. There were some of *Sheffield*'s crew, crazed with drink, some even dancing in their underpants, stained with God knows what, licentiously swaying to the calypso music clasped to the half-naked bodies of Barbadian ladies of the night. Even though I was hopelessly lost to drink, the sight left an indelible impression thereafter, of the low-life enjoyed by our Navy's happy matelots! We were not in a much better state ourselves and one of us had already been sick *and* it was slowly beginning to dawn on us that we were in a serious predicament. Just how were we to get back on board? The lights of *Sheffield* rocked in the gentle swell some quarter of a mile out in the bay... then I had what I thought was a good idea, showing real officer's initiative. Here and there small fishing boats lay beached, all ready for the morning's fishing, and in amongst them small rowing boats were tied up above the high-tide mark... why not use one of these to row out to the ship? We could surely get on board if we were careful enough and had a little luck without being seen by the night sentries on the quarterdeck, by dashing up one of the forward ladders normally only used by the ship's crew returning on late passes, once they had either run out of pay or their supply of French letters. The forward ladders did not warrant night sentries, they were reserved for the officers' quarters aft, below the quarterdeck. It was agreed that it was a good idea.

Stumbling among the boats, we began desperately to look for oars. There were none, so, powered by rum and desperation we tore the thwarts out of one of the small rowing boats and untying the one we had first chosen, and using these short planks as paddles, we set out across the bay towards the lights of *Sheffield*. We made it to perfection, leaping for the forward ladder's platform, with not a soul in sight. Just before jumping last, I grabbed the gangway rope and pushed the gunwales of our small rescue-boat under the dark waters of Bridgetown harbour, hoping to scuttle the evidence of our drunken adventure. Alas, it did not sink entirely, but waterlogged, went slowly bumping down the ship's side towards the quarterdeck. Any moment we expected to hear a call over the tannoy for the emergency watch to turn out. We ducked below to our chestflat and I wondered just how far out to sea the thing might drift. At least we had made it and there were no alarms. Well done Croft! It never struck me that in all probability the little boat had been some poor black's livelihood and that now we'd as good as sunk the thing!

Since the 18th century it has been the custom for midshipmen to write-up their 'journal' every week and we were no exception, having to give details of the ship's passage, peculiarities of harbours and anchorages and so on. Technical diagrams were encouraged, along with the description of any unusual event which had occurred.

Misguidedly, and I can't think for the life of me how I could have been so stupidly naïve, I wrote up in my journal – in a slightly abbreviated form, playing down the fact that it had been a perfectly good boat we had 'stolen' – a description of how the three of us had managed to make it back on board, adding some complicated excuse as to just why we had missed the last officers' launch. I thought it would go down well – initiative and all that! But when I mentioned casually, a couple of days later, to my two friends that I had written something in my journal about our escapade, they went crazy – *'You resign if you like, but don't get us into the shit, you idiot. I hope you didn't say who you were with that bloody night…'* Luckily, I hadn't, and I thought no more about it.

Our journals duly went in for review some few days later, but nothing happened, until one morning I was reading my letters in the gunroom – one from my mother and good news in the form of a letter from Houston – a follow-up to my discussion with Tom Payne, asking me to keep him informed of my situation, which meant he had been sincere in his offer and that things *were* actually going to happen – when over the tannoy came the quartermaster's voice, *'Midshipman Croft to the Navigating Officer's cabin please.'* At least it was 'please', but then it always was, for officers. I once again faced the naval officer (known unofficially as the 'snotties' nurse,' as it was his responsibility to be in charge of our training) whose job it was to inspect our journals and to whom I had made a clean breast of my wanting to resign. Oh God, what now, I thought. It never crossed my mind it was going to be about my journal, it had gone in with all the others, days ago!

He seemed more perplexed this time, rather than fuming; he had difficulty in summoning up the right words to describe just how utterly disgraceful he thought my actions had been, *'Stealing a boat, is what you did Croft. I won't ask who was with you. As to your so-called initiative…'* he was at a loss to understand my behaviour. The result was six weeks stoppage of leave and my reprimand would be noted in my end of cruise report. That last part didn't worry me too much, but what did make me regret what I had done, was that stoppage of leave would mean that I was going to miss seeing Boston, New York, Rhode Island and worst of all, St. Johns Newfoundland – because it was there that I knew there was a chance I might meet up again with a lovely girl I had once danced with at Dartmouth, where at the time her father had been the medical officer and I had heard since that he had been posted to St. Johns. We had done decidedly nice things together I remember, during *and* after the dance put on for the junior cadets, who were celebrating the end of their initial year at the college. Heady memories those can be – puppy love, all of fourteen years old, in your best number one doe skin uniform, clasped to a girl while a Royal Marine Band played slinky music...! Even at that age, the Admiralty seemed to be hoping to give you some grounding in the field of social etiquette and how young officers *should* behave! Some hopes alas! Anyway, memories or not, I was going to miss the chance of any misbehaviour in St. Johns!

As to the flagship's last port of call, at the St. Lawrence, the fact that I was going to miss getting ashore in Montreal didn't worry me in the least – I had heard it was something of a gloomy city anyway – but the thought of the girl and opportunities pained me!

However, it was not all bad news, because as it happened, I did manage to sneak ashore in Baltimore, although I was under punishment and confined to the ship, to explore that part of the city near the docks. We must recently have been paid (a midshipman's pay at the time was just over £14 a month!), because somehow or other I managed to buy a cheap shotgun from one of the several gun shops that were to be found in the rough quarter near the waterfront. One of my pubertal dreams had been to possess a brand new gun to go rough shooting with, as opposed to the ancient hammer job I had, carefully oiled and stacked away in my clothes cupboard at home. Now that I know a little more about guns, I realize just what an inferior product my Baltimore fowling-piece must have been, for something costing a little over $20! Before I was forced to sell it, being broke again, to another of the midshipmen however, it *did* play something of yet another dramatic part in the unfolding drama of my fall from grace...

The other episode for which I remember Baltimore, is that hearing from another of the midshipmen who swore he had actually seen it, was that one of my wilder friends in the gunroom had got thoroughly drunk, gone ashore to have a meal at a Chinese restaurant with some girl he had picked up at a reception the evening before, and had tried to do his inebriated best to shag her behind a carved wooden screen in the corner of the restaurant, much to the embarrassment and in some cases the amusement of the diners. Hustled out by two of the Chinese waiters, while being held upright by his mortified girlfriend, he apparently paused by the door and in a loud and haughty voice, said he was so sorry to have disrupted everyone's meals! It was troubling, many years later, when I saw his photograph in one of the national papers as being the commander of one of our new nuclear submarines, and I thought I should write to him and ask for reassurance that in the event of a confrontation with the Russians, his hands and thoughts might be better employed than they had been on that particular evening. He would have laughed I feel sure.

\*\*\*\*\*\*\*\*\*\*

New York. *Sheffield* was tied up on Pier 90, usually reserved for one of the big Cunard liners. Here I sat moody and disconsolate at the gunroom table, thinking of what I was going to miss ashore. I had been the midshipman in charge of the berthing party coming down the Hudson River and saw the famous skyline dominated by the towers of the Empire State and Chrysler buildings, which must be one of the visual wonders of the world. What a place in which to be under punishment!

The ship had passed close to Ellis Island and I had thought of my father and how he had seen it under such different circumstances. I doubted if I would mention anything to him about it when I got back, especially as I could see through my binoculars the faded remains of the words *'Deportation Area'* on one of the buildings.

As it happened, although I never got out to see Manhattan or to go to any of the city's festivities welcoming the flagship, time in New York turned out to be anything but disappointing.

We had been berthed for four days and I was fed up to the teeth with my additional punishment duties, when one afternoon while on watch on the quarterdeck, gazing enviously towards the city I was never going to see, the officer of the watch came out of the wardroom and beckoned me aside. A call had come from our Embassy. The Duchess of Kent, who was on an official visit to the city, had requested that her daughter, Princess Alexandra, visit *Sheffield* while she herself attended some diplomatic function at the Waldorf.

With two other unsuspecting midshipmen who were still on board, he said that I was to report to the wardroom at 18:00 in No. 1's – our best uniforms – to entertain the girl. A Princess! Christ! Fantastic! Some punishment being in New York!

She was delightful. I wonder if she remembers it. The four of us sat on one of the corner seats, in the wardroom, chatting easily without any embarrassment, about life on board the *Sheffield* and where we had been. She was our age, without the least affectation, had very bright blue eyes and a good sense of humour. Just every now and then there was an undeniable, and I think unintentional, hint as to her royal status, but she seemed genuinely interested in us and she exuded more than a little sex appeal, which would have made it interesting if she had been one of the girls at what had now become boring, official dances and you'd been lucky enough to dance with her. I had the impression the three of us mildly amused her that evening and that she had enjoyed herself.

\*\*\*\*\*\*\*\*\*\*

The city skyline looked as dramatic as when we first steamed up the Hudson, when we left for the run up to Canada before returning home. I was still under punishment.

I thought I might try one last trick to get out of it by asking to see the navigating officer, and to make an emotional plea to be able to go ashore, just this once, so that I could visit old family friends who lived in St. Johns and whom I was unlikely to see again if this chance eluded me. I would show contrition and remorse, standing stiffly to attention and then I hoped I could squeeze tears into my eyes. This was a useful, and I think unusual, trick I had found I could achieve, and I tried it as I stuttered my request. Sure enough he seemed so ill-at-ease, seeing me bite my lip, that in a rush of words he said he would substitute my present punishment by additional watch-keeping on the ship's return across the Atlantic. It had worked like a dream.

In Boston, I watched as the city experienced its first hurricane, dramatically blowing itself out, and bringing down the spire of one of the town's most famous churches. And I was broke. I volunteered extra watches, wanting time to think. I had almost had enough of the endless round of partying, the last of which had been an invitation to go to dinner with Bette Davis and her husband Gary Merrill, in their country cottage in Rhode Island. I was thinking of something rather better than meeting two old film stars. I did go of course, under orders, strange as it may seem, and drank wine by the big log fire in their cottage, and was asked about England and how it felt being an officer at such a young age, which all made me feel a little important, but all the time I was thinking of our next port of call, St. Johns, and the girl there. So much for Gary Merrill and Bette Davis!

After half a day's steaming from the fishing grounds off the Grand Banks, *Sheffield* edged her way towards the jetty of the then small and gloomy Canadian town of St Johns, a town of wooden buildings and not much else, although at the time it was an important naval base. This fact did not interest me overmuch, but what did interest me was the fact that it was here I might once again meet the girl with whom I had first danced cheek-to-cheek as a fourteen-year-old Cadet at Dartmouth. After all, I told myself, I had learnt an awful lot in the intervening years.

84

It seemed that I was not to be disappointed. No sooner than the ship berthed, the anticipated notice went up on the daily orders board, stating that all midshipmen were to attend a ball at Government House, the following evening. There was every chance she might be there, I thought.

She was. Now matured and enticingly lovely. So once again, this time in the grandest of settings, it was very close and cheek-to-cheek – perhaps not quite befitting behaviour for a mere midshipman in mess dress, it must be said! Not in front of the town's dignitaries, together with all the officers from the base. That was perhaps what made it all the more exciting.

There had been crested dance cards for the names of each partner you had chosen for every dance throughout the evening. There was only one name on mine and to my huge delight she agreed there was only to be one on hers. We held each other very tightly and I felt the length of her body pressed very close to mine each time the Marine Band struck up some new quickstep or foxtrot. Those were surely the days… and the dreamy tango, all those fleeting, transient, boyish emotions, forgotten in the heat of the moment, thinking that the girl in your arms was the love of your life! So much for my enigmatic Slav in Trinidad and dreams of dancing to *'Begin the Beguine'* under the palms – so much for everything except the present.

When the ship did leave, I just hoped the Surgeon Captain's daughter would remember a midshipman and his last goodbye that night and how we became entangled in the gear shift of her father's Pontiac, laughingly unembarrassed by the love-stain left on the seat fabric!

The *Sheffield* sailed next morning. Pinned to the 'Daily Orders' notice board in the gunroom were details of this last part of our cruise. It remained only to take on fuel in Gaspe, where three days at anchor allowed time for the ship to be spruced up before passage along the St. Lawrence to Montreal, where we were to 'show the flag' for the last time. Four days there and then it was the Atlantic and home.

I was beginning to be assailed by bleak thoughts of what awaited me back in England – stark reality and whether I had made the right decision, and the finality of actually submitting my letter of resignation, a process which I gathered could be traumatic, long drawn-out and demeaning, with the accusations of disloyalty to what was then called the 'Senior Service'. Worst of all was the thought of having to face my father: the withering look and the none too subtle jibes as to my being feebly introspective and knowing nothing about the real world. I could do without that.

Before reaching Gaspe, on one early morning watch, a young marine about my age, was acting as my quartermaster's mate. I particularly liked him and at some stage I must have told him that I had bought a shotgun and he asked me if he could borrow it, as he had been told anyone could go shooting in the wild country there. It was something I would have liked to do myself, but I was now once again under punishment, so I loaned it to him and on the morning we left Montreal he returned it.

Tradition had it, although not encouraged, that midshipmen were allowed to accept an offer of what is called *'sippers'* (a taste of the seamen's naval rum ration) by way of thanks for some small personal favour the young officer might have given the seaman – in this case a Marine – to be taken in seamen's mess after 'rum up'. And so I accepted the young marine's offer that morning, soon after the rum issue at 11 o'clock. By noon, the ship was humming with activity; the call for *'leaving harbour stations'* was to be at 14:00 and as it happened, I had very particular responsibilities that day, working with the Navigating Officer up on the bridge. But naval issue rum is, or was before the Admiralty thought it best to forget this tradition, incredibly strong. By the third sip I was rendered completely stupefied. Numerous of those famous Barbados Yacht Club rum and fresh limes were like baby's milk in comparison. I was a goner! I didn't even remember climbing from that mess-deck to the midshipmen's sea-cabin below the bridge, (where I collapsed), let alone hearing the call to *'Harbour Stations'*. I just remembered one of the midshipmen shouting at me as he slid the cabin door open: *'Christ Jim, you're meant to be on the bridge!'* A sudden rush of adrenaline sent me stumbling through the cabin door and up the ladder, bursting drunkenly onto the bridge, while the electric voice of the tannoy system barked out *'hands to harbour stations'*. My befuddled brain was struggling to tell me that I was supposed to have been up on the bridge an hour ago, where my duty was to have been to make ready all the charts on the navigation table, ready for leaving the harbour.

I saw the Admiral sitting in his high chair watching proceedings; the Commodore was on one of the wings of the bridge beside the Navigating Officer, who had a megaphone and was giving orders as the cruiser's wires were slipped. Oh God, oh God, I thought to myself, this is the end… I had to do something. I lurched for one of the old wind-up phones to make contact with the engine room to check what revs had been ordered for leaving harbour, one of the vital duties of the navigation officer's assistant, which I was supposed to be! I barely uttered a couple of slurred words before everyone on the bridge knew that I was hopelessly drunk! An instant later the communications officer forcibly took me by the shoulders and pinned me to the back of the bridge, with orders to stay there. The other officers, including Admiral Stevens, just gave me a quick look of disdain. God knows what they must have thought. This was going to be the end of my career; quite unplanned and ignominious in the extreme. Some wretched little snotty who couldn't take his drink and at harbour stations of all times! I stood rigid with fear, in dread of the impending consequences, confidence of any kind totally drained away. I knew it was almost certain I would be discharged for conduct unbecoming an officer as soon as we got to Portsmouth. Shame for the ghost of Captain Babb of the Royal Yacht "Victoria & Albert".

And there I stood, almost to attention, unmoving, waiting for some dreadful naval sword of Damocles to fall, watching the grey point of the ship's bows as she swung round each turning point in the St. Lawrence river, until the light faded. In the dusk, someone, I don't know who, just said: *'Croft, go below.'*

This was not what I had planned. My thoughts were full of gloom. It might have almost been better if I had actually scarpered from the ship in one of those West Indian Islands, as I had on more than one occasion seriously considered, having passed the midshipmen's exams only a few weeks earlier and done rather well, as much as to say: *'Well there you are Admiralty, if ever you want me again in time of war, here's what I was trained up to be so take me back!'* Now it was all down the drain, just when I was going to get my first gold braid as a sub-lieutenant, and that, under normal circumstances, would have been hugely exciting if I hadn't wanted to resign.

I have never had any explanation for the fact that there were no consequences. One of my own theories is that the C-in-C was a very kind and understanding man. Any official report on the event would inevitably lead to my being thrown out and perhaps he, along with the Commodore, thought it best to keep a young and hopefully promising young officer *'in'*, whatever his inclinations might have been at the time, which would themselves in all probability fade away over the next year or so anyway. Or maybe it had been the Commodore himself? Perhaps some very small affinity had existed.

\*\*\*\*\*\*\*\*\*\*

They were not particularly happy days those last few, still unable to believe my actions had been overlooked. We eventually sighted land, past the Scillies, and all the wider view of life I'd been privileged to see in the West Indies and America faded miserably, overtaken by thoughts of possible punishment to come followed by a depressing journey home by railway, through a dreary landscape of still rationed England, and then, finally, the sight of my father pedalling away on my mother's bicycle, wearing his trilby. I knew I would have to tell him everything now.

I had given my home address to Tom Payne and I was now desperate to hear from the Bayshore Oil and Gas Co. to know that the door was still open to me. Once past the deflation of finally securing the ship at her berth in Portsmouth dockyard, my highest priority was to see if there was any mail waiting for me. Anything from Trinidad and, more importantly, from Houston? There was none.

When I finally steeled myself and told my father I wanted to resign my commission and had the offer in America, I got even more of the usual '*You just don't take things seriously enough, do you? And as for all this juvenile introspection and a so-called job in Texas, that's going to do you no good at all chummy*'. Chummy was even worse than being called Jimmy, and was weighted with heavy sarcasm. He wasn't exactly what you'd call understanding.

Now that he knew that I wanted to resign, I tried to be effusive about the last nine months, saying what a marvellous experience it had been, but one thing I decided not to mention was Ellis Island and going up the Hudson. I knew that would set him off against the Americans.

Our relationship was increasingly deteriorating to the point that I avoided being in the kitchen at the same time, if he was there. My mother must have known what was going on and the likely outcome. I just kept on thinking of the number of days it would be before I'd be able to submit my letter of resignation to the Captain of my next ship, now that my time on *Sheffield* was over, so it could be passed on to the Admiralty in the required manner. I knew that events were accelerating. Everything in Folkestone seemed depressingly pointless. I just wanted independence, still hoping that it would be out in Texas, with Bayshore Oil & Gas. I had written once more, telling Tom Payne I was sure it would not be long before I was free to join them. I was desperate to hear back, but I had no letter.

One morning at breakfast while my mother saw to our liver and bacon and prepared the plate of poached eggs for the Admiral, before she took it through to the dining room, my father over-casually asked me where I was off to next. I replied that it was submarines this time, for what the Admiralty called *small ship training*, at HMS *Dolphin*, in Gosport, across the river from Portsmouth, mentioning almost as an afterthought, that I was now a sub-lieutenant – it didn't seem to impress him!

This was all confirmed within a few days when details of my commission arrived, instructing me to serve on H.M. Submarine *Aurochs* for the next six months, together with the usual travel warrant and joining officer's details. The heavy brown cardboard box from Messrs. Gieves arrived at the front door a day or two later with my two new uniforms, each with their gold braid ring on the sleeves all wrapped meticulously in tissue paper, with an accompanying *'With Compliments'* slip. You never seemed to get a bill.

\*\*\*\*\*\*\*\*\*\*

There was a standard letter of resignation that any officer who wished to leave the Service had to write by hand, the first part of which was couched in archaic language dating from the 18th century, to which you had to adhere without deviation, giving your name, rank, your ship and her commanding officer. So mine began: *"I, James Robert Neville Croft, Sub- Lieutenant, H.M. Submarine Aurochs, based at the shore establishment HMS. Dolphin, commanded by - - - - - - - , do hereby humbly submit that I wish to resign my commission in her Majesty's Service, for the following reasons…"* then you could go on to give your reasons – or try to… I always ended my letters with the assurance that I wished to be recalled in time of war.

I wrote the first of my letters on the day I arrived at HMS *Dolphin*, using Admiralty headed paper from the wardroom writing table, once I had checked the name of *Aurochs'* commanding officer from the Orders Board. As bad luck would have it, he was one of the commanding officers who was disdainful of my attitude and made it fairly clear he was not too happy at having me on board his A-Class Boat. (For some reason submarines are referred to as boats in the Navy.) No room for a whinger on *his* boat. Between myself and the other three officers, who all knew of my intentions, a very close bond soon existed and we became great friends. It had been a marvellous surprise to find that one of them had been in the cricket XI with me at Dartmouth, then much senior to me, but now just a friend in our six-foot by eight-foot wardroom. Submariners are a special breed. Individualistic, free-thinking and never keen to abide by what they regard as pettifogging rules. Given the chance, they drink to excess and are womanisers, certainly imbued with an overdose of testosterone, but capable of instant adrenaline whenever challenged. Totally carefree as to dress on board; none would bother to look twice if you even wore drag! In fact, as a mark of having become one of them, I used to wear my mother's old 1920's fur hat very often when we were at sea and I was on watch in the conning tower.

We exercised daily, leaving our berth after we'd taken breakfast in the wardroom, simply walking down to the pontoons by way of the lawns which front the main buildings of the shore establishment, crossing over the gangplank either to go below or take up one's position on the casing or up in the conning tower ready for putting to sea. It was like having a job, when you're back at teatime: a few dives out beyond the Needles, periscope drills a little further out in the Channel, and then back in "Dolphin" Creek, as if you'd just got in from the office and were ready to settle by the wireless and listen to "Much Binding in the Marsh" or, better still, a dance band with Edmundo Ross.

Admittedly, I was always a little relieved to be out of that claustrophobic, cramped and airless war machine, inside which you frequently sensed you were on the edge of danger. One day, when exercising in the Firth of Clyde, the submarine submerged, with air being sucked in for her diesels through the newly-invented *'snorkel mast'*, this new secret piece of equipment decided to shear off with a noise like a small explosion, bringing water cascading into the control room. There followed frenetic moments with each officer frantically doing something while I just stood riveted to the spot, quite useless as I had been given no specific duties, certainly not what to do in any emergency, as the Captain had not considered me capable of taking on any responsibility in his boat! He hadn't taken to me at all!

Like grounding aircraft after some structural failure, although noone was allowed to know it at the time, this episode had meant that all our submarines fitted with the new *'snorkel mast'* – which was almost every one in commission – were withdrawn from operational use.

Happily this little adventure meant we had to make for the secret repair yard at Greenock, not far from Glasgow.

Word had it in those days, that in the cocktail lounge of one particular smart Glasgow fish restaurant, there was almost a certainty that you could pick up the frustrated wife of some local business man who was too bored to go along or still at work. The women, in their turn, must have known they stood a good chance of enjoying an interesting interlude with some young naval officer from one of the ships or naval bases near the Clyde. So going out for a little more than fish and chips was an opportunity you really couldn't miss! And it wasn't missed. Two of us from the *Aurochs* did in fact end an evening by treading the stained upstairs carpet of a seedy hotel, round the corner from the restaurant, drunkenly enjoying the scent of Chanel No 5 and sex with an older woman. When finally we all got back to the boat in the early hours, still heavily under the influence of drink, we laughed at our lurid experiences and agreed that it had all been very worthwhile and for the first time I began to think that being in the Navy wasn't a bad thing at all! It certainly had its advantages.

A very black morning followed. The Captain told me that he had received a signal from the Admiralty, informing me that my resignation had not been accepted. There was nothing I could do. My only option now was simply going to be to turn up for my next appointment, this time the Royal Naval College at Greenwich, and to submit my next letter immediately I got there.

I had heard, by now, stories of officers in the same situation who had taken the step of simply not turning up for their next appointment, only to be ignominiously arrested by the police and escorted back to their establishment for Court Martial, and even after that were only found guilty of 'missing their ship!' and given a reprimand with the appropriate loss of seniority. So had I done this the whole thing would have been a humiliating waste of time and I certainly did not want that. I had no option but to wait.

Little notion did I have before I left the dirty old yard where *Aurochs* was being repaired and I said goodbye to my friends of the last few months, that it wasn't going to be that long before I would be returning to these shipyards on the Clyde. A great deal of dockside property had just been left to decay; space was not at a premium, the big yards were closing down and the Clyde had got tired and when there again, it would be to scratch a living from the muck along her banks, root amongst the detritus of the ship-breakers and in old warehouses that hadn't been disturbed since before the war.

In the meantime, it was back to face my father and yet another confrontation, but this time by way of placating him, at least I could tell him the Admiralty had turned down my resignation, I was still in the Service, with my next appointment the Naval College at Greenwich and my black tin trunk was still upstairs. All along I had known the response I would get when I told him about Tom Payne and the Bayshore Oil & Co. and how I was going to be put through business school and, sure enough, I got it all, again, in the dining room with him sitting in the Admiral's armchair. I tried to explain, but it was completely futile. He thought I was going to become some kind of liability. He asked when and how this offer was going to be legally binding because he wasn't going to let me go on some wild goose-chase at his expense. That was a good one, as if I was on an allowance! But he did know something about the law and people who were under twenty-one being regarded as minors and I was still just under twenty-one, so '*chummy think again!*' And that was it. But I was sure he knew he had lost and I couldn't blame him for the way he got up and stalked out, back to the kitchen.

\*\*\*\*\*\*\*\*\*\*

The Royal Naval College, Greenwich was the naval equivalent of a university. The grand cluster of 17th century buildings, guarded east and west by immense ornamental gates, are only accessible by these entrances or directly from the River Thames in front, from where it is possible to take in the full splendour of Greenwich with the heath rising up behind, all the way up to the Observatory near Blackheath. In the fifties it was still serving as a temporary home for each batch of Lieutenants and other officers who came to be lectured and tutored in such subjects as hypothetical war games, geo-political situations which might involve naval action, together with English history, foreign languages and more advanced mechanical and mathematical studies.

Life there was free and easy, virtually free of discipline, which made for a heady existence, seeing that my pay by this time had risen to just over £20 per month and the Elysian Fields of Knightsbridge and Chelsea were only about twenty minutes away. But this did nothing to change my mind and by the time I had grown accustomed to just what a splendid place it was, breakfasting and dining in the Painted Hall, not to mention simply living in such privileged surroundings, I once again penned my formal letter of resignation. I knew I had totally lost interest in Service matters.

When I was finally called before the Captain and told my resignation had once again been rejected, I recovered fairly quickly from my initial disappointment, on account of life at Greenwich being so pleasurable. However I left the interview as determined as ever, because the Captain had implied I had no idea what I was saying and should instead pull myself together, echoing the words of my father about having no self discipline whatever. So it was on with the easy life of rowdy evenings in the West End, girls and drinking

94

too much and behaving too badly and just waiting... I was still hoping for the long-awaited letter from Houston, or one from Trinidad, but still nothing appeared in the mail.

On one occasion, as usual steeped liberally in alcohol, I took the infamous one-wheeled cycle and rode it almost the length of King's Road with all the traffic backing up behind me, afraid to pass, until the police stopped me for causing a nuisance. Another Sub-Lieutenant in an escorting car – a very few lucky ones by now had one, but needless to say I was not amongst them – explained who we were. It appeared that the police had an understanding with the authorities concerned in those days, allowing them to overlook indiscretions concerning young officers and the episode ended with a mild ticking off, it being suggested that I reserve use of my unicycle for circus performances. The traffic officer at least had a sense of humour!

Too soon it all came to an end. After the start of the second term I contracted glandular fever and collapsed during sports, trying for the javelin record, and left Greenwich for the last time in an ambulance, bound for the Naval Hospital at Haslar, less than a mile from *Dolphin*, looking over to the Nab Tower towards Spithead. From the balcony outside my ward, I could watch the submarines from *Dolphin* going out for exercise each morning and remember time on the *Aurochs*. It gave me a strange feeling and I had a premonition that it was not now to be long before I would be *'out'*. I felt so detached, lying on my iron bed in isolation and musing. I looked at one of the nurses when she came to take my temperature and recalled how one of the Australians had said he'd been in Barcelona for his leave and how he used to lie on his hotel bed while the girl did wonderful things to him with her mouth – now that would be something if it happened here with the nurse I recall, musing. Or perhaps he had just made it up... remember that in the early 1950s sex was very different and only a few of us had heard of the great scandal of a Duchess who had been photographed on her knees, apparently sucking some man whose head was not in the photograph. Besides which even 'sea hardened' young officers who thought they knew a bit about sex, in fact knew very little about its finer points.

Meanwhile I had to endure black thoughts of the unavoidable upcoming postings for specialist courses, due to start in the autumn and it was only going to be then, that I could hand in another letter of resignation. These were the specialist courses, to bring you up to the highest possible level of training before once more joining the fleet. *'Oh my God'*, I thought, *'had Greenwich been no more than a fool's paradise?'* Meanwhile I was not going to be able to send another letter of resignation until I had arrived at the first establishment where these specialist courses were to begin and I was under the command of a new Commanding Officer.

The only good thing about these fairly short courses was that it would enable me to apply for resignation at each new establishment, which meant I could have three or more chances within the next twelve months. I had already endured over two years of this absurd charade, freely admitting to all my instructors that I had no further interest in naval matters and that I now found the fact that I was being forced to stay in against my will utterly unacceptable. The majority didn't understand, some just didn't want to and some were virulently unpleasant in response. God knows, I thought, how much it must be costing the Service to keep me, feed me, let me play on submarines and buy my uniforms at great expense. It seemed to make no sense whatever. Yet who could I appeal to? Who could I enlist to help me? Forget my father. The old Admiral was past it all. My Hampstead godfather was out of touch, of another generation. I didn't want to whinge my way out. A clean break and understanding was all I was looking for.

Released from Haslar early and sent home to finish my convalescence, I drifted into one last summer of tennis and fishing, acutely aware that my father heartily despised my attitude although reproaches were by now left unspoken.

I had managed to borrow £7 from another Sub-Lieutenant and with this I managed to buy an old broken-down Wolsley Hornet. Six cylinders: it didn't matter that it barely went. To have a car in those days was an enviable status symbol – not that I could drive, but I knew I could quickly teach myself, which I did, taking the machine up to Greenwich once – no licence, no insurance, no road tax – so that I could stutter round the establishment's private roads and hopefully impress a few of the other envious Sub-Lieutenants. Eventually after another uninsured, unlicensed trip back to Folkestone the car gave up the ghost and I left it abandoned inside the house gates leading to the old Admiral's garage, much to the contemptuous glances of my father each morning, as he mounted my mother's cycle and pedalled off to his work.

*********

My first course was at HMS *Dryad*, the shore establishment specialising in navigation in all its forms, its aids and their development, including what were in the 1950s new and secret types of radar. The establishment was a large 19th century house, a little way inland, beside the river Hamble. Principally dealing with the sun and stars, along with the natural elements, nautical matters here, I am sure, bred a more understanding and softer officer specimen than say, a torpedo specialist or a gunnery officer. That ordeal was yet to come!

At *Dryad* the atmosphere was more relaxed, coming as something of a gentle reminder as to what life in the Service might be like – member of a boisterous wardroom along with all the other officers – a small room with iron bedstead and Admiralty-issue chest of drawers and stewards at breakfast every morning to prop your paper on its wooden stand; other heads hidden behind other papers, no one talking and the only noise that of purposeful clinking of china cups and saucers.

Here, once again, I carefully penned my letter, humbly submitting etc., etc., and asked permission to see the Captain. In fact it was the Captain's secretary who accepted the letter on his behalf on account of his Commanding Officer being away from base and my interview would have to wait until he returned. At least until then I would not have to face the almost certain indignity of one more confrontation and probable rejection.

I doodled through the lectures, occasionally jotting the odd line of poetry and explaining whenever I could that I was extremely sorry but I had no real interest as I had made up my mind to try for a life outside the Service. I was becoming something of a pariah by now.

I thought I might try ringing the Bayshore Oil and Natural Gas Co. for reassurance, but that I thought, might be pushing my luck and, besides, transatlantic calls cost three pounds or more and anyway I still wouldn't be able to tell them when I would be free to go out to Texas.

The confrontation with *Dryad's* Captain, when it did come, was a repeat performance of all that had gone before – with me doing my best to look contrite but nevertheless full of resolve, while I tried to justify the reasons for my wanting to leave, if perhaps I had not expressed myself clearly in the submission to their Lordships. It was a waste of time. He just looked down at the Admiralty's rejection signal and I heard him mutter *'preposterous, lack of moral fibre'* and then looking up with the slightest smirk of seniority, he simply said, '*Sorry, Sub.*'

\*\*\*\*\*\*\*\*\*\*

After just one week's leave, late one cold March day, I found myself being saluted as I went through the main gate to Whale Island, HMS *Excellent*, the naval gunnery school. The high wall kept out any sight of the outside world where dockyard workers went streaming home on bicycles and caught trolley buses which went whining along all the working-class streets. In 1956 there were few cars about in places like this and any shops there were, were shabby in this part of Portsmouth and singularly uninviting.

Inside those high, dark, brick walls there existed another kind of bleak and alien world where men wore shiny black gaiters and the buildings in which you existed were fronted by one enormous gravelled parade ground some four acres in area. It was here on most days, at some time or other, inescapably, that you were subjected to stentorian shrieks of command which were obviously emitted with cruel delight. Marching, wheeling, halting, drilling; at ease, stand easy, rigid to attention, eyes right, don't move a single muscle, boots grinding on the gravel and gaiters shining.

*Excellent*, the naval gunnery school, was feared and respected by some, loathed by others. All of us had been forewarned that this course was not going to be a very pleasant experience. It seemed that intentionally no improvements had been made inside the buildings since our ships had sailed to Sebastopol half a century before. Stone corridors, cream-painted with dark-brown doors and skirting boards only relieved by an even darker band of green where a dado rail should be. My room, my cabin, the smallest part of my private world where I could think about the Bayshore Oil & Gas Co. and hope for news; stone-floored, no rug, no mat, cast-iron radiator and the usual Admiralty-issue iron bedstead with embroidered counterpane, thin curtains and very cold in late winter. It seemed that someone was out to punish me yet again, regardless of my first gold braid, as if to bring me down to earth, to have me yield to the awful naval stentorian robots who ruled outside on the parade ground. At least being together with the other Sub-Lieutenants through these so-called specialist courses, meant I was with good friends, many of whom sympathised and kept me from falling into a state of abject depression and even after a week's leave it was marvellous to see them again, and to know that whatever lay ahead, it was to be a shared nightmare!

In today's world the regime on Whale Island is epitomised by the performance of the naval gun-crews who smash and crash their field guns with the indescribably precise movements, in their annual display at the Royal Tournament. Not the slightest error nor the minutest deviation from orders is acceptable. You had to run between lectures like automatons, with quick piston-like movements of your arms, fingers bent close to the palm of the hand at the second knuckle. It was so ingrained in some who had become instructors that it was not unusual to see such men in the wardroom bar, so totally absorbed into this alien and desperate world of one man's power over another, standing still, stiff as ramrods, fingers still bent at the second knuckle, while their glasses of 'horse's neck' were raised, as if by numbers, in rigid jerks, towards their lips. It is no exaggeration, I have seen this.

It soon became evident that sport was going to be the only worthwhile relief. I knew our course officer could not refuse a request to leave the establishment at any time in order to take part in some inter-service match. Luckily I had managed to play number 3 string for the Navy squash team, which allowed me the odd day away, sometimes up in London, which came as a soul-saving reprieve from the grinding bestiality of gun-drills. I won no friends among my instructors, who, you could tell, were loath to let me go, although they knew they had to and the fact that I no longer had any further interest in matters naval, riled them more. By now knowing there was little point in submitting the customary letter of resignation as soon as I arrived, I left it some time before going to the Captain to explain my request before he passed it on to the Admiralty, together, I imagined, with his recommendation of rejection. To be truthful, I held out little hope here, at Whale Island, the very core of naval discipline, but to my astonishment this base commander, when I did see him, wore a slight smile as he scanned the letter and appeared receptive to what had outraged those other Captains I had confronted. Without appearing to talk down to me he said he would pass the letter on to the Admiralty, and for one moment I thought he understood the way I felt.

*********

My next plan to get away from this establishment of the damned, might well have been conceived as some April Fool's joke:

it was the first day of April 1956, but inside those high walls of HMS *Excellent* there still existed the whiff of 19th century sadism that made me think anything was worth a try.

My idea was to write to the Lawn Tennis Association, somewhat tongue-in-cheek, it must be said, applying for a competitor's ticket to the National Hard Court Championships, which were due to take place in Bournemouth at the end of April. I was under no illusions as to my standard of play – competent, maybe even to lesser county standard on a good day. These were the days before the game had turned professional and famous players the likes of Hoad, Pancho Gonzales, Laver and Sedgecombe were the leading lights of tennis, touring the world, enjoying themselves, as so-called amateurs, picking up a little unofficial money for travel and hotel rooms.

This tournament was the precursor to Wimbledon and important in the international tennis calendar. Needless to say, I had never come across any of the top players who toured the world circuit in those days. I had played a few matches for the Navy in the past year, but I knew that I was hardly in the same class as the Budge Pattys or Sedgecombes of this world, but this was not going to deter me, I decided. If my application was accepted, I could even be lucky and meet some other unknown in the first round. It was an idea of embarrassing cheek, but one worth trying as, if it succeeded, it would allow me at least a few days out of the Hades of the shiny gaiters world, even if I did get beaten in the first round. And so *'living the dream'* as they say, I applied to the L.T.A., explaining that as I had been abroad for the last couple of years they would not have noticed my name in any of the smaller tournaments, but I felt sure that my old L.T.A. coach of Folkestone days – the delightful little Mr. Gay in his long white flannels – would assure them that I was worthy of acceptance as a competitor.

The gunnery officer of my course heartily disliked me and he made life as unpleasant as he could for me. When I told him that it was likely that I might have to go to Bournemouth to take part in

101

the Hard Court Championships, his reaction was little short of venomous – jealousy and resentment oozing out of his narrow little personality.

When the L.T.A.'s reply came, it was to my utter astonishment and disbelief as their letter enclosed two small round competitor's tags for attaching to your lapel and presumably to your racket bag. I don't think I realised just what I had embarked upon but there was no backing out now!

The tournament started on Monday. Every weekend, rather than stay in the wretched barracks, somehow I had to rake up the few pounds necessary either to get home, which was never my first choice, but cheapest with a rail warrant, or better still to be able to take the opportunity of some free or cheap bed somewhere in London. It was always possible to stay at the R.N.V.R. Club off Berkeley Square for just a pound or two; a small partitioned room and a decent breakfast, but in the heart of Mayfair.

And so it was there that I intended to stay on that weekend before Bournemouth, at the same time wangling myself an invitation to a late evening cocktail party for the Navy Skiing Team in one of the reception rooms, which seemed sure to add some not too expensive spice to my stay.

It had struck me that I would have to do something about my tennis kit as I only possessed one pair of acceptable shorts – in fact, cut down from old cricket flannels, but with a certain touch of class. The others were all absurdly long, a little baggy and looking distinctly cheap as they were my Navy-issue tropical shorts and that was not going to create a good impression on court for sure. As for rackets, I had just one, an off-white Slazenger and that was fairly worn and anyone could see the strings were not new, but I would have time before catching the train to Bournemouth, to go along to the firm's H.Q., behind the Strand and on some pretext try to 'borrow' one or two more; I mean you couldn't turn up for the Hard Courts with just one racket!

No. 38 Hill Street, Mayfair, is a fine 18th century building with columns each side of its wide, black coach-painted entrance door. One of the pillars had a large brass plaque in heavily engraved roman lettering announcing to any passer-by that this was No. 38, entrance to the R.N.V.R. Club.

The hall porter took my canvas grip upstairs, with the handle of my tennis racket poking out rather unceremoniously at one end, whilst I signed in at the desk. It was all rather matter-of-fact at the R.N.V.R. – no frills, and the porters must have been used to young officers coming in at all hours, usually very much the worse for wear. I could hear the rising and falling noise of a hundred voices coming from the cocktail party in one of the reception rooms at the far end of the hallway and after a quick but keen look in the mirror in my room, making quite sure there was nothing like dandruff on the shoulders of my charcoal Gieves-on-credit suit, I went downstairs and joined the hubbub.

I recognised a few faces without being able to attach names, from earlier training days. I took in the usual, obvious, bevy of nice girls who were the kind of Navy camp followers, hoping for a life as an officer's wife. The skiers, tanned and easy, stood out among the other young officers who were probably doing the War Games Course at Greenwich and, completing the crowd, I could clearly recognise maybe a dozen or so typical old Navy hands, who couldn't quite give up memories of the wardroom and now lived with small private means in places like Fulham Road and parts of Bayswater. The centre of attention in a small animated group by the near window was a blonde, late twenties I guessed, somewhat short perhaps and on the plump side, but sensuous, with fantastic legs and an appeal that you could almost smell as she smiled, teasing her admirers. Someone, a little drunk already, passed me and smiled and in reply I nodded back towards the window, saying: *'I wouldn't mind that one, would you?!'* Checking for a moment, wobbling his glass slightly, he told me in a low voice that *everyone* knew her; she was Honeypot Schellenberg. Her brother was our Olympic bobsleigh man.

And thus it was that my weekend began by falling for this twenty-eight-year old and her honeyed charms and I did not have to use my room upstairs, but instead shared a small bed and the hiss of her gas fire in a two-roomed flat off Beaufort Street, succumbing to every kind of scent which lingers once two lovers have shared the sweet delights of sexual nectar. Any thoughts of Trinidad and seeing the last harbour lights fading from sight were long gone, so too I suspect, if I had but known it, were my chances of making my mark in Bournemouth!

By 8:30 in the morning my taxi had made Slazenger's, in the city. The pavements were packed solid with phalanx after phalanx of bowler-hatted men on their way to offices, brief cases and rolled umbrellas part of their uniform, as if to say *'I am a civilian'.* Lesser civilians strode with nasty, long, dull-coloured raincoats and carried newspapers. I felt above all that, not in any unpleasant way but with some quiet satisfaction, it was all too mundane. These men inhabited the world of bank accounts and mortgage payments, about which I admittedly knew next to nothing, but all bound to end in happy retirement after a lifetime of treading these pavements on the way to work. I think deep down my father would have been envious of them, but I was not.

The man at Slazenger's counter seeing my canvas grip with the racket handle sticking out, seemed somewhat perplexed by my unusual and urgent request, but as I had made quite sure that the competitor's label was very clearly visible on my bag, his quizzical look relaxed to a helpful smile and *'Yes, I could help you out'. 'Pity you've left all yours at home, sir – one moment, I'll see what I can do.'* He let me try the balance and the weights and asked that sometime I return them, and wished me luck. So now at least I could make some kind of impression with three rackets and wasn't going to look like some aspiring club fool who was totally out of his depth! There was no time to get any decent shorts as I had to make it to Waterloo, get my ticket for the Bournemouth Belle and find the right platform all before 10:30.

The restaurant car was quite full, leaving me little choice but to sit opposite a slightly-built, blond-haired man about four years older than myself I guessed, who was sporting a tiny goatee beard. He smiled as I sat down and wished me a good morning with a Scandinavian accent. He had an air of delicacy and almost preciousness in his movements, fiddling with his cup and making notes on a small pad. He could have been a commercial salesman for a medical instruments firm I thought.

We fell to talking and it was not long before he asked me where I was going. *'To Bournemouth to play in the Hard Court Championships,'* I replied. At this, he leant forward, looking excited and said that was where he was heading. Astonished, I thought to myself that it might all turn out to be much easier than I had first expected if there were to be a few more competitors like this man; why he was well under six foot, with a pinched face and little goatee beard. He'd have no unreturnable service and he was certainly no athlete, so maybe I *was* going to get through a few rounds.

I purposely steered the conversation away from tennis, afraid of showing my ignorance about what had been going on in the various big tournaments during the winter months, in places like Australia and South Africa. I was only guessing that these had taken place – I really didn't know! So now, thinking it was time for a detailed read of the paper, I rose and offered a handshake saying that we'd meet on the platform on arrival in Bournemouth and share a taxi to the West Hants Club. Even his handshake was limp – he could possibly be *'homo'* I thought – some, after all, must play tennis! As I rose, I noticed under his seat, at least six or maybe even eight, neatly stacked Dunlop Maxply rackets and on the side of each shaft were the letters T.U.

Back page of *The Telegraph* – Tennis – Oh my God! There he was, seeded number three, Torben Ulrich the Dane; player of exquisite touch and elegance, runner up in Cape Town 1955. I felt almost sick with embarrassment at my earlier judgement of the man. I was being taught a very salutary lesson.

Sharing a taxi to the venue, I could do nothing but cringingly apologise for my not being a contender in his class, confessing to my reason for having entered the tournament in the first place; I don't think he understood and it didn't go down too well. Him with his small battered cabin trunk, his eight rackets and me with my Admiralty grip with just one poking out, and another couple under my arm.

It went from bad to worse in the dressing room. It was like living in a terrible nightmare of appalling unease as one after another; bronzed and athletic-looking players greeted each other with huge camaraderie, eagerly unpacking trunks and travelling bags and all the time talking animatedly of recent matches and competitions they had played in. I was learning an unbearable lesson, numbed, trying to do up the flies on my cut-down flannel shorts, wondering if my nerves were even going to allow me to get on court.

Through a mist of deep depression I saw the referees' tent with the match schedule board outside, through a crowd of milling early spectators, looking to see which matches were going to be worth seeing. At least, thank Christ, I was on an outside court, playing someone called Mills, mid-afternoon.

I do not suppose for one moment that the *Telegraph* sports reporter had in fact even seen a single point played on court 12 that day, but his paper the next day said that although Croft had struggled against Mills, in a match of 6-0, 6-0, 6-1, he had achieved deuce in a number of games. I discovered later that Alan Mills played for our Davis Cup team, so perhaps even getting one game in the last set hadn't been bad, but then it might well have been charity, as he is a charming man and went on to run Wimbledon impeccably, for many years.

I handed my score sheet into the referees' tent, but word had got there before me. He took the sheet without even a *'bad luck'* and bitingly said that players at the Hard Courts came to get a match of the expected level – and that was that. The put down was the final straw. I decided I would rather go back to Whale Island and face a little embarrassment rather than face the prospect of being pointed out as Croft, a first-round loser, drab in his the old shorts, who had gone out 6-0, 6-0, 6-1.

**********

Now that the gunnery course was nearly over, three of us decided that an evening out might be a good idea, by way of celebration. Accordingly, after more than a few 'horse's necks' (the usual mix of whisky and ginger ale, at the going rate of 4d. a time in the bar) and an early supper in the mess, we rolled out past the sentry at the main gate, heading for Southsea, where we knew of a drinking-club-cum-coffee bar called the Golden Parrot, where there was always the chance you might end the evening with some cheap local girl – God, what snobs we were! – who was out looking for a good time. On the way we stopped off at the Keppel's Head, known as a favourite watering hole for generations of naval officers, and as good a place as any to get drunk! The trouble was that by the time we reached the Golden Parrot, its doors were shut and the three of us had already had far too much to drink. But we were not about to give up. We could hear the enticing sound of music and laughter coming through the fanlight above the somewhat seedy entrance. The fanlight was open and I don't know whether any of us would in fact have been able to climb in, but anyway we were going to try!

Who was on top of whose shoulders at the time, I do not recall, but suddenly we were aware of a policeman beside us, suggesting that *'we desist and curtail our antics forthwith and be on our way without further ado.'*

As I have previously mentioned, mildly robust drunken behaviour involving young officers was looked upon with some leniency by the police. In this instance it turned out that it was a keen young inexperienced policeman who had arrived on the scene. We weren't to know this and began to grandly amuse ourselves, falling about with laughter, hopelessly inebriated. We could well have decided to push our luck further, but common sense just managed to prevail and we thought it best to call it a night, albeit after some jocular defiance as one of us climbed down and we began to lurch across the road, shouting mild taunts back at the policeman, as we made for the late-night cafe opposite the Golden Parrot.

The proprietress behaved like a bitch from the start. You run into quite a few who probably regard young officers, with their apparently easy lifestyle, as being stuck-up and working-class women resent them. First she asked us to keep our voices down and then she made a point of coming over to our table to wipe the oilcloth clean of cigarette ash, which had inadvertently missed the ashtray. To cap it all, the coffee was vile and all three of us left it in the cup, which did not go unnoticed. We left with heavily exaggerated and sarcastic *'thank-yous'* to the woman and, going out into the street through the wretched bead curtain, I felt someone slip something into the pocket of my overcoat. I looked at him and he just gave a small laugh because I guessed, rightly as it happened, that he had picked up something by way a souvenir of the evening's outing.

What happened next had undreamt-of and unimaginable repercussions down the years. The woman emerged from her doorway as we swayed and laughed our way perhaps a hundred yards down the street towards where our car had been parked, undecided whether to risk driving back to Whale Island or to get a taxi. There was no one about. At this point the bitch called out *'You've taken my ashtray. Bring it back here.'* Looking round, we laughed and carried on our way. Almost immediately, this shout was followed by a man's voice telling us to stop where we were. It was the policeman who had, ten minutes before, seen us trying to climb through the fanlight of the Golden Parrot and now he was jogging towards us. This was fun! This was a challenge and the race was on! We accelerated into a very fit young Sub-Lieutenant's 220yd sprint, laughing as the occasional glance back showed the poor man's attempt to catch us was fizzling out. But then a whistle, followed by another from a different direction from somewhere down the quiet residential seaside avenues. Almost out of breath, we agreed that we should make a last dash to try to reach the main road, hoping we could get a trolley bus, or better still a taxi, before either of the two policemen caught up with us. We were confident we could make it. Before reaching the main road, however, we heard a third and closer whistle, followed not long after by the sound of a police car bell, getting closer. The station must have had a call from one of those emergency police phone-posts, you used to see. It was all becoming like some comic scene of hot pursuit you'd see in the films. At this stage we were running hell-for-leather past a row of terraced houses where two had been left derelict after wartime bomb damage. All of us knew the game was up. Suddenly I remembered the thing that had been slipped into my overcoat pocket. I put my hand inside, grabbed the object and hurled it onto the weed-strewn rubble of one of the bombed-out houses. The police car pulled up beside us, the bell stopped and the awful thought began sinking in that we *were* more than likely going to end up on a charge of being drunk and disorderly, after all.

It was now past midnight. Police stations are not the happiest of places at the best of times and now that adrenaline had soaked up most of the alcohol, the three of us were lined up in front of the station desk to face the sergeant on night duty. He had doubtless seen it all before, and showing just the slightest sense of humour, in a kind of resigned voice he just said, *'Well now, let's see what to do with all this'*. The Golden Parrot policeman was now standing beside us, and sitting on a bench was our unpleasant coffee bar proprietress, looking as unpleasant as ever. Names and addresses were recorded. HMS *Excellent*, Whale Island. The sergeant then went across and spoke quietly to the woman. None of us could hear what he said, then he went to an inner office, where we could hear him on the phone again. On emerging, he said he was sorry but we would have to spend the night in cells as the woman was pressing the charge of the theft of one of her ashtrays. You could tell he did not agree with the decision, but the law in all events had to be followed. In disbelief, one of my friends blurted out he was prepared to pay the woman fifty times the cost of what turned out to be a Brickwood's Brewery ashtray, if she would drop this ridiculous charge. There was no reaction to his offer and the woman just got up and left. Now, all braces, belts and ties were removed and someone who I thought was maybe an inspector out of uniform looked in and nodded to the sergeant who said it was agreed that we should all three share one cell.

Our appraisal of the situation was not a very hopeful one. We knew we were in for it. There could be no leniency now, no overlooking the fact that three Sub-Lieutenants from *Excellent* had been charged with stealing. My God, this could mean anything, I thought, perhaps even court martial and dismissal from the Service. By now it had dawned on my two shipmates that they particularly, having chosen the Navy for their careers, were in dire straits. As for myself, although I never wanted it to end like this, I thought in all probability this was going to mean the end of my own time in the Service and that the acceptance of my resignation would be immediate, if not being given a formal discharge for behaviour unbecoming an officer.

Naval transport with an escorting officer came down to the station to collect us at seven the next morning. The man was seriously not amused. Each of us had no more than a couple of hours sleep. We asked if we could retrieve the car we had left somewhere near the Golden Parrot in Southsea, to which the emphatic reply was, *'No. Your course officer has ordered that you return forthwith to Excellent, change into uniform and muster by the main entrance at 9:15, ready to be taken to the Magistrates Court. Your case is to be heard some time before 11 o'clock.'*

The same, unamused escort officer accompanied us in a dark-blue R.N. Bedford minibus, to the Magistrates Court in Southsea. The full gravity of our predicament had now sunk in. After a brief wait, while clerks to the court, policemen and sundry small-time local reporters passed us as we stood waiting in the corridor we were called forward by a grim-faced usher, through a door out into the courtroom. Four magistrates faced us on their bench, unsmiling, under the Royal Arms which hung on the oak panelling behind them. Two or three policemen, who appeared to serve no purpose other than to add gravity to the proceedings and maybe stop us escaping, stood around, including the one we had encountered at the Golden Parrot. Someone called out – *'Case number four. A charge of larceny. The defendants to the dock.'* At which we were ushered into the courtroom. My brain was going numb, but at the same time I was not aware of a feeling of being cowed, as it all seemed completely ludicrous. First to take oath was the over-zealous policeman who had initially tried to stop us. He recounted the events in sequence in the usual flat monosyllabic police language. Next came the driver of the police Wolsley who again with incisive monotony stated that: *'Whereupon I did see the three accused proceeding in a northerly direction along Beechwood Avenue and I did see the accused, Croft, throw an object into the bombed premises of number 17 Beechwood and after a search of the aforementioned, was found, your worship, exhibit A'...'* at which the clerk moved across to a table below the bench and took up a broken earthenware ashtray, holding it up for all to see. At this point I could contain myself no longer and to the astonishment of the entire court, I burst into laughter! The chief magistrate's gavel hammered onto his desk. *'This is no laughing matter, apologise at once. I will not tolerate this kind of behaviour in my court'.* I could see the escorting officer from *Excellent* scowling at me from the public benches.

A few minutes after my outburst, we were all found guilty of larceny, each fined £5 and, looking suitably contrite, forced to make a public apology to the proprietress of the coffee bar. We were then led from the dock to the rooms beneath the Court, where our combined fine was paid before being passed over to the sergeant whose job it was to fill out the record sheets. Before this could be done, however, one last indignity had to be endured, as numbered slats were passed to us to be held across our chests so that the appropriate photographs could accompany our criminal records. The police photographer aimed his camera and the magnesium bulb did its job and the mug-shots of three upstanding young naval officers had been taken. We were now, by law, each of us a convicted criminal! The charge, according to the records, states that *'we did feloniously steal one ashtray, the property of...'* How times have changed!

Although I have been to considerable lengths to find out whether the records – and in particular those mug-shots– still exist if only to show what a complete 'wrong' un' I had become – the police were sadly unable to unearth them after nearly half a century and I only have a cutting from one of the Portsmouth papers which records this most scandalous of events.

Down in the cells however, the duty sergeant had to some small extent restored one's belief in human nature; at least he smiled and visibly warmed to the absurdity of what was going on under the courtroom as he filled in our record sheets. He looked up with such remarks as, *'Now Sir, what kind of places would you say you frequent? Dog tracks? Billiard saloons? Tattoo parlours? Brothels, Sir? – Think that might be what's called for, don't you Sir? And scars Sir, any razor slashes, cauliflower ears and the like? I'll just put a few of these down sirs, if you agree with me!'* He clearly saw the funny side to it! But little did he realise what lay in the future.

And so it all went down, the three of us agreeing wholeheartedly and with much amusement now that the serious part upstairs was over.

However, going back to Whale Island did not promise to be fun and it dawned on us all that the world of rigid discipline which awaited us was going to be very unpleasant, judging by the unsmiling demeanour of our escorting officer.

We certainly had a tale to tell when all of our course met for lunch and everyone agreed we were in for it but I did detect some slight admiration for the way we had got ourselves into the deepest water possible and had survived this far! Just a little smugly, the general reaction was *'Glad I'm not in your shoes though...'* and I can't say I blamed them! But they were good friends.

I am only guessing that the naval authority had thought that the worst punishment we could endure would be to be left in doubt as to what the final outcome might be, because the only immediate reaction was for us to be confined to base until the course was over, which was only in just over two week's time. After this, with a three-day leave break, which was customary, we were due to meet again in Lee-on-Solent, at HMS *Daedalus*, the Naval Flying School for our introduction to both land-based and carrier operations. There was no mention that the punishment would run on once we got there.

I just thanked God the gunnery course was over! A long weekend before re-joining was better than nothing; I would have liked to head for London, but being broke, as always, I had no option but to take my travel warrant for Folkestone and prepare to face more of my father's withering displeasure. I would not dare to tell him about the larceny business, however fatuous.

*********

There had been two significant developments during my time away at Whale Island. One was that the Admiral's jaunty walks in his homburg, down to the Masonic Lodge, were probably over for good as he had been taken ill and was now in a nursing home, unlikely to return, my mother told me.

The other event was initially exciting, in that instead of a letter from Houston, which was something I had been hoping would arrive any day, a parcel awaited me, with colourful U.S. stamps on it, franked by Customs. I unwrapped it in the kitchen. My father was home from the office and it was with his usual look of disdain and in this case with exaggerated interest, that he watched me take the lid from the large, smart, cardboard box with the name Abercrombie & Fitch, written across the top. Folding back the tissue papers, much to my astonishment I found two beautiful, light-grey Stetsons inside.

It so happened that my father had something of a hat fetish and had more than once mentioned the name of Locks of Pall Mall and Lincolns, of the Burlington Arcade, where some time in the better days of the past, he had been a regular customer. Seeing the hats he gave an unusual smile of appreciation as I took them out to see if either would fit, even before looking for any enclosed letter. Although they came as a complete and exciting surprise, these mementos of *Sheffield*'s stay in Galveston, all I really wanted was a letter saying the offer of business school in Houston was a firm commitment. Unfortunately there was no letter on Bayshore Oil & Gas Co.'s headed paper, only a smallish hand-written note on one of the corporation's cards, saying: *'Thought you might like these Jim. Best of luck – Thomas P.'* Not a single word like, *'When are you coming out James?'* I just stared at the card for a moment: it gave me a cold shiver of finality seeing that typical American writing, somehow telling me that this was perhaps the end of my dream and that if I did get out, I would have no job waiting for me, which was one thing that had always strengthened my resolve to leave the Service. I had simply made them wait too long.

My father's only remark, having glanced down at the note, was a terse: *'Well I could have told you, they're all big talk. It seems to me that you won't be hearing from him again.'* I suppose you had to hand it to him; my father knew more about life than I did although I was loath to admit it. Later that evening I went upstairs to my room and wrote thanking Tom for the two hats, yet again saying that I hoped it would not be too long before my resignation would release me so I could take up the offer of business school in the U.S. I just could not accept the possibility that the whole affair had been wishful thinking all along.

\*\*\*\*\*\*\*\*\*\*

I travelled down to Portsmouth a few days later, taking the ferry to the Gosport side and joined HMS *Daedalus*, the naval flying school, on a late spring evening, pleased in my subdued mood to be re-joining my course companions once again.

The initial outlook for the course seemed pleasant enough, compared to what was now behind me at Whale Island. Our cabins were comfortable little rooms in freshly-painted wartime wooden buildings and the mess had an air of relaxation. No stiffness, nothing over-regulated. It seemed an almost suburban, seaside existence, being able to stroll out of the main gate and down to the beach as the jets screeched out at intervals over the Solent.

I tried to put to the back of my mind the fact that one of my best Dartmouth friends, a few terms senior to me, who had qualified as a pilot only a few months back, had been killed taking off from an aircraft carrier on exercises. He had lived just outside Folkestone with his widowed mother and when I had first heard about the accident, it made me think that life was never that straightforward. I thought his mother was terrifically attractive, and sexy. She must have been at least forty, was very good-looking and had even taught me to slow-foxtrot which had given me a hard-on!

Classes for the first two days gave us a general introduction to naval flying practices together with the theory of aerodynamics. Some were keen to get into the air, but I was more concerned with the possibility of an inter-services tennis match against one of the Hampshire regiments and I found myself enjoying the walk past the grass courts on the way to the lecture room, thinking I could just bear the Service if it was always going to be like this and also I did not feel under immediate pressure to present myself to the course officer in order to go through the usual ritual of request and rebuff, ending up feeling depressed and sidelined. I would wait a week or so for that.

Day three was fine enough for flying. It was time for our first 'practical'. This meant light-khaki overalls, lots of zips and straps, brief explanations as to procedures for ejection seats and parachutes and then out across the tarmac with our instructor pilots – no older than their mid-twenties, leading each of us to their own silver and blue Sea Venom jet fighter. Word had got around that I wasn't exactly what you'd call committed to Service life and my pilot had obviously heard about it too, as no sooner than we had both strapped into the side-by-side seats of the trainer, just before starting up the engine, without a smile he said *'Well, let's give it a go, even if you aren't interested, shall we?'*

The exhilarating power of the jet's Rolls Royce engine soon had us airborne, climbing away from the Solent below, with the entire landscape of Hampshire flattening out like the page of an Atlas. It soon became clear that my instructor had no sympathy for my obvious nervousness as the jet banked and rolled. My hand gripped the shared joystick firmly and my feet were attempting to follow his instructions, but my mind was in another world. Memories and thoughts took shape as landmarks far below marked events which had taken place across the last ten years.

Tilting below the aircraft's wings was the coastline of Christchurch leading on to the broken cliffs not far from where my prep. school had been. As we banked again, beyond Southampton I could see Portland Bill and the snaking road that led to Portsmouth. Now, right underneath the slowing jet, lay Southsea, scene of my recent infamy and then the back reaches of the great dockyard creeks where spectral lines of our mothballed fleet lay anchored, now home to *Sheffield*, empty of its happy crew and our handsome Commodore Campbell-Walter – all of another time and another experience, as were the awful blockhouses of the gunnery school, Whale Island, which I could see, looking out across the black creeks towards that dead fleet of ghosts.

Had the day been one of perfect visibility, to the West I could almost have seen the edge of Somerset and the countryside bordering the great estate of Earnshill, with its parkland sloping down to the little River Parrot, where I used to watch semors fishing for dace, before prep. on late summer afternoons. Eastwards, had the sky been clear I would have seen the tip of Dungeness, not far from Folkestone – all the last fading memories of youth, until, with a screech of tyres hitting the runway, I was back in the world of my mine-sweeping uncles, living near the Finchley Road, and the old Admiral dying, together with my own frustration, and the fading hopes of my father.

Day four at Lee began with the customary newspaper propped in front of you at the breakfast table, nobody talking, while the stewards served up kedgeree or sausages, and if you nodded, quietly refilled your coffee cup.

Nine o'clock and the tannoy sounded the bugle call for colours when, by tradition, the establishment's white ensign was run up to the masthead, at the start of every day. On once more with the flying suits and into the pre-flight briefing in our Nissen hut classroom, where our instructor began to explain in detail how best to appreciate the exercise we were about to undertake – stalling, at 20,000 feet! *That* was something I was not looking forward to! All of a sudden, there was a rap on the door and our course officer put his head inside, apologised for the intrusion to our instructor and beckoned me outside. Standing in the corridor, the officer read from a sheet of signal paper: '*As of noon, May 26th, 1956*' – one day after my 21st birthday – '*the officer currently attached to Royal Naval Air Station, Lee-on-Solent, James Robert Neville Croft is discharged from Her Britannic Majesty's Service at his own request.*'

It was just after ten o'clock. I had been due to fly in half an hour. Standing in that green and cream-painted corridor, my life, at one sweep of the second hand had irrevocably changed. I recall shivering with excitement and the lieutenant telling me to get my things together, ready to go to Whale Island for my discharge papers, back pay and travel warrant home. I had no time even to look back through the glass door and I left my friends listening to the fading sound of my black shoes on the cement floor of the instruction hut.

On arrival at Whale Island , still in my Sub. Lieutenant's Uniform, I remember walking purposely very slowly across the dreaded gravel parade-ground, in full view of anyone looking out from the Gunnery School buildings, on my way to draw my final pay, change and pack my grip. Just a few weeks before, I would have been running, arms piston-like, fingers bent at the second knuckle and it was not many moments before I heard voices shrieking... '*at*

*the double that man there…at the double, report to me, now, at the double!…'*
My only response was to carry on calmly walking, without so much as a turn of the head, smiling.

I had been told the Commanding Officer wanted to 'have a word with me' before I left and wondered what he might have to say…

Once changed, my uniform stuffed into my black tin trunk, ready labelled to be sent on, PLA, and my grip ready, I again took in that awful smell of antiseptic mixed with polish, as I set off down the corridors towards the Captain's Office.

*'You're going to find life very different outside you know Croft. My son Gervaise went to Downside and became very interested in the theatre, so I do know that the Navy doesn't appeal to all young men.'* At that he smiled and shook my hand and the act seemed both warm and sincere. In that moment it became clear that I had him to thank for recommending that my request to resign should be approved and also, in all probability, why the criminal record episode in Southsea had been so relatively lightly treated. *'Thank you, Sir,'* I said, turning away, and that was it!

I closed the door, even a little sad: that man had been kind. There could have been so many crueller ways to end my naval career and going out through the gates of Whale Island on my way to the station meant nothing. I got a salute from the sentry, and went to wait for the Fratton Park to Upnor trolley bus to take me to catch my train to Folkestone.

\*\*\*\*\*\*\*\*\*

I have always liked train journeys, however this was like no other, so agitated was I with excitement, tinged with worry and foreboding, my mind flooded with desire to wallow in non-conformity and enjoy the individuality that all those naval minds had found so out of place.

Apprehension crept in on my journey to Folkestone. There had been no news from Houston. I had no bank account, no driving licence, no qualifications worth speaking of and a father who'd had to take all my Post Office savings, leaving me with just about enough money to last two or three weeks. On top of this, I was going to have to face him. I just wanted to get away, go abroad, anywhere, until I heard from America. I'd sell the old Wolseley Hornet, sell any item of uniform I could, maybe even try to write an article for a paper or a short story on the portable Olivetti I'd bought on instalments, hoping to get down some of my poetry.

When, later in the day, my father pedalled in from the office, he was not only shocked to see me, but he brought with him all the expected reactions to what he called my absurd, irresponsible, juvenile behaviour. We sat in the dining room and as usual he went through the entire gamut of the Americans being unreliable and how I would have to pull myself together – just look what my brother had done ... got his house near Fareham and soon going to be a Senior Lieutenant. Maybe I should think about taking up teaching. I could have hit him when he said I'd better just forget about America. He said he knew someone at a firm called Gabbitas & Thring, where they specialised in placing unqualified and down-at-heel members of the gentry into the teaching profession. He particularly relished saying the bit about 'down-at-heel.'

Yet again, I had pissed before my water came it seemed and he wasn't going to help me out!

My old Wolseley went – towed away to the breaker's yard – £3. Clothes and a few pairs of black navy shoes, all in the tin trunk, wheeled by bike down to a second-hand dealers not far from the harbour, £12. With this, together with the remainder of my last pay, I felt ready to equal Hemingway on his epic wanderings around Spain and the Mediterranean. I would take my Abercrombie & Fitch Stetson, I'd take my typewriter, get a ticket to Paris, get out to the suburbs and then try to get a lift to anywhere in the south. This seemed a good idea, but in the two weeks before I took the boat train out of Folkestone Marine, I kept my plans to myself, trying to lie low.

The old Admiral had apparently become very frail by now and barely recognised my mother whenever she went to see him in the nursing home. Occasionally now, we used his sitting room, rather tentatively just in case he suddenly revived and came in to discover how we had all abused his hospitality in his absence. I particularly liked the two armchairs and how one could walk straight out of the French doors right onto the lawn, rather than go round the back path by the coal bins. My mother did a little gardening and I knew she was upset about me, but said nothing. She was a good woman and it must have been difficult living all those years with my father. Years ago I had discovered a leather box full of old love letters under their bed and I knew there were a pair of riding boots in her wardrobe, so she must have enjoyed better times and been happy before the war.

I could not resist one last fling on the tennis courts down at the Pleasure Gardens Club, and there one afternoon I joined a group of members at the clubhouse window, watching a sun-tanned girl playing smooth, classic forehands with impressive ease on one of the shale courts. She turned out to be a Dutch girl called Elna and I managed to get an introduction.

We played each day until I left. We liked each other, we both loved playing tennis and it became clear that our involvement was going to lead to more than just tennis. Our encounter was brief but serious and she said that if I ever came to Holland to get in touch, as her family had a private court at their summer house on the coast.

Luckily I did not have to wait for a passport and there was therefore nothing to delay my departure into the wider horizons of my imagined Bohemia. I also had a plan. Yet again, in a foolhardy and impractical way, it all revolved around a girl. Not the tennis player – she would have to wait! – but another, this time, a ballerina, who danced for the Ballet Rambert. Her company happened to have been performing in Havana when *Sheffield* had been there. We met at one of the receptions and found we shared an outlook as to how we thought life should be – painted with a broader brush than most would appreciate once you gave your emotions and imagination a chance. All hopelessly sentimental stuff of youth! I had told her about how I was hoping to leave the Navy and spend time, quite free, doing something like *'bumming around the Med'*, and after that I was going back to America into the oil business. I had hoped I might see her in London, where she told me she had a flat in Ecclestone Square. I would have done once the cruise was over, but I hardly ever seemed to have the fare to get to London, let alone enough to give the girl an evening out and I never saw her again. But I did remember her name – Phillida – and the name of her friends, who she said owned a yacht moored down in Cannes, where she was sure they would welcome me as a friend and find me useful, crewing for them. So that was where I would head to.

I left the house before my father was up. A stylish-looking plastic American-type valise, with a few clothes, Stetson and typewriter, together with the tennis racket Slazenger's had given me a few months before, made up my baggage.

After a few mild adventures, I arrived in Cannes, where I found a cheap room for the night not far from the waterfront.

With limited money it was imperative that I make a move to find the yacht Phillida had talked about. I had already spent more francs than I had bargained for, first in a smart restaurant I had dared step into, near the Carlton Hotel, where I had some kind of cocktail and watched the women, hoping I looked at ease in such opulent surroundings. And then, everything going to my head, I foolishly went to Juan-les-Pins and into the as yet only dreamt of world of Casinos! This was the life! There, even more of my meagre assets were dribbled away at the roulette tables. And this was on day one! The only trouble was I had stupidly forgotten the name of the yacht! At least I knew the name of her friends and I felt sure it was not going to be too difficult to find them.

I was up early and headed off to the harbour. Trying to appear as casual as possible, I asked the first person I ran across speaking English, and asked him if he knew Rex and Barbara Leppard. I had forgotten the name of their yacht, but the ballerina had told me they were almost certain to be in the harbour throughout the month of June. In fact, the man, who spoke English, was a Dutchman, whose own small yacht was moored alongside a converted MTB, with the name "Ginasal" on its stern. He seemed very friendly – yes, he knew the Leppards. They owned the "Dawnlight", but they'd left for the Greek Islands the week before. I must have looked crestfallen. *'Hoping for a bit of crewing are you,'* he said smiling. *"The Ginasal might take you on. Camper Nicholsons Yacht Agency up the town's the place to ask. The captain's another Dutchman like myself. I think they've been chartered by some old American widower who's a cripple. He'll be rich: it's worth a try!'*

I saw the agent at Camper Nicholsons and was duly taken on by the skipper of the "Ginasal", as crew.

Now an invalid and long retired, the old American had once owned the Penny Bank of some town in the mid-west. Sitting in his wheelchair, he was wheeled along the jetty by his nurse companion, a woman of about fifty, who together with help from me and the other temporary crew member, a wandering Scot, somehow managed to get him aboard, where he sat propped up in the large stern cabin. I was told we were going on a two-week cruise, down the Italian coast.

Within no more than a day or two, a vicious hatred developed between "Ginasal's" captain, a Dutchman by the name of Boomkens, and myself – he was uncouth, unpleasant and worst of all, incompetent. As so often it all began with jealousy. He loathed me for having ingratiated myself with the American and his nurse. I became their friend and was almost constantly in or close to their cabin chatting about America or helping them by translating if they managed to get ashore to do some shopping.

It came to a head in San Tropez, where I had been asked to go ashore and get some special food the old man was asking for.

Boomkens' wife was the cook and neither he nor she took kindly to being sidelined by a fresh-faced young Englishman, especially one who professed to knowing something about the sea. Boomkens warned me off and implied that it wouldn't do my pay any good if I insisted on spending most of my time aft. The poor Scotsman told me that he'd had no pay for more than a month but this didn't overly concern me, as meanwhile I was kept happy with the almost daily 'tip' from the old man, along with the leftover change from shopping ashore, which I was told I could keep, so things could have been a lot worse.

Before the end of the first week, the "Ginasal" had only reached San Remo.

At the start of the second week, "Ginasal" still lay in the port of San Remo. Clearly we weren't going far. The nurse told the skipper to return to Cannes, as the old man had had enough. By now I knew I couldn't take much more abuse from Boomkens, and I made up my mind that as soon as I got paid, I'd get out of Cannes and take the Blue Train to La Hague, contact Elna and spend some time playing tennis. I had already phoned her once from Cannes and she had sounded odd on the phone, at one stage starting to cry. I thought no more about it on that occasion, but when I rang her for the second time, saying I was still hoping to get to Holland for a while, she barely made sense, saying things like: *'If they're nasty to you and say you can't go to the summer house, or I won't be there, don't worry and be sure to try and come.'* Odd!

Back in Cannes, the old man was taken to his suite at the Carlton. There was no mention of any pay. I wanted out, so I decided to force the issue by going to Camper Nicholsons. I made no mention of my intended visit, either to the Scot or of course, to the Boomkens. The agency manager's reaction seemed detached and he merely said he would get in touch with the owners, who *'would sort it out.'* It struck me as suspicious and anyway I wasn't waiting around for someone like Boomkens. I decided I would confront him: as skipper, it was his responsibility to see that his crew were paid.

I got back to the "Ginasal" to find that Boomkens' wife had already served lunch in the wheelhouse. Our skipper had been joined by one of the other charter captains I had never seen before. Making up the last of this four was the Scottish deckhand. The conversation was amiable enough, Boomkens even bothering to include me for once. I was desperate for an opportunity to broach the subject about the pay. Trying to keep a calm voice, almost as if it was an afterthought, I said I had been to Camper Nicholsons.

What happened next could well have come out of a 'B' movie. Boomkens went absolutely puce, his veins stood out, his cropped hair, I could swear, bristled as his shoulders heaved forward. Rising, he grabbed the wine bottle and breaking it on the chart table, swore he'd kill me as he lunged forward holding the neck of the bottle in his fist. In the few seconds he was temporarily held back by the other skipper and the Scot, I slid off my stool and ran, just as he broke free.

Over the gang plank and down the jetty, the uncouth Dutchman screaming oaths, attempting to catch up with me, all to the astonishment of the quayside strollers. The situation, apart from being unreal, was serious, but I was very fit and made it to the streets well before he had given up the chase and I saw him walking back to the "Ginasal". I almost collapsed into the first café I saw, trembling, mouth dry, desperate for a beer. There I took stock of the situation.

All my things were still on board: my passport, typewriter, the little money I had, all in the valise, stuck up for'd in what had passed as my cabin for the last couple of weeks. My thoughts were racing: what the hell was I to do? I was alone in this predicament for sure. Then I noticed the telephone inside, beside the bar. Suddenly I knew the answer – the Consulate of course!

The man's voice that answered my desperate call was smooth but uninterested. *'But this, this…'* I stammered, *'This all happened on a British registered vessel!'* hoping mention of something British would stir him into action. *'Surely, you've got to do something about that?'* A slight pause and then, tiredly, he said he'd make a call or two. *'If you have any more trouble get back in touch … "Ginasal" you say?'* He said there was an international regatta the next day and things were a bit difficult. He obviously thought I was making it up or at least exaggerating wildly and I blurted out: *'But I'm a naval officer.'* A fat lot of good that was!

I was calm enough now to buy another beer. I had six francs left in my pocket and I was wondering just what I could do next, when a man came over. Apologetically he said he had overheard my call, and he thought he might be able to help me. He was a Norwegian reporter, working for the Oslo press, in town to cover the big international regatta. News opportunities interested him – maybe even *'Englishman stabbed to death in Cannes!'* He seemed the kind of man who would have known about tight corners.

*'Look,'* he said, *'nobody would dare to do anything if I came along with my camera. I'm sure I can get your things off for you all right. You must certainly get your passport.'* So, one more beer to re-establish some kind of equilibrium and we set off for the quays. It would now have been twenty or thirty minutes after my escape and by now a small crowd who had seen the incident, had gathered by the "Ginasal" to see if anything else was going to happen. My Norwegian friend made a point of being seen, pushing forward to take photographs, because there at the head of the gangplank stood Mrs. Boomkens, herself a hefty woman, scowling menacingly, blocking any possible access to the boat. And then, on the jetty, to my utter relief, I saw my things – valise, typewriter and even my tennis racket. I thanked the Norwegian profusely, reckoning that this had been enough for one day, but there were further twists to follow.

Going back into town to find somewhere to stay for the night, I passed my friendly Dutchman from the yacht which had been berthed alongside "Ginasal", who agreed we share a beer. So sitting out on the warm pavement under a café awning, I told him in detail what had gone on earlier in the afternoon. He didn't seem surprised. Boomkens was known in the port as a very unpleasant and unpopular skipper, only hired as a last resort. There were rumours hinting at a Nazi connection in the past.

He asked me what I intended to do now. I told him I was hoping to get to La Hague to see a girl I'd met in England. Casually he asked me her name as if by chance he might just know her. *'It sounds awfully grand actually,'* I said *'it's Elna Van Hoveltot Westerflier.!'* At this he half laughed and at the same time looked amazed. *'Wow!'* he said, *'With that name she must be related to the Dutch Royal Family! How the hell did you come to meet her?'* His look varied between one of disbelief and amazement as I recounted the details of the day I had seen her playing tennis at the club in Folkestone and what happened afterwards. I knew that the Dutch Royals were the most straight-laced and dreary bunch in Europe and I had often wondered what on earth the lovely Elna had been doing in a town like Folkestone. It had never occurred to me to ask her! One suggested explanation is that she was staying with the Radnors – Lord Radnor's family owned most of the town and a good slice of the county and judging from Debretts was pretty high in the pecking order of the English Establishment. I shall never know the answer to that one!

Just how I intended to get to The Hague I was not certain however, let alone find the wherewithal on which to exist for the coming weeks. I had virtually no money left, there was no way of getting the pay owed me and after what had happened I had no inclination to hang around Cannes. So after finding the cheapest room for the night, I had an inspiration. I confess I had a pang of guilt when I conceived the idea, which was to go along to the Carlton and ask to see the old man and his nurse and, rather than actually asking for anything, suitably crestfallen, I would tell them I was going to be stuck in Cannes as the skipper didn't want me any more, ending up by saying I hoped things went well for them and how I'd enjoyed doing things for them on the yacht. And just to rub in my predicament, I would mention a fictitious girl I wasn't going to be able to meet, all because the charter company had failed to see that the crew were paid properly, me included.

I think it was the bit about the girl that swung it or perhaps my well-rehearsed 'faltering' voice as I said it, but whatever it was, my plan worked to perfection and I left the Carlton not only with what I said my pay would have been, but also a generous tip from the Penny Banker. I didn't feel the least guilty. He said he knew that things like this happened and thanked me for all the help I'd been.

Next morning, I headed straight for the station to book my seat on that evening's Blue Train to The Hague. Travelling on the famous train heightened my sense of adventure and excitement. But, things did not turn out at all the way I had expected.

Even today I can hardly believe what happened to me on arrival. On presenting my ticket at the barrier, two men moved forward from the waiting crowd and with the words, *'Are you Mr. James Croft?'* took me gently but firmly by each elbow, moving me aside. I stood bewildered, heart pounding, as they asked the purpose of my visit. Before I could answer they suggested that I return to England immediately. That, considering the reason why I had come to The Hague, was a suggestion I was NOT going to take from anyone. I demanded an explanation. Unsmiling, they moved me further aside, as I expostulated fiercely that I held a British passport and had only come up to see a girlfriend. One of them then said that was *'not a good situation'*. I was struck dumb at this, again asserting my rights and saying I would go immediately to the British Embassy if they did not let me go at once. Mention of the Embassy seemed to do something, as one of them let go and went across to one of the station telephones. *'It is not a good idea,'* he said, coming back, and instead of releasing me, he suggested it would be best for everyone if I went with them. *'I have been told you can see Miss Westerflier. You can see her for half an hour. That is all we are permitted to allow you.'* Incredible! How could they know she was this girl I had come to see and on whose orders were they acting?

Out of the station, I was led to a large Mercedes with the blinds pulled down, told to get in and in an atmosphere as cold as ice, I was driven for some twenty or thirty minutes, unable to see out, until, arriving at a large house in what I took to be the suburbs of the city, I was guided inside into a gloomy and cavernous, panelled hall and shown to a door behind which I could hear someone crying.

There was poor Elna, standing motionless, except for heaving sobs, and quite unable to speak long enough to give any explanation as to why she had been told not to see me again. All I could do was to hold her hand while she carried on crying uncontrollably. After thirty minutes, the door was opened and I was firmly asked to come out to be taken back to the city from where I could make my way back to England. Once back in the car, in a last desperate attempt to avert what I really knew to be inevitable, I refused absolutely to leave in this manner, at least until the next day. The men had a brief discussion and I was told they would take me to a hotel, which they would pay for, but I was to leave without fail the following morning.

To say that I was overwhelmed by a feeling of anticlimax and depression falls far short of describing how I felt on my way back through France. I sat in a state of stark and gloomy mortification, realising that what was to have been a dreamy and idyllic summer had suddenly become a nightmare. My father would be vindicated. The uninspiring countryside of northern France slipped by the window as I sank further into a state of dejectedness.

**********

Back in Folkestone I very soon understood that matters had not improved during my short absence. My father had opened two letters franked with the Admiralty anchor, which he pushed in front of me. Only one had been addressed to him. This one referred to him as *'guardian of a minor'* and stated legal action was being taken to claim back a very substantial sum of money for various uniforms supplied during my training. This certainly would have made him furious as there was no way he was going to be able to stump up. The second envelope just contained printed papers. I read these with incredulity. They were call-up papers for National Service! Were *'they'* trying to teach me a lesson and humiliate me? It could not have simply been some clerk's mistake, coming as it did so soon after my discharge. The call-up age was something like seventeen and here I was, aged twenty-one, already having served eight years and as technically qualified as it was possible to be.

I hadn't expected that my father would be exactly overjoyed to see me. His mood after he saw the impression the two letters had inflicted upon me, was one of resigned irritation, as if to say: *'I knew all this would happen'*. He was scornful about everything – especially the fact that the yacht owners in Wisbech had found some reason not to pay me. I'd told him about that, hoping to evoke a little sympathy. At least he did say rather grandly that he would do something about that. He rather fancied himself with litigation and, sure enough, within ten days he produced £45 which he said was all they had sent through to settle the matter, although I'd said they owed me at least £70 for my time on the "Ginasal". I wondered if they had, in fact, sent the other £25!

When he mentioned the Admiralty claim, he thinned his lips with exasperation. He told me I'd have to go to Cripplegate and see someone in a firm called Birkbeck, Julius, Coburn & Broad, his solicitors, with whom he'd spoken already.

As to the matter of the call-up papers, they were my affair, he said. Call-up was the law and my eight years in the Navy didn't count, he added by way of rubbing it in. I decided there and then to go and see the town's MP, Sir Harry Mackeson, about the matter. This I did and the whole thing was very quickly brought to a satisfactory conclusion much to my relief, but I still had no prospect of a job.

As by now I had still not heard anything from Houston, I finally came to terms with the realisation that my job in the oil industry was never going to materialise and that my father had been right all along – it had just been American big-talk. At least I still had my Stetson!

My journey to Cripplegate, to see the illustrious firm of Birkbeck, Julius, Coburn & Broad, was, at a stroke, going to change the entire direction of my life however, because it was in the restaurant car of the 9:05 from Folkestone Central to Charing Cross that attendant showed me to a seat opposite a woman.

\*\*\*\*\*\*\*\*\*\*

**One of M's boys helps remove a ships wheel**

*'What luck,'* I thought. I was in for a pleasant journey tinged with a little excitement, with all the possibilities that sitting opposite such an attractive woman might bring – it was easy to let one's imagination run riot when you are twenty-one! She smiled at me as I sat down and I secretly watched her as she demurely raised the coffee cup to her lips. I could not but help noticing how high her cheekbones were and how her mouth was wide and generous, her lips full, red and voluptuous, enticing enough to give me an instantaneous frisson of desire. Smiling back, I rather rigidly said,

*'Good morning'* wondering whether I would pluck up enough courage to speak to her. As it was, it came easily and it was not long before we fell to conversation and I recall how her eyes, together with that enticing smile, appeared to radiate amused interest as, hoping to impress her, I told her a little of my life so far, which seemed to me to be a natural enough thing to do under the circumstances.

I summed her up as being in the prime of her sexuality, with the kind of classic English good looks of a woman whose portrait you might see on the inside page of *County Life* magazine, indicative of a certain background. We chatted on and it was not long before she told me she was married and I thought I detected the merest note of sadness and indifference in the tone of her voice as she went on to tell me she now had two boys at prep school, as if to say somehow she thought life was passing her by. This made me wonder. What I was sure of was the way a deliciously warm current of mutual attraction seemed to exist between us whenever our eyes met and there was no denying my urge to glance at the seductive cleavage between her breasts, showing above her light summer dress.

I told her how I had been to Dartmouth and served as a midshipman out in the West Indies and how I had tried to write poetry and sometimes, when on watch, I used to scratch pictures of whales and sailing ships near palm-fringed islands on the lids of my Benson & Hedges cigarette tins to while away the hours – this clearly amused her a great deal – any my attempt at poetry seemed to arouse more than a little astonishment. She in turn told me she lived barely a couple of miles from the old Admiral's house, along the coast at Seabrook, in what had years ago once been a Victorian seaside villa, overlooking the sea. I thought to myself that was only fourpence on a 103 bus to get there from the edge of Folkestone, where I was living. Just fourpence and anything might happen! Her husband was currently away apparently, serving some sort of short service commission in the Army. He had been to Marlborough, which I knew to be one of the most exclusive public schools, and after that been wounded in North Africa in the war. When that was over, he had taken up gentleman farming – I think that's what she called it, although I was not sure exactly what she meant – somewhere near Tunbridge Wells, not very far from Chartwell where Mr. Churchill lived. Sounded all very posh to me and very different to the world I knew. The farming had not been a success, children had come along and he had returned to the military. From the way she told me this I had the impression there was some regret she had married at all – the war, pity for a wounded soldier… maybe I was wrong.

The grimy outskirts of New Cross meant we were nearing our journey's end. In all likelihood I was never going to see her again. Little would the uniformed restaurant attendant have guessed that he was unknowingly witnessing a seminal turning point in my life as he might have watched us getting off the train that morning.

Just before returning to her carriage, much to my delight, she said how much she had enjoyed our meeting and hoped our paths might cross again sometime. I doubted it. And then to my surprise she said, *'You could drop in for tea or a drink if you're ever down in Seabrook. I'd like it if you did.'* And then, scribbling something on the back of her discarded bill, she added, *'This is my phone number. It would be nice to take up where we left off. I'd like to see one of your poems if you've kept any.'* And with that she was gone.

On the platform at Charing Cross I did catch one last glimpse of her. I thought even from behind how elegant she looked, dressed so well, carrying a small oval case which appeared to be made of crocodile and wearing tan and beige high-heeled shoes. Out of my league, but lovely! And then she was swallowed up in the crowd going out towards the Strand.

Later, she was to tell me she had in fact been on her way to an assignation with an architect, with whom she was having a brief affair. Had I known this at the time I would have been consumed with jealousy and hated her, but nonetheless she told me she had looked out for me on her journey back later that evening.

All the way to Cripplegate to see the lawyers, I kept thinking about out meeting and if she really had expected me to keep in touch; after all, she must have guessed we did not have much in common, but then I remembered those urgent pulses of attraction I had felt during our conversation and I made up my mind I *was* going to see her again.

Once back in Folkestone I let a day pass and then braving a rebuff from such a sophisticated, older woman, I put two penny coins in the public phone from where I customarily made my telephone calls and rang her number. Alas, there was no reply. Perhaps she was still in London I thought. I wandered back past the privet hedges of the houses leading to where the Admiral lived, feeling dejected, and then thought perhaps she had just been out. She had told me she had an old lurcher she had rescued from some gypsies; maybe she was walking him along the beach. Or perhaps she was just outside, hanging washing or doing something in her garden – after all, that's what women did. I'd take a chance; I'd put on some decent casual clothes, go along to Seabrook and simply turn up. Her house would be easy enough to find from what she'd said.

So, decked out in my best suade shoes, cavalry twills, crisp white shirt, complete with home-made cravat, I duly caught a No. 103 bus from the stop opposite the Metropole Hotel at the top of the road which led down to the Admiral's house, feeling slightly anxious and hoping I was not going to make a fool of myself by just arriving out of the blue.

I found the house easily enough and I could hear the waves breaking on the beach below as I stood on the path leading across the lawn up towards the house, wondering whether I should go on or not, when she suddenly appeared at an upstairs window. *'Well this is a nice surprise,'* she called out with a broad smile. *'I'll be right down,'* and as she came out through the garden door, I know I blushed and said, *'Well, you did just say "just call in", but I don't even know your name – neither of us thought to tell the other on the train, if you remember.'*

*'No, we didn't did we,"* she said, *"but let's not be too formal, I'm Mamie*

*– what's yours; I'm not going to have to call you midshipman poet am I?!'* and I knew at once she had a sense of humour, making me instantly feel at ease.

*'Mine's James,'* I replied, not telling her everyone called me Jimmy – James sounded so much better.

The house, with its delicate ironwork verandah, was Regency, she told me. Once inside, I knew I had not be in a home like this since the time I had gone with the squash team to play at a fine old country house near Budleigh Salterton. Oil painting and hunting prints hung on the walls, rugs and carpets covered the floors, everywhere there were delicate ornaments, china and cut glass and all the furniture to me seemed exquisite, all of which told me that Mamie was a woman of taste apart from being exceedingly attractive.

She brought tea into her drawing room and we sat side by side on a small sofa which faced the window looking out across the sea. Are men enchanted? – I think *I* was. I was certainly spellbound, as I sat wondering what to say next while she poured the tea from a white china pot, decorated with coloured birds and flowers – somewhat different to the old brown earthenware pot my mother used. As she offered me the sugar bowl I noticed for the first time how delicately long and slender her fingers were, each tipped with a well -manicured nail she had painted red.

Our conversation carried on from where we had left off in the restaurant car. We talked about life, hopes and expectations, sad and happy experiences and all the time I thought how tender and unusual her feelings were. By this time I felt it was possible that a warm current of possible sex and seduction existed and I found myself holding my breath each time I looked at her. Sex with a woman like this would be magnificent, I was thinking, *But...* did I detect, or imagine, for a split second before it began, her look of surprise: or was the look some kind of warning that this was a danger-line, not to be crossed, saying *'I have a husband, I am married.'* In that same instant came a softening look in her eyes, which told me to take the risk, and on a heart-quickening impulse, I drew her towards me.

Unresisting, bringing with her a soft and subtle smell of perfume, she moved forward into my arms, as with open lips we kissed, while our tongues probed deep into each other's mouths and, pressed together, she helped me as my fingers fumbled for the buttons of her dress and I felt her bare breasts exposed for me to caress. And as I did, she sighed, pressed tighter and my mind blurred into a state of pure delight as the two of us yielded to the power of lust. Her silky suspender belt fell and her hands moved urgently, feeling for me; our bellies touched as her arms wound round me and I was just conscious of her murmuring *'baby boy'* as we both melted into a passionate swoon of delicious sexual excitement, sliding together onto the floor for our first ecstatic act of lovemaking.

It was not long after, as we both lay sated with desire, close and happy in that tangle of discarded clothing, raising herself, she glanced down on me smiling, with her eyes half closed. *'What a clever poet baby, that was marvellous!'* she murmured. Then to my astonishment I felt her fingers encircling that still excited part of me which she had just enjoyed – or so I hoped! – and I looked down to watch, as she bent over, her full breasts brushing over me and with her red-nailed fingers, gently guided the object of her desire between those sensual lips, deep into her mouth. I lay awash in a sea of ecstatic disbelief as she slowly took me to yet another climax of carnal pleasure. What unimaginable bliss!

Oh youth – what to be twenty-one years old once more!

It was at this stage that I must have known I had crossed an unknown Rubicon, some normally forbidden line, on the one side of which was the world of raffish boyhood with all its passing infatuations, and on the other, the adult world of marriages, of motherhood, respectability and secret adultery. All I knew that afternoon was that I adored this lady from the 9:05 train to Charing Cross and this was going to be the start of a new life, one of which I

had no conception, but it was something I had always longed for –
to start again as James.

From then on, over what seemed those long and deliciously
enjoyable summer months and into that autumn, I began to be
drawn inexorably into Mamie's life. I met her boys; they seemed to
like me. I got one interested in butterfly-collecting and they liked to
hear about the Navy. We walked together along the cliffs above the
harbour; once I went to one of the children's sports days, where
Mamie won the mothers' race and sometimes we swam from the
shingle beach below her house after making love in the afternoon. It
was an idyllic way to spend a summer. Like most privileged people
of the upper middle class, she enjoyed searching out nice things with
which to decorate her home. She knew antique dealers and with one
had become extremely friendly – this was helpful. We made forays
in her open Bentley, rummaging through the post-war junk shops
together and seeing what was going in the local salerooms,
sometimes buying, sometimes selling on when something better
came along, and I began to learn a little. This was how I became
involved in the rather disreputable world of 'antiques'. It was all far
more stimulating than having to think about the next watch or some
navigational error you had made and certainly more entertaining
than tipping back a horse's neck in the gunroom.

Mamie had no money herself and lived solely on the somewhat
diminished allowance her husband thought sufficient; after all, the
boys had to be educated. Things had not turned out the way he had
hoped and he had made bad investments. There was no room for
extravagance. As to her Bentley, it appeared that this was one
extravagance he had given way to on one of her more forceful
whims, which allowed her to buy the romantic old 1937 tourer.

But the storm clouds were gathering. By now I was finding it
increasingly difficult living at home, hanging about, waiting for some
kind of hopeful development by way of work. I barely spoke to my
father by this time. He must have wondered where I went to most
days and on occasion I had to give some pretext for having to go to

London. These were the days when I went with Mamie of course, to meet her coterie of friends, in whose company she veritably sparkled, which captivated me. It also made me feel proud, being so comfortably accepted as her new lover and being able to mix with whom to me were rich people who had probably inherited family money and who spoke of the arts, new plays and books or had their own businesses and enjoyed meeting in good restaurants in Knightsbridge and at those fashionable little eating places down the King's Road or off Sloane Street. These were the first of very special days and nights and it was not unusual to find ourselves having to share a single bed, after some party or other, in an elegantly furnished flat, much to the relaxed amusement of our broadminded hosts, close friends of Mamie, and who generally lived in the smarter parts of Chelsea or South Kensington.

One particular weekend, when I managed to escape from life in the Admiral's kitchen on some pretext, much to the annoyance and suspicion of my father… with Mamie looking more attractive than ever at the wheel of her open Bentley, she drove me over to West Sussex to stay with one of her closest friends of those days. I was simply bound to like her, she told me. The two of them had met at a party in Chelsea the previous year. This friend had a cottage near the sea, in some rather exclusive enclave, which had a private beach. The thought of it made me feel nervous that I might feel out of place and make some social *faux pas* and perhaps embarrass Mamie, in the kind of surroundings I was so unaccustomed to. In fact I need not have worried.

The place was called the Witterings, not far from Chichester, and the woman who came out to greet us, along with her two sleek looking salukis, was, apart from being stunningly good-looking, clearly at pains to put me at my ease, eager to learn as many details as she could with regard to this new liaison, which Mamie must have told her about. Any nervousness I might have had soon evaporated as I sat in the small drawing room, wondering what kind of world I had wandered into, going for a weekend to stay with someone called Vanessa d'Arcy-Lascelles!

I very soon sensed the two women had much in common, both more than a little attractive, in their early thirties, who were used to the well-heeled kind of society of which I had so little experience. Both sexy – you can always tell that from the look in a woman's eyes when she smiles, I had discovered! Not least was the fact that they both adored animals, which was clear to see. Vanessa, with her red hair and ravishing figure, had until recently been the mistress of Max Rayne, the City tycoon, Mamie told me later when we were going to bed. Everyone had heard of him, even I had! By now I was beginning to think things could hardly get more exciting... talk of the City and tycoons, salukis – *and* bed – incredible!

*'John's on his way down from town,'* said Vanessa, looking over at Mamie. *'You remember him, don't you!'* and Mamie replied with a knowing smile that said a lot. *'Come on, its such a marvellous evening, let's go for a swim. We can change on the beach. I've got some things you two can wear.'*

And so it was that the three of us wandered down the long lawn and out onto the sand, just before dark. The shoreline was deserted and lights were just beginning to go on in some of the big houses set back from the beach. We heard a car arrive and Vanessa said that would be John. We were already in the water when a man appeared and waved to us. *'Don't hurry; I'm fine. I'll sit here and have a smoke,'* he called. On hearing her man's voice, Vanessa stood up in the water wearing only her bikini shorts. I had noticed this, very much to my own excitement before we had plunged in. What we nowadays dismissively refer to as 'topless bathing' was something considered daring beyond belief in those days. Her body was, I must say, beautiful – Max had been lucky! Now it appeared it was John's turn!

I could never have imagined I would be swimming under such circumstances – with the woman I had fallen for, and the other, a half-nude beauty who had once been the mistress of a millionaire industrialist!

Now, she was affording her new lover a little pre-dinner titillation, showing her wonderfully pert breasts, as she splashed in the shallows! What a day it had turned out to be. To say the very least it had been somewhat different to the lifestyle I had grown used to living in the old Admiral's house. It turned out this new man of Vanessa's drove an E-Type Jaguar. I saw it in the morning and wondered whether I was ever going to be lucky enough to have a car like that – or any car for that matter! Over dinner I learned he owned a linen mill which, I later discovered, had gone bust not very long after that weekend. Vanessa moved on to richer pastures and out of Mamie's life but what a truly extraordinary two days those had been; I thought to myself it had only been a matter of months since I had been stuck into the co-pilot's seat in a Sea Venom, on my last day as a naval officer, flying over this very part and would most probably have been able to make out Vanessa's cottage as a mere speck on the coastline. A time of my life when at best, I might be looking forward to guest-night in the mess and afterwards, if I had managed to turn on sufficient charm, I might screw some amiable, but vapid girl who had managed to wangle an invitation through her father who was on the town council. One had heard that in the 'good old days', girls like that would have 'followed the fleet' with aspirations of becoming a naval officer's wife. What a thought! Better, some more feisty girl, like an aspiring young actress from the local rep., if she had somehow got invited and let the wine go to her head – a girl who you knew you would never see again because it was said that sort always drift off very quickly, going up to Town, only to disappear on the fringes of the London stage. With her, it might well have been possible to enjoy the quickest of sexual thrills in someone's parked car, if you knew the owner well enough. Little could I have possibly imagined what lay in store for me then.

My last memory of the Witterings, deep in the night, sensually entwined with Mamie and sated with delicious lust, was of hearing our hostess and her new man making love in their bedroom across the thickly carpeted landing. That is how it was then. But sadly, I knew, times like that were not going to last.

There were to be only a few days before Mamie's husband came home on leave and anyway I had to make some money. More and more time I was spending away from the privet hedges of gentility surrounding the old Admiral's house. Although by now I knew I had the knack of picking out saleable things we came across in the old junk shops – copper bits and pieces, the odd brass candle-stick or pewter mug, but things like that hardly meant real money.

I was worried as to what would happen when the inevitable introduction to her husband was going to come. Mamie told me not to worry and that it would be all right as she had asked me to help with the boys' French and do useful jobs at the house, painting the verandah, re-laying the paving in the backyard – everything would be all right, she assured me.

Now that my money was running out, I had made a few exploratory trips to London, hopeful that I'd hear of some lucrative employment, like getting into commercials for the telly, but this was all wishful thinking. On one of these trips by chance I had run into four young BBC trainees in a coffee bar off the Edgware Road. They were a good crowd, all with the type of background I understood. One happened to be John Dunn who became one of the most well-known of all the BBC announcers and it was he who offered me the share of a mews flat off Southwick Street, just off the Bayswater Road, if ever I found myself in London, with nowhere to go.

I was nervous the day before I knew I was going to have to meet her husband, but Mamie was particularly loving, reassuring me once again that everything would be all right, and the day before her husband's return, in the afternoon, we drove to Dungeness to walk the shoreline where wild flowers grow amongst the shingle almost to the high-tide mark. It is magical, desolate and beautiful. Along the shore a few small fishing boats still afforded a living to the last of the inshore fishermen. Most of their sail lofts, tarred and bubbled by the alternating sun and salt winds, were now deserted and the winches which had once hauled the fishing boats up the shingle had been left to rust among the wild vegetation.

An old man in a blue jersey was scraping an upturned boat. He must have been one of the last inshore fishermen. Not many people walked that part of the remote beach and he raised a hand to us as we passed. His sail loft looked as if it had been abandoned. The door hung open, askew, on a single hinge. Narrow and in proportion rather tall, the building appeared intriguing and I felt an immediate urge to go inside, as I had done in the old farm sheds down in Somerset as a boy, just to see what I might discover. Before asking if I could look inside, I enquired about the prospects of fishing, now that the government was beginning to regulate and interfere with what he and his forefathers had been doing for generations. This I hoped would break the ice.

Yes, he knew all about this, and as a result, his smack was now beached and permanently lay shackled to a rusty cable near the water's edge with its planking drying out. His own days of going out were over. He said there had been some compensation, but most of the boats were laid up like his. It was said they were going to build a power station out on the point and that would finish everything for good. I told the old man I had been at sea, throwing in a few nautical expressions like *'running before the wind'* and *'taking bearings'*, and talked about the tide and sizes of boats' cables, and the all-important bond was made.

I had no idea what I might find inside the sail loft, but intuition told me that it might be something good. In the initial darkness, out of the sunlight, I did not at first realise the full potential of what lay in front of me. In fact it was a scene that was going to repeat itself time and time again over the coming months and years, always with that smell of tar on the nets mixed with lamp oil and diesel.

Here lay a jumbled heap of all the nautical paraphernalia with which fishermen surround themselves. I had already seen things, similar to this, in some of the antique shops Mamie and I had been to. Amongst the heap of nets I could see an old life-belt and a small wooden wheel, a pile of lamps lay heaped in a corner, dark with verdigris, while against these was propped a rusty small boat's anchor, still attached to its line, neatly spliced at one end. On the bench, scattered haphazardly, lay shipwright's tools, an open box of netting needles, together with an oil-covered copy of *1951 Tide Tables*. Under the bench, more boxes and fish baskets, wedged tightly between bales of faded sailcloth. From the beams hung more lamps, oars and, to my surprise, a brass Verey Pistol used for firing distress flares, hanging on its own nail beside a small brass oval porthole. The last thing I noticed lying at the end of his bench was an antiquated boat's compass, still with its brass gimbals.

I knew that almost everything in there would be snapped up by antique dealers, if I could somehow get the old man to let me buy. You must however, I had learnt, never appear too keen when you're wanting to buy something – just start off by saying something like *'That old oar would look nice over our fireplace; any chance that I could buy that...?'* gradually working up your enthusiasm as each new item seems to increase its appeal as a possible ornament for your home ... because, deep-rooted in the English psyche is an interest in the sea and all the traditions which surround it.

In a situation like this, it was no good if you gave the impression you were up to something – taking some kind of advantage: you had to be fair, at the same time realising that most of what you see in front of you was either destined for the scrapyard scales, as would be the case for the lamps and anything else made of copper or brass, and the rest for a bonfire on the beach, or, at best, taken to some marine stores dealer and sold for a pittance.

And so it was with this first and intensely exciting deal, with Mamie watching, standing on the shingle, looking out across the Channel, the old man's weather-beaten face lighting up at my suggestion I buy all that he wasn't going to find a use for any more. He liked the idea that it was all going to someone's home and I am sure Mamie's presence had something to do with it. I knew that he would only get a few shillings, by weight, for the lamps and brass things and probably no more than £10 for everything else that had ceased to be of use.

Thirty pounds bought the lot. The old man was obviously delighted and thanked us both. I said I would be back to pick up what I couldn't get into the car. Luckily he didn't see the Bentley which we had left where the beach road petered out. I'd hire a van maybe. He said he would ask along the beach to see if any of his mates were clearing out their lofts. I am happy to say some did and the final yield from that afternoon's business was almost £92! Mamie took £20 and insisted that I had the rest.

Almost immediately after this the storm clouds began to gather.

By now we were seeing each other whenever we could, but her husband had written to say the Bentley was an expense he could not afford and that he was not going to accede to yet another of her arty whims, so it was eventually to go, to be replaced by a Standard Vanguard.

The affair was now becoming more serious and I had no doubt as to how happy she was in those early days of our relationship. We were both enjoying every moment of our happy and abandoned sex, which we indulged in at every opportunity, oblivious to surroundings.

As to her husband, I sensed his initial suspicion, but she was so casual about her explanation – the French tutoring, and what a help I had been at the house, not to mention that together we had made a little money by selling a few antiques we'd found. It was made easier because I overheard her telling him something about my being a poet, who'd got out of the Navy and he said, judging her by the other lame ducks she'd picked up, I was probably a *'homo'* who had been kicked out.

So I became accepted and any joint venture of ours was actively encouraged if it was going to be profitable and wasn't going to add to his expenses. I didn't feel guilty. The marriage would not have lasted anyway. She would probably have gone off with some brother officer of his and spent years of tedium in married quarters, bored by the artificiality of mess nights and more affairs.

Actually, he was fundamentally a decent man, if rather haughty and given to pomposity. He seemed an unlikely partner for high-spirited unconventional Mamie. He seemed disillusioned with life, melancholic and unable to cope with everyday matters of family life. In fact, I rather liked him, this man, whose wife I was calmly stealing, this rather crestfallen, misguided person who was the product of one of England's finest public schools, who had worn an Eton-style collar as head of house, before going off to war. No, it would never have lasted even if there hadn't been the 9:05 to Charing Cross.

By this time my father knew I was up to something. Why hadn't I got on with something through Gabbitas & Thring? The term would be starting soon. He was fed up with seeing me hanging about with nothing in view. Then one day he exploded.

That morning, not unusually, I got up late. It must have been time for him to pedal off to work, but now I heard his heavy tread on the stair runner, coming back upstairs and then the noise of his Veltschoen brogues on the lino in his room – he must have forgotten something, I thought.

Coming out of my room, I saw him standing on the landing and through the window behind him I noticed it had been raining. He must have come upstairs to fetch his mac. He was standing there, waiting for me to come down, giving me that sneering look of utter disapproval as I reached the landing.

'You just use this place as a hotel, don't you?' he snorted.

For a moment I tried to disregard him, but then, only half-trying not to barge past, it was my turn now to give him a look of disdain. He grabbed me: *'None of that chummy –- none of that dumb insolence! Not with me, you don't…'* he blazed, trying to push past me as I turned my back on him to go downstairs, all but coming to blows. He shouted at me to get out and not come back until I had learnt some self-control. *'Yes, that's right, get out,'* he thundered, before ramming on his old trilby and bursting out of the front door.

144

And that was the last I saw of him for eight years. By which time, *he* would be teaching Latin in a girls' school and from time to time, working for *me*!

My poor mother was in tears. The whole thing was a mess, but I am sure she understood. I wasted no time in packing my few things and I walked out to take the train to London. I'd find somewhere: there were my friends at the BBC, who'd said I could have a share of their flat in Albion Mews off Southwick Street – I'd try that first. I'd have to take up the teaching job from there, which I did, Gabbitas & Thring finding me work for a term, teaching French and games, at the same time asking John Dunn if he could keep his spare bed available for me to have during the holidays. The deal was £1 a week if I agreed to help out with the cooking from time to time. Looking back, I don't know how he put up with me. My head was full of a rag-bag of ideas, none of which were what you'd call practical. All I was certain of was that it was going to be difficult living like that, haunted hour to hour by thoughts of the woman I loved so much, from whose bedroom window one could hear the watery rustle of a calm high tide, washing gently up the shingle beach.

I wrote to Mamie every day and much to my relief she came to pick me up at half term. Her husband was away on exercises and we spent three happy days buying from the junk shops and hoping for a repeat of the afternoon near Dungeness, as we worked our way through the small fishing villages from Hythe to Hastings. We nearly always found something and I discovered one marine stores dealer who said he nearly always had Admiralty-pattern lamps for sale – I knew that they were 'sellers'. I had begun dealing, even picking up a little of the 'trade' lingo.

I bought a few rudimentary books on antiques and looked through them in the caravan which was my school accommodation. They didn't help much, just showing choice examples of such things as sets of Chippendale chairs, Georgian library steps, Derby Porcelain and Battersea snuffboxes and so on. Things I knew nothing about whatsoever and wouldn't recognise if I saw them.

One term's teaching was enough – so reminiscent of the seediest world of Waugh's 'Decline and Fall', transported to the late 1950s, headmasters who were little more than con-men, teaching wrecks, with soup-dribbled cardigans who taught divinity. Dormitories, which by day became classrooms and food of the vilest and cheapest kind.

Once more back in London, out of touch with my family, I was taking any job, from emptying the coins from the new-fangled scent machines, which gave girls a squirt of cheap perfume for one shilling and were installed in all the best pub lavatories. Those were the days before the arrival of the French Letter dispensers, which when they did arrive, soon put them out of business. I worked on building sites, washed up and even aspired to become something of a waiter in a basement restaurant off the Cromwell Road. Who cared, it was independence!

There were times I was able to afford to make the trip to Folkestone to see Mamie, where I began staying in cheap boarding houses. And happily there were times when, on some pretext, she could join me in London for the night. By this time I had taken a single room in a house owned by the Church Commissioners, in Southwick Street. All I had in it was a pine chest of drawers, which had cost me £2, a cheap bedside lamp along with a bed I'd bought in Camden Town. *And* my very first item of antique furniture which was a chair with a caned seat and the frame in what one of my books described as 'simulated bamboo'. But it was the bed that really mattered! Mamie christened the place '*Bella Vista*', as its only window gave onto the backs of adjacent houses, with their down-pipes and areas full of dustbins. What a honeymoon we enjoyed in Bella Vista!

On the strength of our joint small successes in dealing, I decided it was time I got my driving licence, buy some kind of car and try my luck properly all round the coasts of southern England. Mamie agreed. She let me use the Vanguard. I took my test in and around the roads where I might easily have caught sight of my father on his bicycle. I passed, and a whole new era began.

Back in London, thinking the world was wonderful, with £185 in my pocket, I found a motor dealer in the Edgware Road, who specialised in what were advertised as *'good condition, second-hand cars'*. I bought a light-brown Bedford Dormobile van, with windows in each side and slatted seats in the back (the earliest attempt at a 'peoples' carrier!') I bought it on hire purchase to conserve my capital, and this meant I had to open a bank account, which was something I had only dreamt of doing until now. My capital was the small wad of notes, kept in my hip pocket. Duly, sitting in the Manager's office in the Notting Hill Gate branch of the National Westminster, my job or profession was noted on the necessary paperwork as *'antique dealer'*.

Around this time, Mamie presented me with a six-week-old mongrel puppy to keep me company. I called him Jarvis, after a new-found contact from Camden Town, who had a small metal-polishing business, becoming as time went along, a close friend of mine, always ready with common sense advice.

Up to now I had simply sold on everything made of copper or brass, caked with layers of paint or encrusted with verdigris, before I realised that if only I could get them polished, the profit would be far better. Hence I made enquiries and ended up in a mews, off the Brecknock Road – number 100, Camden Mews – where Jack Jarvis had his business. The mews, now gentrified, was then a burrow of small workshops of every kind: panel-beating, plumbing, general handymen to upholsterers.

Metal-polishing involved first dipping the article into caustic soda to remove the paint and verdigris and then holding it to the polishing mop, which ran off the spindle of a 3hp motor. Messrs Cannings, down in Clerkenwell, who sold polishers' sundries, supplied what was known as *'soap'*, a solid brown bar of hard, waxy substance which was applied to the mop before the polishing began. Use of the 'soap' meant that what had once been a wholly unattractive and grimy metal article was quickly transformed into a shining brass or copper ornament. The only problem was that as the mop reduced in size with the pressure of the polisher, everything except the thing being polished became covered in particles of clinging filth – mop, soap and metal. To save expense on shampoo it was customary for all polishers always to wear a hat made from folded newspaper, which looked something like a child's paper boat.

In any of the Italian cafés in that part of Camden Town you could always pick out the polishers by their distinctive headwear quite apart from a hurriedly-washed, still filthy face.

I was to become quite adept myself at the polishing wheel before too long... young Jimmy, sinking even further!

It wasn't long before I tried the entire Kent and Sussex coast, from Newhaven to Dover and on up the Thames estuary. Ships' oil lamps were the most saleable items I was finding, coming from boat repair yards in small harbours, from yacht builders in the Thames side-creeks and from old-established ship's chandlers along the river. Much of what I was finding was government wartime surplus – sometimes never even used, in original wrapping, dated variously from pre-First World War. One batch of lamps I found in Dover, although rusted badly, had an unexpected elegance ... no wonder, they were stamped *'Bulpit & Co Birmingham 1893'*. Government surplus.

Now I was travelling further afield. Early morning starts, 4:30 in the dark, deserted streets, with a stop at the soup machine in Parkway. Out through the trafficless City to Edmonton and then the open road towards the east coast fishing ports. It was a time of staying in cheap bed & breakfast lodgings which catered for commercial travellers and where the eiderdowns smelled and you had sterilised milk for breakfast in the morning. I had no roots - just Bella Vista and Jarvis, my dog, travelling companion and link to the other world.

Good days would end with the back of my Dormobile beginning to fill up with my finds, hands dirty and my wad that little bit thinner, before trying to find a suitable-looking B&B for the night and then finding a phone box to ring Mamie, excited at the prospect of hearing the voice I loved, which brought with it a wonderfully reassuring feeling of excitement and elation, knowing that she wanted me to succeed, wherever I was. Usually that was in the rundown part of some coastal town, in circumstances very different to her own, at home, in comfort, with her young family

By now I had established a loose pattern of a week away, leaving Bella Vista on a Monday concentrating at this stage on the east coast towns; back to Camden Town for the weekend to unload all the brass and copper lamps and other bits of nauticalia, for polishing in Jack's workshop the mews, before going down to Seabrook, where with any luck, if the coast was clear, I knew that no matter what time of day it was, I would soon be in bed with my lover. After that it was once again back to London, to sell off what remained of my finds, and the items my good friend Jack had polished up while I had been away, happily enjoying wonderful adultery! *'Jim,'* Jack used to say, only half smiling, *'it'll get you into trouble one day!'*

Really good pickings were to be had in the East Coast fishing ports. Yarmouth and Lowestoft had once been renowned for their fleets of drifters and trawlers. Now, the whole fishing industry was in decline and life was draining from the fish docks – new regulations and quotas meant wharves were lined with old steam drifters, rigging wires hanging limp, deck-houses brown with rust, laid up for the last time before being towed away for breaking. Long gone were the days of Yarmouth bloaters! Dockside buildings had become emptied of life, with trawler owners' office windows void of notices of any kind or requests for deckhands. Only a last handful of family-owned businesses seemed in operation. I was told: *'Get further up along the coast if you want to do any good; all the breaker's yards are further north, they'll have all the stuff you're looking for – Grimsby, Hull and Newcastle.'*

So one day, having exhausted working along the quays in Yarmouth, I decided to act on this advice as it didn't look as if I was going to have much luck there – the thought of Grimsby had somehow always appealed to me. However, before taking the road north in my Bedford, I struck it lucky for one last time just outside the town. Here, in a sheltered inlet, in the early 19th century, Fellowes & Co. had established their shipbuilding firm, renowned for many of the fine trading clippers and barquentines they built, many of which later became the subject of fine nautical oil paintings, which even *I* knew, were in very high demand. With the coming of steam, the firm had struggled on, building small coasters, until after the war, with the contracts to the Admiralty gone, the business began to founder. There were no longer the big trawling fleets calling for repairs and the firm's equipment had become outdated. The last of their customers, the small merchant cargo lines had all but faded away. Their yard, I noticed, now bore all the signs of decay and dilapidation. Like others I had seen, the office window with the name 'Fellowes', was now filthy, the gilded letters peeling. The place looked hopeful and sure enough, there in the dirt-covered window was a reminder of the firm's illustrious past - the model of a sail – *and* – steam trading vessel of the late 19th century, in a glass case. This was just what I wanted to see!

The office manager sold me the model. *'Here,'* he said *'if you like that kind of thing, take this as well.'* At which he took a water-colour painting of the ship, still in its frame, from the back office wall. *'She was one of our best in her day. Best keep the picture along with her model.'* I was well in and after a little of my now well-honed gift of the gab, I found myself being asked if I might care to see if there was anything in the store sheds which might be worth something.

I wish I still had the things I found that afternoon. I was still too green to appreciate their value and rarity. Almost certainly the contents of the shed had remained untouched since the early 1900s. Instinctively I knew I was looking at real value: a teak binnacle mounted on dolphin feet of cast bronze, exquisitely pierced brass cabin lamps, small copper lanterns set in gimbals, even an early octant made of ebony and a sextant still in its box. There were boxes of nautical trivia: voice pipes with trumpet ends, hand-carried candle lamps, copper pans from some galley. I found boxed compasses, white faces yellowed with age, a ship's chronometer in a brass-bound carrying case. I could hardly believe my luck! Last of all and something personal and touching – a fine teak shipwright's box with spliced rope handles and the name "Thos. Pollard" on the front, inscribed on a brass plate. Each tool was in its allotted place, each boxwood handle was marked T.P. – so evocative of those old days.

Needless to say I bought the lot, the office manager seeming only too happy to have the stuff cleared out, but I have the feeling that I sold off everything far too cheaply.

Grimsby and the North were going to have to wait for another time.

By now I was keeping both Jack Jarvis and his apprentice, Buddy, busy at their polishing wheels. Jack and I had taken to each other straightaway. He was of the N.C.O. mould, with a marvellous sense of humour and, unlike Buddy, who was a cockney kid, Jack had a slight aura of having come from something better – worldly-wise, a warm and kindly man. He had a couple of contracts to polish small metal components for the electrical trade down the Farringdon Road that sometimes had him working well into the night to make ends meet, always wearing the metal polisher's obligatory paper hat, with a roll-up often tucked behind his ear, his face almost black with filth from the mops, with just a little pink round his eyes and lips, but his advice was always worth listening to.

If I was stuck in London, I might well try my luck along the Thames or the Essex creeks again beyond Thurrock where they broke up barges and where unskilled shipwrights sold patched-up yachts and motor cruisers to unsuspecting would-be nautical types in caps.

Relentlessly I pursued my scavenging throughout the late 1950s and on into the new decade, where there was a whiff of change in the air and I was learning fast. The commercial world was becoming aware of the value of space – disused buildings were being torn down and cleared of anything old and unwanted. There was time for ordinary people to think about new ways to decorate their homes and new ideas were in the air.

By now I had moved up another notch and bought a brand new Bedford van, and it was in this that my dog and I cruised innumerable working-class streets, back alley warehouses and dockside scrapyards, in search of a deal. In fact, old copper and brass ships' lamps and fittings had become virtually the only source of income for me and all the while my little wad was growing.

Much to my advantage the Elder Brethren of Trinity House, together with old fogies at the Board of Trade, who both made and enforced our maritime laws, were still living in the past luckily for me. Oil-burning lamps they considered still to be the primary source of all lighting aboard ship. Of course electrical systems had long since overtaken the old oil and colza-burning copper and brass lamps, which had remained unchanged in design since the mid 1880s but these were still having to be carried by law, meaning that any vessel arriving in the breaker's yard was sure to be carrying a complete set somewhere on board if you could root them out. That, or you could find them already taken off and lying about the jetty, and if the yard was busy and several ships were in for breaking, you might turn up twenty or thirty – all made of copper! To the ship-breakers they simply represented a mere few pounds weight of 'non-ferrous', at around 1/3d. a pound.

On this occasion, I had spent two days rummaging round the fish-docks of North Shields and the breaking yards along the Tyne and my van was filled and my wad depleted as I finally turned into the cobbled mews well after dark. Bud and Jack were still working – paper hats on, their spindles humming, lit by the dim glow of the three 100 watt bulbs hanging in a halo of suspended filth from the mops.

Normally, my return would have been greeted with raucous cockney oaths and jokes. But no, not this time. The two spindles did not stop immediately and they both bent over their work as if not pleased at all to see me. After a worrying pause, I saw the two black faces staring at me with a look which could mean that something calamitous had happened. Suddenly they both started talking at once; Jack asking what I had done, Bud saying *'they'* – meaning I presumed the Police – *'had been searching the workshop since early afternoon.'* *'Who were they?'* I asked, knowing the answer, heart quickening with a sinking feeling, utterly bewildered. Jack said, *'Four police in plain clothes came asking for Mr. Croft.'* One of them had left a note for me to ring a certain number as soon as I got back to London. I took the note. At the top was the name of a detective, a certain sergeant Lawless, (ironic under the circumstances!) and the contact number Whitehall 1212 – extension 269. A few minutes before I had been desperately hungry: now the pit of my stomach vanished into a nothingness and I began to tremble. *'There must be some awful mistake,'* I said, but I could see that Bud and Jack thought otherwise – the posh bastard who'd said he'd been a naval officer and was having an affair with some toff's wife and who'd now deceived them. The police visitors had been tough and uncompromising, obviously about some very serious business … *'Just what have you done?'* Jack asked in desperation. I was terrified – what HAD I done? Fear of the unknown was worse than the fear of being found out for something I knew I had done. Was it anything to do with Holland or anything I had done in France? I stood speechless, unable to give any satisfactory answer. I saw my world, everything I had worked so hard for, about to be snuffed out. I wouldn't see Mamie any more – my inspiration and my anchor. For the first time I succumbed to a violent wave of guilt – maybe it was Mamie's husband behind all this. He had found out finally and appalled at my adulterous deceit, had found some way to frame me. I'd eaten at his table, met his friends and even taken the boys on buying trips with me.

There was no phone in the workshop. There was nothing I could say to Jack and Bud as we unloaded the van: this was probably going to be for the last time. I couldn't get the things off quickly enough – I had to get to a phone to make sure this was just some terrible dream. There was one I knew, down Camden Hill, which I would pass on my way back to my basement off Parkway.

I rang the number. A terse voice answered, *'Flying Squad'*. I started to say something, but no words came out. *'My name?'* the voice asked... Sergeant Lawless was out on patrol, he was unable to be contacted. It was past eleven o'clock. Falteringly, I said I would go down to Scotland Yard first thing in the morning.

Well before nine, without breakfast, now not having eaten for almost twenty-four hours, I drove down to Westminster and went into the Metropolitan Police buildings. The man at the desk checked some kind of logbook and it seemed as though he knew I was expected. I waited for what seemed an interminable two or three minutes, before a tall figure, carrying a thick file in one hand, approached from one of the wide corridors.

After an unsmiling, insincere *'Good morning,'* he beckoned me to follow him down to the basement and the interview rooms. A door was opened to a small partitioned room, where another officer already sat waiting.

I sat facing the two men. There was a pause while they both looked at the file, then began their questioning. It was clear they knew a lot about me. They knew who my parents were, where I had been to school and that I had lived in Folkestone, joined the Navy, been through Dartmouth and had left in 1956. At this point there was a long pause, but still no accusations, nor any response to my repeated demands for an explanation as to why I was being grilled like this. Very slowly a slight, wary, feeling of relaxation came over me. It was clear they were fishing and seemed to be uncertain whether they had anything against me or not. My mind cleared somewhat and I began carefully to follow their line of questioning. They really were not that bright these two from the Flying Squad, but they were frightening enough! *'Yes, I had been to ship-breaking yards.' 'Yes, I did deal in old ships' gear.' 'Yes, my brother was still a serving officer in the Royal Navy.' 'Had I ever bought ships' compasses? Did I ever sell any of them in London?' 'Yes.'*

Then I knew. I knew what it was all about!

The week before, responding to the pleas of my mother to keep in touch with the family, I had called in see my brother, down near Fareham, before pushing on to Portsmouth, where I bought thirty Admiralty-pattern small boat compasses from a scrap business by the name of Smith & Leak, which dealt in surplus from the naval dockyard. They were all in their original wrappings, painted grey and never used. I had seen such things in antique shops, polished up as ornaments, and I knew they would be a good buy, especially since they were unused. I might even be able to sell some back to maritime suppliers down in the London docks because I knew a likely place near Fenchurch Street Station, where they sold charts and navigational supplies – probably compasses as well, so I had gone to have a try.

A be-suited manager seemed interested and came out to look in the van to see just what I was offering. What he saw was row upon row of what was normally a commodity in short supply. He bought the lot. What a deal! Later – and this I know for certain – he suddenly came to the conclusion that he might have been buying stolen goods, they had been so cheap – the dirty van, the dog, the unlikely young chap in the chukka boots – and duly rang the police to clear himself, just in case. The police, in turn, had checked the records – Croft, J. R. N., naval officer, charged and convicted with larceny 1956 – well, well, onto something here they must have thought. Living in Camden Town, a pretty rough area, no known job, this could well be serious… and hence the raid on 100 Camden Mews.

It was almost eleven o'clock and I had been in that basement for almost three hours before finally with weak begrudging smiles Sergeant Lawless said *'I think that'll do for now Mr Croft. You can go.'* All that remained to do now was to eat and then ring Mamie to tell her about my experience. It felt marvellous to be free and even better that I loved the woman whose reassuring voice I heard once I'd pressed button "A".

\*\*\*\*\*\*\*\*\*\*

Grubbing along the fringes of the early 1960s antiques trade, I had by now learnt the various types of dealer I was likely to encounter. There were the hard-bitten types – maybe whose families had originally started off as rag-and-bone people before bettering themselves in the 20s and 30s. They'd try to outwit you, trading on your inexperience. Others, just like any shopkeeper, fair and even positively friendly, reckoning it might be worthwhile to cultivate such an odd young man with his clean shirt, posh voice and cavalry twills – perhaps a bit of his family silver might be the result. Some even bothered to point out things amongst their own stock, saying if I ever found anything like that, be sure to let them have a go at it. One of these, in Crawford Street, said he thought I might well come across what he called 'military' furniture – mahogany chests and desks with inset brass handles, used by officers on board ship and by army officers while travelling on campaign. *'Well worth keeping a lookout for anything in that line: very much in fashion,'* he told me. His advice was going to pay off!

There were *'knockers'* you ran across, who held no stock but just sold on everything their hyena nostrils scented whenever they called on some unsuspecting householder. Everyone seemed to look down on them. Their dubious method of buying was to call on elderly couples, or better still, single old ladies who might have seen better times, finally leaving with some valuable possession which they had inveigled out of the poor owner very cheaply.

Then there were the *'runners'*, van owners, like myself, who went from one antique business to another, very often taking things away on a sale or return basis, using their knowledge to get a better deal from the next man The horrid thought occurred to me that I might be referred to as a *'runner'* – I wouldn't so much mind being called a general dealer; in fact I rather liked that although it sounded about as low as you could get. After all, everyone in those days had heard of Dawson, the king of post-war junk and government surplus and he'd made millions – the difference was he bought a thousand old Matilda tanks and aerodromes full of mothballed *'Liberator'* bombers … at one go, or the entire contents of army depots … come to think of it, one of the yachts moored at Cannes had been his!

By far the most important dealer to me, to whom I was selling the majority of my stuff, was a tough-looking, one-armed American from the Bronx, called George Knapp. He bought to fill containers to ship out to the States. Everyone knew him. He combed all the markets, buying in enormous quantities and he always paid in cash. I had bumped into him in Bermondsey antique market. All the foreign dealers, or their buying agents would be there – it was a place where you made contacts. By some ancient law, Bermondsey market had the distinction of being the one place you couldn't be had for receiving stolen goods and this accounted for a good number of very doubtful types whose vans were always the first to arrive in the dawn light, spilling their contents onto the pavement, while the shady owners stood hopefully by.

Having seen what you had to offer, Knapp liked to buy the lot. Unsmiling, just one offer, fair, and that was it. Standing in his Frank Sinatra porkpie hat, he'd extract a huge wad of £1 notes from his coat pocket and with a conjurer's dexterity, cut the wad, judging the thickness to tally with the cash he owed you. He was rarely more than a few notes out!

If he wasn't around the markets, you'd find him holding court in a seedy hotel called the Westland, at the less salubrious end of the Bayswater Road. Here dealers would call in the hopes that he would be interested in what they had to sell. He'd get up from his usual corner table in the lounge, in summer with the short sleeve of his left arm flapping empty, and go outside the hotel entrance, look into the van or at whatever had been dragged out onto the pavement and that was how you had a deal with George.

Selling in the road like that wasn't exactly going to make me rich but I still had visions of one day being able to buy a house and asking Mamie to live with me. Sometimes being able to sell almost everything in one go when I got back to London meant I had time on my hands with which to dream up some additional way to make some money with more opportunities to get down to Seabrook to see her.

**Rummaging in the graveyard of forgotten fairgrounds in Bloxwich**

I decided to make cannons. I had always been interested in them. The more exclusive dealers, who advertised in the *Field* or *Country Life*, were always keen to buy early firearms. I knew a bit about casting from my days in the engineering workshops at Dartmouth and how to achieve a hollow barrel, by making something foundry-men call a core. Once this was done, these would have to be mounted on wooden carriages, with proper fittings, but that wouldn't present a problem as by this time I knew a blacksmith who was helpful with metalwork problems.

Cheap and crude ornaments were being turned out in Birmingham for so-called antique shops – horse brasses, toasting forks with goblin handles and many other supposedly antique-looking knick-knacks for the mantelpiece. I had even seen small cannons from the same source, small and badly cast, with no appeal at all. Mine would be in bronze, quite big. I would get plans from the naval archives held in the National Maritime Museum then make exact copies, scaled down. Having checked the going rate for bronze casting – the most desirable metal in the antique trade – I reckoned I could produce a 24 inch for well under £150. I had seen similar, real ones, advertised in antiques magazines for well over £500.

A little market research was needed before launching into this new idea.

Therefore, before going to Seabrook again, I thought it would be a good idea to go along to the Portobello Road to get a feel of what was happening and to see if there might be the possibility of selling cannons to the dealers there. In most of the adjoining streets and part of Westbourne Grove, an entirely new area was being taken over by dealers, some of whom sold every type of antique including what was referred to as *'pop art'* – amusing or decorative everyday articles which essentially recalled a past era when England had an empire – not necessarily antique, but what we now know as memorabilia: old shop fittings, enamel signs of the kind you might have still seen on railway platforms, stone jars with *'tapioca'* or *'lentils'* written on them, wooden butter pats, dairy churns and so on, some of which might only be forty or fifty years old, some less. Someone might have a buyer for old sewing machines, others might take a fancy to old tea tins or old tin toys or even a colourful railway signal arm. In particular I had heard of a shop called 'Dodo' where you might see anything from an outsize wooden boot from a country shoemaker's sign, to well-peppered duck decoys, enamel advertising signs, or even an old weathervane. That might be the kind of shop which would take a few cannons if making them turned out to be a success. It turned out that more than a few places were interested in the *'bronze cannons I thought I could get hold of…'*

Step one was to make an exact, scaled-down version of a naval cannon, taken from the National Maritime Museum's archives. This done, the step meant finding someone who had a lathe and could turn the barrel pattern, exact to the original plans. It wasn't gong to be a problem I could easily crack up in London so I decided to try first Folkestone and then Dover. And this found me one afternoon, drifting from one likely-looking place back to another, making enquiries. Yes, there was a small foundry, but a business which used lathes – a problem. And all the time I was doing this not far from where I knew my father worked and I had the strangest of feelings that I might catch sight of him, or see my mother's bicycle leaning up against the wall outside some building. I didn't see him and eventually my efforts paid off. I was directed to a firm called Channel Woodcraft, where I was told one of their foremen might be able to help. After work was finished for the day, I could find him at home. The office gave me his address.

Just before what they call 'teatime', I found myself walking up the path of a semi-detached council house, home of David Richards, who I had been told was the foreman cabinet-maker at Channel Woodcraft. I explained my problem to his wife, who said she was sure he wouldn't mind if I went down to his workshop to see if his lathe was what I was looking for and that he would be back very shortly.

And that five-o'clock meeting turned out to be the start of an association that was to last more than twenty years. It was to be his unparalleled expertise and capability to use just sufficient imagination in the wildly improbable tasks I was going to throw at him that not only earned him my undying respect, but millions of pounds for the eventual business that blossomed from our meeting that afternoon.

I liked him at once.

I could understand his initial suspicion that I was out of my depth, and he out of his, with my talking of the trunnion bearings and recoil rings of an 18th century ship's cannon and I didn't blame him as his had been a world of nothing but wood machinery, window frames and door lintels up to that afternoon. I showed him the drawings and asked if *I* could use his lathe for making the pattern for the barrels *and* if he would be able to find time to make the carriages. Quietly, with a professionalism I could detect, he said he was sure he could. So that was it, the idea was up and running.

It remained only to find a B&B for the night and to start work in his shed the following morning, which I did, finishing by midday. The only imperfection occurred when I fixed the trunnions across the barrel with some plastic wood, which shrunk and in fact was a give-away if the barrels had ever been closely inspected underneath. Luckily this never happened! In all other aspects the wooden pattern looked exactly like a small 18th century ship's main armament cannon. It only remained for the shellac to be applied to prohibit the sand from sticking and it was ready for the foundry.

I was told the first of the 4 barrels I ordered would be ready in a week. I needed to fill in time meanwhile. I couldn't hang about. Mamie was away, staying with army friends and wouldn't be back for some days. With all my stock sold off, I decided to make a quick trip once again to the fishing ports on the Norfolk coast. Before leaving Folkestone I called at the old Admiral's house to see my mother and let my dog enjoy a wander in the garden. I knew that my father would be at work. These fleeting, secretive visits to what had once been my home, made me feel very strange and completely detached from all the years that had gone before – school, awful adolescence and the Navy. All gone.

I also intended to try to make an exploratory call at an old-established engineering firm near King's Lynn that I had heard about, where I had been told they used to make steam traction engines and equipment for the Army in the First World War. This sounded very interesting: certainly not somewhere to be missed out. What I didn't know was that on account of this venture, my cannon scheme was going to be considerably delayed.

Yarmouth this time yielded very little, so I made an early start the following morning, taking the Norwich road, towards King's Lynn, as usual keeping a keen eye open for any interesting-looking features, such as old-style shops with traditionally sign-written fascias, or run-down business premises with yards beside them, where anything might go on, or be found. A stone-masons might yield up something by way of a garden ornament. Somewhere else, in dilapidated sheds, you could well find old pre-war motorcycles being mended and parts of cars being sold – even pre-war cars, the names of which have been long forgotten. In somewhere like that you might well find an old radiator emblem or motor horn – everywhere had its possibilities.

With this in mind, I made my last call at a small Norfolk Broads boatyard. Nothing doing. Then turning in the direction of King's Lynn the open road lay ahead, except for what looked like a smallholding, with a horse grazing outside an enclosure of corrugated tin, from behind which I could see smoke rising. I slowed and saw three men standing round a fire. Behind them were some sheds, beside which were two wooden-wheeled caravans – not the gypsy type, these were simply painted in maroon, lined in gold, with cut-glass windows and each with lettering on the side, saying *'Button Brothers, Showmen of Repute'*. This looked interesting.

I stopped the van outside the gate and tentatively approached the men who appeared to be throwing what looked like a large wooden ostrich onto the fire. I could scarcely believe my eyes – it was surreal!

I said I couldn't help looking in as it seemed such an extraordinary thing to have seen through an open gate. With keen naïve interest I asked them what they were doing. Gradually at first, they explained that it was not extraordinary at all. Showmen up and down the country were doing this, now that the county fairs were declining because of the telly. Times were changing and they were making everything in fibreglass now and it was lighter and didn't need the repairs like the traditional old wooden animals for their rides, and besides they sent their remnants up to a gold refinery in Watford, who gave them £7 per hundredweight for the ashes. I was transfixed as I listened to all this. *'Yes, you see guv'nor, over the years apart from repainting our gallopers and ostriches every end of season, some of the decoration has always been best gold leaf, sheets and sheets on every animal and that's why the ashes are so valuable … at £7 per hundredweight.'* I wondered how many birds they would have to burn to achieve just one hundredweight of ash!

The showman went on, enlarging mournfully on the slow demise of the travelling fairs. Stalls like coconut shies and shooting galleries were going – not worth the weight in the trailers with the cost of petrol being what is was. Swing boats were all but finished and nearly all the showmen were stripping down their carousels, scrapping all the old carved and gilded ornament parts, as he called them and going over to fibreglass. *'The old days are finished, Guv'!'*

This was all spellbinding information.

The opportunity that presented itself seemed one not to be missed, although I had no real idea whether I was on to something or not. I managed to convince them that I would be pleased to pay a decent price, just to see the birds saved, it seemed such a pity to just burn them. Of course my *'just to save'* really meant there might be something in it for me. There was little doubt they thought my proposition peculiar, but the sight of a bundle of notes being taken from my hip pocket just as another bird was about to be thrown on the pyre, convinced them I was serious and yet more ostriches were dragged from the sheds together with a bear, on all fours with a single saddle carved on its back. This was their last Russian Bear they said, but the ostriches were two-seaters.

I loaded one of my newly-acquired menagerie into the van and said I would arrange to have the others collected by B.R.S. – they offered me tea in their living wagon and seemed like honest men, down on their luck, and with a handshake, I was on my way to King's Lynn and the old established engineering firm of Savage & Co.

On the way I remember looking into the back every now and again, speculating as to the best way of capitalising on something as unusual as six-foot high ostriches and a five-foot long wooden bear … as it turned out, I need not have worried. Without knowing it, I had struck into a hitherto untapped vein of gold. The world of Fairground Art.

Getting into shipyards and shipping offices did not present any problem, but getting into a place like Savages was another matter. As opposed to the scrapyards they would not expect casual visitors, let alone anyone poking about and wasting their time. So a little subterfuge was called for.

Whatever the business, I usually began by saying I hoped that I was not disturbing anyone, but I would be grateful if … and in this case, thinking it wise to try and bypass the main offices, I would ask if there might perhaps be some foreman in the yard who could spare a few minutes on account of my writing a thesis on the development of agricultural machinery. Thesis? The gatekeeper probably had never heard the word and it wasn't one of my often-used words either. He could hardly refuse, my final persuasion I liked to think, was the cultivated Earnshill accent. I just hoped he hadn't seen my van with Jarvis looking out of the window!

He picked up the phone and I heard him say, '*Someone to see you Fred.*'

The man called Fred was the general workshop foreman – heavy lilting Norfolk accent, brown overalls and balding, with a micrometer sticking out of his breast pocket.

I put my problem to him as we walked towards the factory buildings and I tried to steer the conversation towards the possibility of looking at some obsolete or outdated equipment. He replied he was sure the works had some things still lying about, which might help me with my thesis. He was proud of his job and his father had been foreman before him, but now there were whole parts of the enterprise which were being closed down. Originally the firm had made steam traction engines and had only recently reconditioned the last of their steamrollers, made well before the war.

He continued. In the 80's and 90's when travelling fairs were at their height and huge fortunes were being made on the fairgrounds, they had specialised in the construction of steam-driven carousels and showmen's living wagons. Those were the days when Savages' gallopers had been famous for their elaborate carved decoration. The firm had made up the carcass of each horse or other animal and then, his father had told him, all the carving had been done by a travelling band of carvers from the continent – the horses, the panels and the framing, all in extraordinary detail, scrolled and bordered with elaborate decoration of the highest quality, which was then painted and gilded by local signwriters and artists. Sometimes the carvers would stay all winter, if business was good, at other times they might move on after a few days.

I hung on his every word.

Savages, he said, had made circus wagons as well for travelling menageries ... and come to think of it, there were still two or three painted panels from the side of a beast wagon in one of the buildings. I could hardly contain my excitement as the rusty bolts of one of the sheds were drawn back to reveal two incredible oil paintings on canvas, stretched across an ornamentally carved board, one depicting lions snarling ferociously while the other showed tigers cautiously stalking their prey, each of them in the artist's imagined jungle scenery. Beautiful quality, even *I* could tell that, now browned with layers of deep varnish.

Beside that shed was another, larger, with flaked and faded lettering above the doors, now obviously unused, the word FOUNDRY just visible – and that could well mean treasure! Perhaps there were some old wooden patterns left, from which they had cast things like brass letters, even mundane engineering items such as cogwheels. Made in wood and polished up all this seemed to have become all the rage for décor.

By now Fred was beginning to hurry: it was nearly clocking-off time. He was proud to have been able to show me round and tell me all the things that had gone on there when his father had been foreman. Yes, of course I could have the old animal paintings and yes, if there were any of the old wood patterns left in the foundry shed, I could have these too. He had no need to ask the main office he assured me.

I think I gave him £10. That would have been just about his week's pay packet and he beamed as he hurried off and left me to take my booty out to the van.

I thought what a day it had been. First the extraordinary bonfire of the ostriches, and all the possibilities which that presented, now just a dozen miles down the road, the coincidence of turning up more fairground remnants as well as a bundle of interesting-looking patterns. Almost too good to be true!

Now just the run on through to Peterborough and the main road back to London and a really slap-up Indian meal before going back to my basement. It would be the *Star of India* in Paddington tonight, fried rice and two meat dishes, parathas, the lot!

But things were not going to turn out quite as I had expected.

The flat Fenlands road runs almost in a dead straight line from the outskirts of King's Lynn to the village of Eye, some miles short of the county town of Peterborough. Feeling that I had had a productive trip, reckoning that this new type of stock, come across so unexpectedly, might lead to new and remunerative niches in the London market, I happily rattled into the open countryside.

The road was absolutely devoid of traffic – no car, no lorry, not even a single tractor in sight. In the distance I saw the outskirts of Eye, houses on the left, some trees on the right and little more than an approaching speck when I first noticed it, what appeared to be a motorcycle, heading towards me out of the village. As I was doing about 50mph and the oncoming motorcyclist, I imagine, doing somewhat less, our closing speed would have been near to 100mph.

Almost level with him now, suddenly, just before my van reached the first of the houses, I passed a gateway and saw some caravans and at that instant the man turned across my path. However quick my reactions, there was no conceivable way I could have avoided him. My brakes locked, throwing the wheel over, my van hit the stone curbing and with that dreaded crashing sound of a human body intermeshed with metal tearing apart, his cycle was smashed, sending his body flying past my driving window, his head catching the projecting mirror which was splattered with blood.

It seems strange to say, but I was more worried about my dog in those first few seconds, than I was for the poor human being who must have been dying a matter of feet away. Almost paralysed with shock, I must have become catatonic. I remember nothing in detail; a mist descended and I heard an ambulance as someone sat me down and gave me tea laced with some kind of spirit in the council house outside which the accident had occurred. A policeman was standing beside me, but I have no recollection of what he said, or asked me, I just recall him being calm and understanding.

Then, without warning, he was gone and there I was just left sitting in the council house in a state of shocked suspension, asking the kind occupant who had given me the tea, if my van was badly damaged. *'No,'* he said, *'it didn't look too bad at all, except for the right wing.' 'Was the man dead?'* I asked. He said he thought not but his head was pretty bad and my dog was still in the van. Could he help me? The awful thing was, he said, that the man's son had been killed by a car on that exact spot only three weeks before.

After starting up I realised the steering had gone. To go straight I had to steer to the right – but I had to drive, whatever my own condition. I had to get to Peterborough and somewhere where they could fix my van – without it I was sunk. With almost full right lock I managed to get going – the front suspension had obviously been broken. Had I been doing more than 50mph? … had the police measured my skid marks? If I had been, I could be on a manslaughter charge … oh God! If only I had Mamie with me now, but I had no one who I could ring to come and help me.

Just before closing-up time I found a garage and in virtually incoherent language tried to explain what had happened and how urgent it was to have the van repaired and how I would have to take my dog back to London on a piece of string – did they know where the station was? It must have struck them as being all more than a little peculiar and that something untoward was definitely up, with me in a state of near collapse and such odd things in the back of my Bedford. So, without my knowing it, as soon as I had tied my little companion up to his piece of string and headed off towards the station, they apparently had rung the police.

At least I had my wad in my hip pocket and this always gave me a sense of security, but it did little to allay the morbid thoughts flooding through my mind as I stood on the platform, forlorn, with my dog on his string, waiting for the London train.

I had taken the risk of ringing Mamie from the station kiosk, hoping against hope that her husband would not answer the phone. It was late in the day by now and he might have been back and I certainly didn't want to arouse any suspicions – at this juncture. There had in fact been just a few over the last couple of years. Luckily he was late and she gave me what loving consolation she could when I told her the predicament I was in and said she would get to London sometime soon if she could.

Two men approached me. Jarvis ironically wagged his tail when one asked '… *Mr Croft?*' Dear Jesus, they were going to charge me right now – the man is dead – they have to be the police – or the things I had got from Savages; someone had been looking out from the offices and seen me loading the van – no permission … I had stolen them. Christ help me … the policeman went on, '*A garage tells us you're in a bit of a state … is there anything we should know about?*' '*Yes, yes, absolutely yes there is,*' I exploded. '*You would be in a state if you'd just had an accident with someone who had probably been killed, with his brain on your wing mirror. You just ring your traffic people.*' One went away and soon came back – he nodded and he took me gently by the arm, apologising and saying that they understood. They even wished me luck.

Back in London, finding it impossible to shake off the gnawing agonising certainty that the worst was going to happen and that I was going to be held responsible for a fatal accident, I could barely gather my thoughts, let alone think about trying to do any business before I knew what was going to happen. It was as well that I had no phone in the basement as I wanted to know whether the man had died or not, but I had been told that whatever I did, I must not on any account ring the hospital as this could be taken as an admission of guilt.

I spent the ensuing days on tenterhooks, hanging about the mews, watching the polishing wheels, waiting for mail, as I had given the workshop address as my place of residence; the awful foreboding of the brown envelope which I knew would come sometime soon from Peterborough haunted me day and night. Some entire days I spent walking aimlessly up the roads beside Primrose Hill but I remember little.

Jack by now had the phone going properly and had taken a call that the van was ready and soon after that a letter from the coroner's office arrived, summoning me to the inquest in Peterborough, the following week. The poor man had survived for two days. The coroner was sympathetic. I gave as precise and accurate account of what had happened as was possible and he thanked me, finally giving a verdict of death by misadventure, mentioning the possibility that the man's actions had probably been influenced by the death of his son only three weeks before.

Exiting the court that afternoon, I had a feeling of elation: even the Peterborough air smelt sweet. I was liberated.

When I collected the van, with all my haul still safely in the back I noticed to my horror that there was the smallest smear of blood that appeared to be between the silvering and the glass on my wing mirror, but even that ghoulish reminder, put into perspective, was nothing now that I was exonerated, free at last, clear-thinking and with a new type of goods with which to test the market back in London.

**********

I could have sold everything twice over. The travelling menagerie paintings were seized upon at once. Looking back, I know I sold everything far too cheaply. Dealers broke their golden rule of only appearing half-interested in their eagerness to buy. Something told me that these fairground things were exceptional, something that they had never seen before.

So the sixties began with my hopes running high.

Although the easy pickings from the shipyards and breakers were not quite as they used to be, I now had the showmen's world to exploit once I had made the contacts. And at last the castings idea was paying off nicely; the cannons were more successful than I could have hoped for and I started to produce smaller models and also had a variety of doorstops cast in bronze. Bronze was the key to a sale! I had to be careful selling the cannons and somewhat subtle as to which businesses I tried to sell them, in case word got around. I usually approached the rather grand country dealers, whose businesses I could check out from the *Antiques Year Book* to see if they mentioned antique firearms as one of their specialities. I always rang first, sometimes putting on the slightest stutter, which always went well with a refined Earnshill accent, saying that my parents suggested they might be interested in a pair of bronze cannons, as they weren't going to fit into the new house. The mention of bronze always did it. However, I thought it as well to mention that my parents had had the carriages rebuilt some time ago and that meant the sale was guaranteed. A little rubbing round the edges and varnish cracked up with a blow lamp worked wonders on Richards' mahogany woodwork, while the polished bronze barrels fooled all the greedy dealers! Or just maybe they didn't fool them, but were good enough to be passed on to the hapless private buyer, who accepted them as genuine. I was learning.

In total, the cost of producing a pair, complete with their carriages, turned out to be just over £80, so there was a good margin to play with so far as the dealer was concerned, as I was happy to suggest perhaps £220 for the pair! I'm sure my fictitious family would be happy!

Still on a learning curve, I soon had another way in which to make money. The disparity in price between identical items, one made of brass or copper, the other made of steel or tin plate, was enormous and I discovered that by the comparatively easy commercial process of having the latter brass or copper plated, it was easy enough to ask the price of something made of solid brass or copper. If the quality of the plating was good enough, then you could more than quadruple your profit on say a tin lamp, which you'd had plated.

On the strength of this discovery I bought 2,000 small Admiralty hand lamps from a yard up on the Forth, for 1/6d each. Their scrap value was maybe 3d. Plating each cost a mere 4/9d and the dealers couldn't get enough of them at £4.10; somewhat more than quadrupling the profit! Not that opportunities like that arose very often.

In another amusing incident when scratching round in a ship-breakers in Southampton, where they had recently broken up a liner. The yard men, inadvertently had undervalued an enormous number of jelly moulds, thinking they were tin. They had been consigned to the 'light-iron' heap. But their dull soft touch told me at once they were, in fact, made of copper which, as food containers, they had had to have been tin-plated. Needless to say I did not enlighten the foreman and a few pence each was transformed into as many pounds once the polishing wheels had buffed off the plating!

What with deals like this to be had occasionally, the bronze castings selling well and now the potential of a new income if I bought more fairground gear together with a still incessant demand for ships' fittings and lamps, it was all starting to be serious money for those days. It was a satisfying thought that I was now probably making four times as much as those sub lieutenants I had said goodbye to down at Lee-on-Solent, not that long ago.

There was never any shortage of buyers. I had by now sorted out the better ones, most of them in London of course, along with others in what would be referred to as 'smart county areas' not far afield. London, in and around Portobello, remained the easiest place to get rid of stuff. Then came the King's Road, Fulham and around Sloane Street. The search for goods to buy I found exhilarating: it took me down some bizarre alleys, both physically and metaphorically. If you could call it work, then I loved working. It was a challenge to be able to root out enough stuff to convert into hard cash by the week's end, month in month out and the reward was the exhilaration I felt with every small success.

It might have been just too easy to drift along, continuing to comb along the coasts, the country scrap-yards and seedy second-hand shops, but as time went on I knew the pickings were bound to diminish and then what? Perhaps the best I could have hoped for would be to make a good living as a general dealer, maybe just a shade better than the sad little marine stores dealers who sold any conceivable bit of rubbish for a profit in the dockyard towns. Not a happy thought. My father would have been right: my efforts in the end would amount to nothing. I would be a failure.

There was no course of action I could plan. Pure chance dictated the way things developed. My life was haphazard and unconventional, but in the sixties anything seemed acceptable, even having an affair with an older woman, married, with boys and under whose demure exterior lay an unconventional bohemian as headstrong as I was then, in my mid-twenties.

I really had no ambitions except to be free from service life and to make enough money to buy a house and convince Mamie she should leave her husband and live with me. No harm in dreaming those kinds of dreams in the new age of the early sixties. One felt anything was possible.

**********

**I look on as my dog, Jarvis, enjoys a ride on the famous 'Juvenile'**

As it was, in the course of events, I was soon most unexpectedly to encounter and finally join, the world of serious business with its public-school educated entrepreneurs, their offices where architects and designers were planning and devising new hotels and themed eating houses, both here and across the world, along American lines, and who were propelling business with an altogether new face into the new decade. Fresh ideas and exciting new trends were at last coming to the fore and my destiny was going to be part of it all.

Meanwhile with occasional time to spare, knowing I could unload the majority of my finds onto one-armed Knapp, or an Indian whose shop was at number 69 Portobello Road, I could spend more time with Mamie. The Indian had bought some of my first cannons. He was as dark as pitch and seemed almost oiled – how he came to be an antique dealer I never knew. He stood outside his shop, with an air of confidence in crocodile-leather shoes and a starched white shirt. The stock was mostly brass: fenders, umbrella stands, goodish reproduction lamps and the kind of furniture referred to as 'military', with brass straps and inset handles.

Through all this, Mamie was never far from my mind. Unashamedly I had accepted my new position as 'friend of the family', sometimes even taking one or other of the boys on buying trips with me and even being included in the odd supper party whenever the unsuspecting husband thought that an ex-naval, homosexual poet might be an amusing asset to the evening. It was a dangerous and shameless game, but at least I became comfortable with drinking a good red wine and eating avocado: that was sophistication in those days!

Stubborn pride, together with the futility of it, prevented me from looking for any rapprochement with my father, but I did nevertheless always call to see my mother whenever I went to see Mamie and I knew he was away at work. She looked sad and tired and before I left, I always slipped between £10 and £12 into the pocket of her apron that hung on the kitchen door, without her seeing.

On these visits to the coast I invariably stayed at a genteel guesthouse offering B&B a mile or so down the road towards Hythe. The landlady and her ancient mother, who hovered in the kitchen in her slippers, were kindly and always gave me one of the front rooms overlooking the sea – sadly no substitute for Mamie's bedroom – but it meant that almost every night of any visit I would be kept awake by her be-pimpled son of about fourteen, who strummed discordantly on cheap guitars with two friends. It was only years later that I realised the kindly landlady's name had been Mrs Redding and that her pimpled son, Noel, had gone on to become lead guitarist for Jimi Hendrix – and who might well be featured in a music magazine, seen cruising Beverly Hills in his white Rolls Royce!

Years later I bumped into someone who had known the family and learnt that his mother used to travel the world with the group until it was discovered she was acting as their drug mule and was locked-up in Maidstone prison for three years. By this time Jimi Hendrix was dead and I don't know what happened to the pimpled youth who kept me awake so many times in the past.

**********

**The 'Artist' with a couple of things destined for Trad**

I decided to try the Cornish ports, on the way down making enquiries as to anyone who might know of any travelling showmen in the area, hoping to repeat the success of my chance encounter with the ostrich burners in Norfolk. Before leaving Somerset, I did run to earth one outfit, the Coles brothers, who were well-known as the leading showmen in the area, renowned for a famous switchback ride carved to look like Venetian gondolas.

Friendly enough, they implied there was a good chance I might do some business with them if I could get back to them after the summer season, when they'd once again be in their winter quarters on land rented from a farm. Now was not the time; everything was packed ready for the road and the first spring fair. Well there were a few pieces of the old style carved stuff they weren't taking with them on the trucks this time – too heavy. They were the gondola canopies off the 'ride' as he referred to it, which had always been called the Flying Gondolas – apparently unique. Sounded interesting. He then beckoned me towards one of the barns and opening the weathered farmyard doors, he showed me what he meant. They were the kind of thing you might expect to see in some Italian palace, surmounting a Doge's throne; entirely gilded, more ornamentally carved than anything I had ever seen. I knew that I was on to something, but as usual acted rather vaguely, saying they looked nice and how much did he want for them. There were about twelve in all. Rather daringly, not knowing what use they could be put to, I agreed to pay £15 each, saying that I would have British Road Services pick them up in the next day or two. One I hoisted onto the roof of my Bedford to take back to London as a sample. As it happened, I showed this one to Mamie, before getting back to London to try my luck with the dealers and she at once saw its potential apart from its purely extraordinary decorative value. She said it would make a simply stunning bedhead and she implored me to keep one, which I did, and she was right, it did eventually make an absolutely unique bed head for one of her boys.

Rather than thinking about potential use for his discarded Gondola canopies, Mr. Coles was more interested in the fact that I seemed to know about how all the old rides were going out of date and how fibreglass was now the thing: and yes, they could well have things to sell, come the winter. For the present, they gave me one or two other names of showmen it might be worthwhile trying once the season was over, mentioning that even now, I might try the big static fairground on the pleasure beach at Barry Island in Wales, which had been going for donkey's years. They were modernising and going in for new types of rides, all swish and working on hydraulics. I made a mental note. They also said there might be a chance at the permanent fair in Battersea Gardens, as the Collins family who ran it had been some of the oldest travelling showmen in the business and were still in a very big way in the Midlands.

As it was, the Cornish ports yielded very little. They were predominantly ports for lobstermen and small inshore fishermen not yet affected by the shrinking fishing industry as were the large commercial companies who were having to lay up their vessels – these were my main sources. I left Falmouth thinking I would have better luck in Plymouth, which was one of the largest naval bases and was certain to have surplus dealers handling every kind of redundant Admiralty stores. Maybe even more compasses.

Just when I had given up any hope, I passed a notice, Private Road, Penryn Ship Repair Co. Worth one last try, I thought – think positive.

It was what I had seen a hundred times before: a small yard, obviously lacking business. No sound of riveting. The main jetty quite near where the brick offices stood with one letter missing from the name Penryn painted on the red-brick front. Not a soul in sight, but some interesting-looking masts with tattered rigging, in what must have been a small dry dock because I could see no hull on the other side of a short swing bridge. Worth having a look at, I thought.

My usual naval patter achieved the desired result in the office … I said I'd seen the masts of some kind of vessel which had interested me and I wondered if I could have a look. Just a brief look. What I really wanted was the chance of having a poke about in the sheds and buildings down the yard, to see if there was anything I could buy. My request seemed innocuous enough. I was told to be careful, but by all means to go and have a look.

On my way to the swing bridge I tried to get a look inside the wooden sheds and lean-tos where odd tackle would be stored, but I had the feeling it was going to be unrewarding, as the emphasis of the yard appeared to be of repairs and heavy ironwork. The steam crane, the stacks of heavy steel sheets, the welding bottles, a coaster's anchor, a rusty generator, told the story – I was not going to be in luck.

I had seen the film Moby Dick, but I had not seen the film that had been made one year later by the production company that had rebuilt the hull of *Pequod*. Without knowing it, I was now looking at her! I was to learn that *Pequod* had originally been bought as a wreck from a north Devon yard at Appledore and fitted out as a whaler. What I was looking at now was a vessel which had been rigged along the lines of an 18th century sloop, the chequered black and white painted gun ports, still visible, though faded now by the sun and a superficial paint job. There were ten, obviously mocked-up wooden cannons along each side of her upper deck. Fallen rigging lines hung like a spider's web across the deck houses which appeared to be made of thin ply, with painted portholes. The deck planks were beginning to open for lack of sea spray and attention to caulking. Like theatre scenery, the ornamental rails along her high poop deck sides were simply fretted from nothing more than half-inch ply and yet the hull, now naked on her supports for all to see with her rudder hanging loosely beneath was what had been intended to look like a grandly carved and ornamental stern board. What had once been her trompe-l'oeil painted poop cabin windows, now looked like the white of a blind man's eyes.

What on earth was she?

I stood fascinated, imagining the cost of something like this. To what use had she been put? At over a hundred foot in length, in the open sea she would have been an extraordinary sight, evocative of buccaneers trading in the Spice Islands in the days of our illustrious Navy's supremacy. Now my imagination was getting the better of me and I had to remember that I had left all that behind: now I was just a general dealer, picking at the bones.

In the office on my way out, the man I took to be the manager, warming to my, in this case, sincere interest, launched into a potted history of the vessel's past. The vessel had originally been a trading schooner. The hull or what was left of it had been found in

*A rare 16th century carved wood
stag, bearing a collar of fleur de
lys, with original white painted
decoration.*

*Base width 48 in.    17 in.
Overall height    4 ft. 6 in.*

Fine carvings such as these were made in my country workshops from the early 1970's. Note: the above (stag) is stated to be 17th Century. Below (Ships Sternboard, in the American Museum, Bath) is described as 19th Century. Both were made to order.

Examples of decorative relief signs and painted furniture, hitherto never made, sold throughout the antique trade and are now copied widely.

Appledore by an American location team who acquired her for rebuilding as the *Pequod*. Filming over, no further use was foreseen for her until another film company took her over and re-rigged her and superficially refurbished her to look like an 18th century privateer for a low budget movie. The film had been shot along the Cornish coast and the ship was finally laid up in the Penryn yard. That had been two years ago. No word came from the film company as to their intentions, except to say that the engines be removed and sold to defray the docking charges. The Hollywood offices were duly sent a quarterly invoice, which was always paid punctiliously by banker's order, under a note headed 'retained props' and there the story ended. Nothing more. The manager was of the opinion that the boat had been written off and the Penryn yard's invoice was simply sliding through a huge corporate account without ever being queried.

It was certainly food for thought.

Patient Jarvis had been waiting in the van for over an hour. I was back in the real world. I stroked him, deep in thought and started up for a night's B&B somewhere in Plymouth.

Thoughts of what I had seen in the Penryn yard haunted me, but for now it was once more back in to the world of junk.

I struck it lucky in the most unusual way in Plymouth. The largest of the surplus dealers not only had two brass-bound military chests, but also what would have amounted to two truckloads of red-painted, ex-Admiralty fire buckets beginning to rust out in one corner of the yard. Like so many other everyday items the Admiralty had made under contract, their design must have originated way back in the 19th century. They had a pronounced taper to a narrow base and were slightly bellied, exactly like the earliest leather fire buckets, which if you were ever lucky enough to find one, commanded a considerable price.

I remembered the dock full of leather cordite cases I had seen in Bermuda. Then I had thought what a waste of a hand-made, traditional receptacle, which for the lack of leather polish, might have been transformed into a smart waste-basket. I recognised at once the possibilities with the buckets. I knew if I could in some way get them covered in leather – better still, embellished with a Royal Crest transfer, then I would have a highly saleable item. I could take off the metal handle and replace it with one made of leather and then I would have something worth anything up to £25 or more. The surplus dealer's price I clearly remembered was 3/6d each.

I wasn't taking that much of a chance. I managed to get eighty or ninety into the van, feeling certain that I would be able to crack the problem of the leather-work. I left a deposit of £20 on the remaining lot and said I would ring with instructions on having them collected in the very near future.

Back in London not far from Camden Town, it was not difficult to run to earth a family of Cypriot shoemakers – one of them had a kiosk mending broken heels and cutting keys, outside Kings Cross station. This led on to uncles and cousins, who I imagine lived three or four to a room in a rundown street at the back of St. Pancras. They took happily to this extra business of covering the buckets with heavy leather hide, which by sheer luck could be bought at Messrs. Connolly & Co., the country's foremost leather suppliers, whose premises were situated nearby only two streets away from Kings Cross station. I bought 'seconds' because they were cheaper, with slight inperfections, which actually helped the buckets' look antique. Finished off with a line of hand stitiching, top, bottom and along the seam, with an all-leather handle fixed at each end with a broad copper rivet, they looked as if they might well have been made in the 1890s.

I got to know the counter men at Connollys very well after a time and sometimes they would throw in an extra hide for nothing. The little band of Cypriots became real friends and there were many evenings when I would call in to find them all sitting, backs against the wall around their big living room, buckets between their knees,

182

furiously working away, chattering happily in Greek and then in English. *'Ah mister James, leather handle look real smart with big copper rivet – good idea.'*

Much as the attraction was with something being bronze, it was the additional touch of applying a transfer of the Royal Crest that made the buckets a certainty. Although not strictly permissible for anyone except holders of a Royal Warrant accredited by the Royal College of Arms to attach a crest of this kind to their products, I did not find it difficult to persuade Messrs. Butchers of Birmingham, the oldest established transfer makers, to provide me with a limitless supply of suitable 5 inch x 6 inch water-slide transfers. They also were obviously feeling the pinch of the dying trades. The transfers were childishly easy to apply once you sealed the leather with a quick coat of instant drying shellac.

The first batch was a runaway success. I even sold some to Libertys, putting on an extra fiver. And long after they were finished, I remembered a buyer called Stribling used to call me from time to time, asking if there were any more. I had all the others brought up from Plymouth by B.R.S., bought some more in Portsmouth and as time went by, some more in Chatham and even a batch down in Wales. Then the supplies dried up.

To some dealers I became known as the *'Bucket Man.'* It amused me. I didn't mind, why should I? I was making at least £10 on each and selling them in batches of twenty to thirty at a time.

Being the *'Bucket Man'*, if only for a while, was certainly helping to swell my account at the bank. I was, however, about to have my first introduction to serious men of business. Events in my life seemed so often to go from one extreme to another!

After concentrating on the bucket idea for a while, my thoughts once again focused on the germ of an idea I'd had concerning the wreck of the old *Pequod* I had seen in Cornwall several weeks before. I knew that the previous year Whitbread had been sponsoring sailing barge races in and around the Thames Estuary and south coast. I had seen one of the barges, with its ochre sails, lying off Harwich, with the name *Whitbread* emblazoned, along its hull.

What better, I thought, than to have a Whitbread privateer, moored off shore? A floating pub to visit, a pub flying the famous logo of the company from her mainmast. However unrealistic the whole idea might seem now, I therefore decided I would offer an absurdly low price to the studios in Hollywood who owned the *Pequod*, in order to take it off their hands, *'now that it was little more than a wreck'.*

The yard agreed to my idea knowing full well that if I bought her, a great deal of profitable work was going to have to be carried out, and on my behalf they put in a bid of £1,000, subject to an option to purchase within two months, which was going to give me a way out if the scheme failed.

I was going to try to sell the ship to Whitbreads!

The first part of the plan went without a hitch. Someone in the petty cash – or was it props – department in Hollywood was apparently only too pleased to have the liability written off. The yard manager told me they appeared to have been unaware of the ship's existence. To them, presumably, one small payment a month going off to England meant nothing.

I knew this might be a one-off chance. I couldn't think of any set-up which might be more likely to be interested than Whitbreads, given their current maritime connection. A few extra thousand to them, was neither here nor there.

Accordingly, I carefully typed out a letter on my old Olivetti, giving as my address the damp basement in Gloucester Terrace, just hoping that the recipient would not know Camden Town too well! I addressed it to the Publicity Department, saying little except that I had an interesting promotional idea that I would like to discuss.

I must have struck the right chord. A reply came back by return of post, signed, to my disbelief, by one of the directors: he would be more than pleased to meet me to discuss what I had in mind, adding that the company was always keen to follow up new ideas.

It seemed strange to be visiting one of the largest and most prestigious breweries in England, smack in the middle of the City of London. As soon as you got anywhere near Chiswell Street in those days, the yeasty smell of fermenting hops filled your nostrils and if you had not already seen one, you would have had your first sight of a brewer's dray, loaded with barrels, pulled by magnificent Suffolk Punch horses.

The great brewery buildings were impressive, broad and tall with barely a window and the all-pervading smell announcing just what they were.

The name of Whitbread was synonymous with every aspect of traditional English life. The master brewer's half pint on the village green after a cricket match, the pubs with their old-fashioned swing signs – all stood for continuity of a way of life. Bearing all this in mind, I reckoned that I should be able to pull off what I hoped was going to be the deal of my life. I would ask £8,000 for the *Pequod*. Ten would have been greedy. This price would be trivial to them. Promotional budgets would probably have run into hundreds of thousands, so a mere four to five thousand to bring the old ship back to life would be easily accommodated.

The inner court, beyond the twelve-foot high entrance doors, was cobbled and the all-pervading smell of yeast hung in the air. Two dark maroon Daimlers stood waiting at the side. Number plates, ALE 1 and ALE 2. I could just hear the noise of machinery and the barely audible clink of glass coming from the bottling plant. A porter in livery behind the desk in the entrance hall politely enquired my business, glanced at his daily log, nodded and led me up the staircase to a panelled gallery. Along the walls hung portraits of the founder and other members of the early Whitbread family, ending at the far end with more recent paintings of the company directors.

I must confess to feeling somewhat nervous and overawed as I was shown into the director's room – 'office' would have been the wrong word to describe such a beautifully furnished place.

Smiling, a tall, elegantly-dressed man of some fifty years, wearing a charcoal-grey suit and old Etonian tie, got up from his desk and extended his hand and I felt instantly at ease. I think he was slightly amused at seeing someone as young as I was who had had the temerity to think he could teach an institution like theirs anything about publicity.

'*So, now tell me about this idea of yours,*' he said, beckoning me to sit down.

I began by saying that when I had been at Dartmouth I had seen a small, square-rigged ship lying in the river Dart and had thought at the time what a marvellous way of advertising it would have been, if she had been flying a pennant from her masthead bearing a company's logo. It was such an eye-catching sight anyway, fully rigged, lying below the wooded banks of the river, that everyone would have taken notice. And what better than a marvellous 19th century sailing ship, a Whitbread ship, to complement the small fleet of barges which the company was presently sponsoring and which were such a feature along the estuary and the south coast.

My hopes rose as I could see he was genuinely interested, nodding in an affirmative way with that amused smile. But sadly, he explained, the company policy had changed and the previous year had been the last of their coastal advertising schemes. However, he said, pausing, my idea might well bear some fruit with a friend of his, who owned the Gore Hotel in Knightsbridge. He knew that he was looking to open the first restaurant which the LCC had given permission for, to be moored in the Thames off Battersea and furthermore, he knew he had so far been unable to find any suitable vessel. My *Pequod* might well fit the bill.

Saying this, he reached for his phone and put a call through to the Gore Hotel while I sat rapt in excitement. I could hear the positive tone of the voice at the other end. He laughed as he hung up, saying he thought I might well be in luck – his friend would be delighted if I could get down to the Gore around teatime. It seemed he was definitely interested: during the conversation he had mentioned the price I was asking and there had appeared to be no problem there and that was the most important aspect so far as I was concerned.

On my way back to Camden Town, I wondered whether I was out of my depth, but self-confidence told me I could cope and that all being well, I was on the verge of carrying off a coup that might well alter my life – with £7,000 profit I could buy a cottage and a car instead of a Bedford van.

The rush-hour traffic was just beginning soon after 4 o'clock, as I drove down to Knightsbridge to find the Gore Hotel. I had heard of it as being one of the exclusive places where Americans could dine on roast swan.

The smooth hotelier wasted no time in his questioning – what length was the ship, what beam? Was there one main saloon below decks? Had she ever been fitted out with a galley, did I know? To all this I gave as authoritative answers as my guesswork would allow, adding that although suffering from a little drying out, her hull was in good condition. Was it, in fact, I wondered? I had my doubts, but this was certainly the wrong time to air them. He listened intently.

*'Right, we'll go down tonight. There's just one chap I'd like to go down with us who knows a little more about boats than I do. Could you be back at the Gore just before seven o'clock?'* Could I!

I didn't say I would have to go back to Camden Town and leave my van and get someone to look after my dog for the next day or so! I hoped I was giving the impression that he was dealing with an already established young entrepreneur. I very much doubt if he fell for it!

The drive to Cornwall took over six hours. The two men in the front of the Rover discussed the restaurant project as if it was almost certain that they would be buying the *Pequod*. Sometimes one of them would ask me something and at one stage Dartmouth came up in the conversation. What did I normally do? The hotel owner asked. To this I dressed up my reply a little, suggesting that most of my searches were for stage props, but that I was more interested in all the various aspects of sea life on account of my family connections with the sea, like the old navigation instruments, ships' figureheads, models and marine paintings … and lamps and ships' wheels and early compasses. *'Early'* was a good word to use!

He was asking, he said, because a nephew of his, Mark Maley, worked for Bass International, who was developing a line of traditional British pubs in the States, Hong Kong and probably South Africa and he knew that one of the main themes was going to be nautical, so it might be worth getting in touch with young Mark. He'd gone to Sherborne and, in fact, must have just missed being there with my brother – and was doing pretty well and worked from the Bass offices just off Piccadilly.

Well into the early hours we arrived at St Mawes, where we were going to spend the night. The Gore man obviously knew his hotels: the place was small but sumptuously appointed. Although desperately tired with the long drive in my overexcitement I lay awake thinking of how events might unfold in the morning.

The three of us had early breakfast, ready to make a prompt start for the Penryn Yard, just twenty minutes further down the coast.

As the four of us stood on the dock looking down at the decaying vessel I was worried that the yard manager would say something about the *Pequod* which would upset the deal. The last thing I wanted was to be the pushy salesman … 'Pretty extraordinary, isn't she,' was all that I said, hoping against hope that my prospective buyer would fall for it as I had.

With a length of a hundred feet or so and a beam of eighteen, it was just about perfect for what he had in mind, the Gore owner said, making notes with a silver pencil in a small, leather-covered notebook. I couldn't hear what he was saying to his friend who was the one, he'd said, who knew about boats. Luckily the yard manager had just wandered off to check some rope or other and then waited on my side of the dock while the two men went on talking on the far side.

After a few minutes the hotelier and his friend rejoined the yard manager and me. Then the hotelier turned to me and said, plain and matter-of-factly, he'd have her! The only proviso was the vessel's draft – it needed three foot under her keel at low tide. He wasn't sure that the Thames at low water off Battersea would be sufficient for her keel to be clear of the mud – but he thought it would be all right. I just couldn't believe it!

On the drive back to London I could barely contain myself. I knew the Gore man would have someone down on the river some time soon to check the depth off the pontoon. Everything hung on this.

By the time we were back in London the rush hour had started. I shook hands with the owner outside the Gore Hotel. He thanked me and said he would get back in touch. Meanwhile I could not wait.

By a stroke of luck, low water was early that evening. I had string and a weight. With my heart in my mouth, I stood on the pontoon's edge and plopped the weight down until it hit the mud. I withdrew the string and laid it on the pontoon, feeling along the string to check where it had become dry. It was nine inches short of the depth required. I almost broke into a sweat, trying once more to see if I had made a mistake, but I hadn't.

The episode taught me a great deal. I had new connections to take up and it never does you any harm to live with disappointment from time to time. It makes you keener to succeed in the end.

I had experienced two other somewhat similar finds, which I thought at the time were going to make me rich. The first one, in the Balls Pond Road, was when I had bought an old nest of drawers, like little spice drawers which, once stripped, look very attractive for the kind of trendy kitchens shown in *House & Garden*. Unfortunately all the drawers were jammed shut from being damp. Putting them into the back of my van, I heard something rattling inside. I dried them out in front of Jack's workshop heater and eventually managed to prise them open. I found three small, stained brown-paper packets. Written in careful Victorian script on one were the words: 'Kimberly – north face', on the second 'Blomfontein'. The third I couldn't read. I tore them open. They contained uncut diamonds, thirty or forty in each packet. Jack said only I could have that kind of luck!

I went to Hatton Garden, and walked into the first diamond house I saw. Yes, they were diamonds, but only industrial quality, worth maybe a few pence each. It occurred to me that I was being chiselled and tried another house. I got the same answer. I kept a few for a while, telling the story and giving them away. With the largest I made a ring for Mamie. I think the first one I gave her. I made it in Jack Jarvis's workshop with the diamond mounted on a bit of copper. She still has it.

The second debacle happened in Lowestoft, on one of my usual ships' lamps expeditions, when I called into a small scrapyard where I had become friendly with the dealer who was in the habit of saving the odd unusual item for me. As I settled up in the office for a couple of copper bits I had rummaged out, he reached up to a shelf and took down a life-sized bronze head, covered in verdigris. It looked Roman. Without saying anything, he put it on the desk and beside it placed a newspaper cutting from the *Lowestoft Argus* with a picture of the head on it. The title read: *'Treasure discovered in trawl by skipper of Sirius. Curator agrees it came from one of the many wrecks off Dogger Bank…'*

Astonishingly, the scrap man didn't seem to attach much importance to it. I hardly dared ask what price he'd take, if indeed he was prepared to sell it. There was no way I could make a mistake, if the price was reasonable. This was a museum piece. Without much bargaining, the scrap-dealer took £30 for it.

Once back in London, I took it along to the Victoria & Albert Museum and there I handed it to the porter behind the enquiries desk, who duly took it away to somewhere in the bowels, where I imagined gnome-like specialists with encyclopaedic minds held sway in their small worlds, smelling of salts and decaying bandages.

One finally emerged, archetypely small and bearded.

*"Well, what you have here is a late 19th century Italian copy of a Greco-Roman head of the wife of Diogenes, the original unearthed during excavations at Pompeii in the 1860s. Several hundred thousand were turned out as novelty pieces, suggesting their owner might have taken the Grand Tour, and were very often found as wig dummies in the window displays of genteel coiffeurs!'* Ah well… I thought, the scrap-man couldn't have been such a fool! I left it lying about the back of my van and sure enough, within a few days a rather grubby dealer, who bought anything and was clearing out my dross, saw it. How much would I take for the old head, his eyes lighting up: *'Well,'* I said, almost too casually *'I'll take £68.'* He said he'd give me £65 and pretending to be dejected, I agreed. It was of course, not even bronze, but made of a bronze-coloured spelter – a very cheap base metal – filled with a patented compound which gave it the feel of weight and quality.

All part of the learning curve!

\*\*\*\*\*\*\*\*\*\*

I had far from forgotten the chance encounter with Archie Coles, the showman I had run across in the West Country, who had sold me the amazing carved Gondola Canopies from his switchback ride. My hunch had been right that they might be acceptable to the dealers who had bought my first roundabout animals. They had been a terrific success and I sold them all very easily for £200 a time

– except the one Mamie eventually made into a bedhead. I remembered Mr. Coles' answer to my question as to whether he knew of anywhere else I could find bits and pieces from old fairs and he suggested it might even be worthwhile trying up in London, in Battersea Park, where Collins had the Big Dipper and a few other rides, as he called them. *'Way back, the Collinses ran all the fairs up North and where they were in a very big way. You might be lucky,'* he said.

The day I crossed from the Chelsea side of the Thames to the South Bank, looking through the windscreen of my Bedford, things didn't look too promising. I could see the fairground, dwarfed by the Big Dipper, standing somewhat incongruously in the orderliness of the park and the neat rows of terraced houses, looking exactly what it was: a run-down relic of the, then exciting, Exhibition of 1951. This wasn't the London I knew. I was familiar with the world of Clerkenwell and Farringdon Road, the 'ins and outs' of all the small streets up to the Balls Pond Road and on over to Hackney and the marshes. Those were the areas where you might come up with something - traditional businesses which had hung on since the early 1900s going bust, strange workshops and the inevitable junk dealers in a side street.

This was all very different. Getting closer to the amusement park, it didn't look hopeful. At first sight I could see nothing looking old. The only roundabout had poorly-modelled wooden motorcycles, covered here and there with flashy chrome. Some of the stalls were shuttered; a few desultory punters were ambling about. The Big Dipper didn't seem to be in operation, ice-cream wrappers and spent candyfloss sticks littered the ground, but I might as well give it a go, I thought.

A stallholder told me go to the office, if I wanted to see the man in charge. The office was part of a pre-fab on the edge of the show-ground. A large plastic nameplate on the door read: *'Collins Amusements, Bloxwich Ltd.'* Behind a cheap-looking desk sat a man counting piles of two-shilling pieces. He had on an oil-stained pair of brown overalls; an empty bottle of Watney's Ale stood on the windowsill. It didn't look encouraging.

When he'd finished counting he looked up at me. I said I wondered if there was any chance of seeing Mr. Collins. No chance of that, he said, his boss was in South Africa on his yacht and he rarely came to the U.K. nowadays. He added that he would be over for the Nottingham Fair, and before Nottingham he would be making his usual week's stay in London and with luck I could catch him, here in the office, in just over two weeks' time – a Tuesday morning might be best.

Without showing any emotion, the money-counter said his boss, Mr. Collins, was a superstitious man. He always wore the same silk suit and had an aversion to the colour green. Whatever it was I wanted I'd not have any luck for sure if I wore anything of that colour. Otherwise he was easy to get on with and talked straight, coming from 'up North', and didn't like anyone wasting his time – so watch out!

When the day duly arrived I remembered about not wearing anything green, so it was cavalry twills and a brown sweater. The door with the plastic nameplate on it was open when I got there. I could see the man in brown overalls was talking to someone who I presumed to be Collins – light grey silk suit, not tall, tanned and fleshy in the face, with hair a little sparse and brushed straight back.

Calling me *'lad'* in his North Country brogue, he asked tersely how he could help me. When I told him the sort of things I was hoping to get hold of – old stuff from a fairground – he looked quizzically at me, paused for a moment before saying: *'Right lad. I think there might be something. You get up to my old winter storage place in Bloxwich; Charlie here will tell you where it is and how to get there. See if there's owt there you want and then get up to the Nottingham Fair. You'll easily find my wagon, my Bentley will be outside. It's a big fair, but everyone knows me. We'll do a deal all right – OK lad?'* Just as simple as that!

The uninviting urban sprawl, which I encountered trying to work my way towards Walsall, was intensely depressing. Mile upon mile of working-class streets, every other building appeared to be some small manufacturing enterprise – anything from ashtray spinners, clock-hand stampers, tinsmiths, fishing-float makers, metal turners to paper novelty makers. Somewhere on the outer edges of all this was Bloxwich – dirty, poor, home to lorry drivers and shabbily-dressed working women who wore their headscarves wrapped like turbans and served as cheap labour in all Birmingham's small cottage industries.

A small Victorian brick gatehouse with misaligned net curtains stood at the entrance to what Collins had referred to as the old winter quarters. What a place to have to spend a winter – acre upon acre of broken tarmac sprouting grass, sheds and lean-tos half overgrown with brambles; small brick buildings with broken doors half open, slates missing from their roofs and some partially collapsed, a row of engineless lorries, their multi-coloured lettering and decoration peeling, their metal rusting. The scene of dereliction covered an area that might well have accommodated two or three large football pitches. I neither saw, nor heard anyone, nor incredibly was I going to during any of the subsequent visits I was to make there in the coming months. It was a bizarre feeling to be standing in this lost world.

I did my best to focus on just what to do. In between two of the largest sheds, stacked one upon another, were what looked like old open landau carriages, about 15ft long, without their wheels – every inch of their sides covered in deeply cut, scrolled carvings. Where passengers had once sat, three rows of seats still held traces of the horsehair stuffing. Two were still fitted with enormous dragon heads at the front; other heads and broken pieces of heads and necks lay scattered nearby. I guessed each one of the carriages must have weighed over a ton; now they were stacked like cars in a breaker's yard, black with the filth of a thousand Birmingham chimneys. These I later learnt had come from Collins's famous Dragon Switchback ride.

In a state of disbelief and astonishment I began wandering in this surreal graveyard of long-departed fairs. Skeletal remains of steam traction-engines, almost overgrown with elder and stinging nettles, stood, rusted through, beside even more extraordinary bits of machinery which at some time must have been part of the workings of steam-driven rides. Poking with a stick amongst the vegetation by the buildings I turned up rows of rotting boards, most of which were curved and stacked in piles, partially overgrown. It struck me that these could once have formed the canopies which revolved on the old roundabouts. I tried to move one, interested to see it was covered with the remains of canvas, which appeared to have been painted. It was too heavy; it must have weighed at least one hundredweight so it was impossible to see other than the top one of each pile. On one I saw what I thought was the remains of a steeplechase scene and on another an imaginary scene of a buffalo stampede. Little did I know then that I was looking at what showmen call 'rounding boards', which did in fact form the revolving canopy on the old rides, and which were invariably painted by journeymen artists with scenes like this in the 19th century. Only a matter of a year later each board would have fetched several hundred pounds, but in my ignorance I left them behind to rot quietly away. On a smaller flat one I thought I could make out what appeared to be a lion attacking some kind of prey, with small diamond-shaped mirrors set into the carved scrollwork along the edges. These I discovered later had in all probability come from what used to be called the Beast Wagons of some kind of travelling zoo, which was always a big attraction in Victorian times. All I did know was that everything was in such a pitiful state that it had gone well beyond the point where repairs would have been possible. If I picked something up some part of it would fall away, soft with rot. Piled together I found three of the ostriches I had once been so lucky to find, lying as if in some dreadful execution pit, legs gone, bodies half rotted. Hidden beneath an old tarpaulin I found numerous diamond-shaped panels each with a cut mirror in the centre and the edges glittering with gold leaf, and stacked in a corner covered in filth there were twenty or thirty wonderfully carved animal head masks.

I began looking in the outbuildings and the sheds. I was overcome with astonishment for here was every conceivable kind of painted and gilded carousel animal in every kind of condition... horses, pigs, flying cockerels and what the Yarmouth showman had called a Russian bear. Some with single saddles, some with double, each with its carved fringe, the seats worn smooth by years of use, last put away God knows when. It was all incredible. Several of the horses stood higher than the others as their heads had been substituted with carved figures of the famous Boer War generals. Like ships' figureheads – unbelievable! There were gilded columns, stall-fronts embellished with ornate triple-shaded lettering, boards with mirrors set in deep-cut scrollwork covered in gold leaf. I turned over some small oval boards and found on each a lion's head mask and then other shield-shaped signboards which were the finest examples of the signwriters' art, lettered *'6 throws 1d'* and one which read: *'The world's finest shooting gallery'* with an American-style eagle carved along the top. There were jungle scenes on long canvas-covered panels, imagined herds of stampeding buffalo being chased by Wild West riders some advertising *'Collins Renowned Stampede'* and again lettered in that fantastic showmen's style, in gold, red and deep-blue shaded letters eighteen inches high.

Still more. Behind one of the dilapidated sheds were the skeletal remains of what had probably been some kind of swinging-boats when fairgoers had sat in their hulls shaped like ornamental replicas of some kind of 19th century sailing vessel. In every shed and lean-to were different pieces from the travelling shows of a hundred years before, all exquisite examples of the finest showmen's art, abandoned as worthless. I hardly knew where to begin to assess what would be best for me to buy. Nothing had prepared me for this astonishing discovery in the back streets of Walsall. Intuitively, I realised all this must be worth something, all the gilt and the ornate carving and painted artwork. But in those days I knew nothing of what they refer to as Baroque carving, nor did I know what acanthus leaf scrolls were or egg-and-dart carving. In fact, I was looking at what today would be millions of pounds worth of historic, fabulous artwork. I was too young, too green, to appreciate what the discovery was eventually going to mean not only to antique dealers and the art world but also to some of the museums in this country. The incredible creative talent and imagination of the men who had dreamt up the steam-driven rides and the wondrously decorative side-shows would have been forgotten. Similarly the skills of the carvers and lettering artists would have become nothing more than a fading memory to anyone born before the death of Queen Victoria had I not happened on the burning of the ostriches in Yarmouth which had led me here. Only photographs of the great fairs would have remained. As for the rest, it would have been most likely destined for bonfires and the gold refineries in Watford as the struggling showmen were simply unaware of the treasures they had. Their only concern was that it was too heavy for the limited space of their lorries and anyway was out of date now that the new age had arrived with its gadgetry and fibreglass.

No scholarly work was done on the showman's art until the 1970s or any definitive work published on the subject in this country. When I did eventually read *Fairground Art* by Geoff Weedon and Richard Ward, I was amused to see a considerable number of pieces I had turned up that day in Walsall and elsewhere in the ensuing months.

So, there I was in Walsall, Jarvis my mongrel travelling companion, as ever patient in the Bedford, and myself uncertain what to do. I quickly gave up trying to be selective after I opened one shed to see fifteen of what looked like figureheads, all gilded, each carved in the likeness of a leading figure of the early 1900s – Edward VII, his Queen, at least one Prime Minister, generals from the Boer War, all in astonishingly good condition. Obviously, I wasn't going to be allowed to buy things like that, but I thought it might just be worthwhile to put one on the van if only just to show the kind of things which interested me the most. So I did. I loaded an ostrich onto the roof rack with some of the cockerels' heads and, into the van went two horses, one of the figures that looked like a ship's figurehead and lastly a random lot of the smaller carved panels, some gilded, some tapering with mirrors in them and one last board with some scenic painting on it. Even if Collins let me have only these at a decent price, it would all have been worthwhile.

Could he really have meant I could have anything I wanted? No one appeared from the gatehouse. I expected at any minute to hear a voice shouting *'Oi! It's just the bits outside for you.'* But nothing.

By now it was midday. It was a good hour's run over to Nottingham and on the edge of town I found the fair in full swing. The afternoon was vibrating to the sound of loudspeakers belching out ersatz steam-organ music. It turned out to be easy to find Mr. Collins. I could see the showmen's living wagons, as they called them, drawn up at the fair's edge. Sure enough, there was a dark maroon Bentley S3 drawn up outside one of them. I would have expected him to be staying in Nottingham's best five-star hotel, knowing how he spent half his time in South Africa or on his yacht. But all this must have been in his blood, the noise, the money and the camaraderie of the other, less fortunate travelling showmen who brought their stalls along and paid him rent for the week.

My blue Bedford looked somewhat incongruous beside his Bentley. He broke off from the two men he was talking to when he saw me approach and looking over at the van said *'You've got a nice little mutt there lad... 'ast been to Walsall then?'*

I explained I'd brought a few things along for him to look at. He could not have missed seeing the ostrich and cockerel's heads on the roof rack. I opened the doors of the van to the wheezing sound of some thunderous waltz coming from one of the rides nearby. *'Great old tune that,'* he said, looking at the various boards I had packed in and at the animals, which I had put in carefully to show their broken parts. I pulled aside some of the gilded panels with mirrors in them so he could just see the one gilded figure I had brought along in the hopes he'd let me buy it. I think it was one of

Lord Kitchener. He hardly looked. *'That all lad?'* He queried, seeming a little surprised although I had packed in whatever I could.

*'Well to be honest,'* I explained *'there were lots of things I would like to buy; nearly everything there had looked really interesting and colourful, especially the small boards with all the writing on them.'* I didn't want to appear greedy and he didn't appear to take much interest in my attempt to describe the relics I'd seen.

*'Let's get down to it then lad. How much for the lot?'* Supposing he meant everything in the van, gold figure and all, on the spur of the moment a price came to mind. Falteringly I said I thought I could pay about £168 for the lot. Of course in truth, I had no idea as to the value of any particular item apart from the ostrich. Pausing for a second before answering, Collins said: *'Make it £200 lad and we'll have a deal. Go back to Walsall and take whatever else you fancy!'* I could barely believe my ears. This was mad! This deal implied that I was going to hand over £200 not only for the things in the van but anything I wanted from the decaying yard at Walsall.

I counted out the notes, we shook hands and he turned back to the two men. *'Cheerio lad,'* he said. In that instant I realised he had no interest in what had been abandoned in Walsall and most probably had no idea of just how much there was there. His world was bigger than all that. To this day I can hardly believe I made the trip to the Goose Fair and that all the relics I wanted in his yard at Bloxwich were mine for the taking. What's more, he had told me he thought there was some more stuff in the old Pleasure Dome at Sutton Coldfield and I could clear that as well if I liked and all in the price!

I hope Mr Collins enjoyed the rest of his life as he most certainly had enriched mine that day. It was the stuff of dreams.

The London dealers descended on me like carrion crows whenever I arrived back with the Bedford loaded with the carved and gilded treasures from the yard: the dragons' heads, the carousel horses, the carved columns, the ornamental boards with inset mirrors – treasure after treasure – and throughout all my extraordinary plundering no one had ever emerged from the gatehouse. I never saw a single person in all the times I went up to collect my spoils. It was almost unbelievable.

It is the lore of 'The Trade' that no dealer ever asks another as to the source of any particular acquisition, but I could tell that some of the dealers I was selling to were tantalisingly close to begging me to tell them from where I was buying such a spectacular variety of wildly decorative objects, if only because it all seemed too good to be true!

My clientele quickly became the smart coterie of discerning dealers whose speciality it was to offer unusual and decorative artefacts for home decoration. They also sold to the many interior designers who were emerging in London in the 1060's and were dictating the trends and, by chance, now it was I who was helping them in establishing a new and exciting vogue and in developing new decorative themes.

The fabulous gilded figures I sold to Christopher Gibbs, one of the kindest and most friendly dealers I ever met. Eminently civilised, he was in fact the nephew of the same Governor of Bermuda who came aboard *Sheffield* that evening in Greenock on his way to take up his post in the colony and who had laughed so much at my antics on the unicycle. I learnt later that the figures were used to decorate the dining room of a wealthy Chinese businessman who had bought a house near the Royal Pavilion in Brighton. For all I know, they may still be there. As for Christopher Gibbs, he established one of the most elegant shops in New Bond Street in the 1990s.

No one haggled when I arrived with my van full of decorative carvings – it was just too easy. Everyone wanted to buy. I could sell the animals almost anywhere. Any number of decorators took the odd and unusual pieces. On two of my return trips to the Bloxwich yard, I even took a lorry, filling it with every conceivable thing I imagined the market might find interesting now that I was beginning to know the foibles of dealers' tastes.

It's sad to think I had to leave many of the larger things behind to meet an unknown fate – the great dragon cars and parts of what looked like ancient ornamental sailing boats, early 'swing boats' which I later saw in Weedon's book of *Fairground Art* and even some of the heavy and cumbersome carved boards. Even so, well on into that summer and into the autumn, I was able to satisfy an insatiable demand, interspersing trips to the Midlands with my scrapyard visits and scavenging the coastal towns which all along had been my staple diet.

Often, I would sell my entire load either to 'Dodo' in Westbourne Grove or more likely to Lord and Lady Bangor, who had set up 'Trad' at the top of Portobello Road, next door to my crocodile-shoed Indian from Madras, who by now was doing very well with his nautical lines.

Lord and Lady Bangor's interest in all the fairground things I was bringing them had by now reached fever pitch. Some of the unusual things they kept for themselves in their Devonshire Mews house, some they sold and the remainder they stored away at the back of 'Trad'. Lady Bangor had an eye for business. The shop in Portobello Road was not only a good investment but by now had become one of the 'in' places to go and to buy from. Lord Bangor had been a prominent war reporter for the BBC and Lady Bangor, before she married, had been a leading columnist. Both were tough and worldly with impeccable taste, and they set about achieving a near monopoly of what was referred to as *Fairground Art*. It was not long before we became good friends.

So that they could have the first offer of anything I had bought they wooed me shamelessly often inviting me to dinners which made for memorable evenings in their house in Devonshire Mews. They had a remarkable collection of 'pop' art in every room, which was all the rage then, but also a good number of the fairground pieces I had sold them since my first discovering the Bloxwich graveyard and which appeared to be highly prized! No more than a few guests made up those parties and you could be sure to meet some interesting people, mostly connected to the Arts and Entertainment. If the woman I was in love with had found some pretext to spend a couple of nights in London, she came with me. She revelled in that easy sophisticated atmosphere. I remember one evening watching her chatting away, full of animation, to the old actor Vincent Price while I was fascinated by the stories Robin Day recounted of his recent trip to the States. Amongst others he had interviewed President Johnson and come to the conclusion that although Johnson had achieved a great deal, he was, in Robin Day's opinion, verging on being a very astute crook in many ways. When I asked why, Robin Day laughed that laconic laugh of his and said Johnson had a way of manipulating government funds to the advantage of the Johnson family – even down to having a number of special executive chairs made, which if you pressed a button on one of the arms, a can of his favourite fizzy drink rose silently from the upholstered depths. It was the kind of evening seldom enjoyed by itinerant junk dealers such as I!

One day, the three of us were in 'Trad' with Eddy and Marjorie Bangor talking excitedly about how their collection of Fairground Art was burgeoning – *'Thanks to you James'*, his Lordship had said, giving me a very rare slap on the back. That meant something was coming… I knew they had a house in France and in fact they almost insisted that I must go down there later in the year. Then they came to the point. Eddy asked me if I would like to go to Paris with them. A friend of theirs had told them some rare fairground organ figures had turned up. *'What about you taking your car; we'll pay,'* he said. By now I had moved up to a second-hand Peugeot *'There's the air ferry from Lydd so we could pick Mamie up on the way. It would be fun!'* From the start they had accepted my long-standing affair as perfectly normal and liked Mamie, but somehow I felt their offer to include her in the trip was yet another sweetener so that they would have use of my car. How convenient it would be to get a few organ figures back if I took my Peugeot – no nasty little shipping bills, no delays, and surely no problems with the customs when you're in the company of a Viscount. Graciously, I hope, I declined their offer, as I knew the business world did not appeal to Mamie and this was after all just a business trip.

With all this interest in Fairground Art, I recalled mention of the long established funfair at Barry Island in South Wales. Marjorie was keen to accompany me; I felt she liked the idea of descending into the murky world of failing showmen.

It was easy for me to chat my way into the confidence of the rough diamond who owned the place once we had arrived, by using my Collins connection. But as ever, it was important to be vague as to just why you wanted to buy anything. I had told Marjorie to say as little as possible if a deal seemed on. The impression one hoped to give was that here were a couple of posh idiots who simply wanted to stop things being thrown away! It didn't take long before we were shown into the storage sheds where all the out-of-use carousel animals had been dumped. The best things were the two-seater Russian Bears – I had begun to pick up the lingo of the show grounds by this time and I knew the names of some of the long-vanished firms whose carvers had made them. Apart from Savages of King's Lynn, there had been Orton & Spooner, somewhere in the Midlands (perhaps the most illustrious), and Andersons down in the West Country. The bears were Orton & Spooners' and I could tell Marjorie, who now knew a lot herself, was tremendously excited at the thought of my small coup. A few of the animals were left behind to be brought to London by B.R.S. While I loaded what I could into the car from which I had already ditched the back seat a week after buying it, I remember her Ladyship saying she wondered how on earth I managed to get them up on the rack single-handed, they were so heavy.

So it was, with her Ladyship in an excited state, that we began our slower return journey now that we had an extra three or four hundredweight on the roof. We got slightly behind and were still about 80 miles from town when it began to get dark. I was really tired after the early start, having left my dog with Jack soon after five that morning. I was trying to keep my concentration on the fading light when, perhaps by accident, her hand touched my thigh and she said she knew how tired I must be after such a long drive and perhaps it might be sensible to stop for the night, rather than pressing on all the way. It was probably my imagination but alarm bells rang. Could this be the hint for an even sweeter sweetener?! I shifted slightly in my seat, saying that I felt quite fresh still and that I thought we would make the Mews by half past ten, when Eddy would surely have knocked up a meal for us.

The remainder of the journey was slightly tense.

Much to my relief we did make Devonshire Mews safely at last and I was right, Eddy had knocked up a meal for us and the incident seemed forgotten when Marjorie smiled at me and said how much she had enjoyed the day.

In the morning I ran the bears over to the shop, Eddy settled up for the lot and Marjorie agreed that the outing had been fun. It had had its amusing moments and led on to yet another one.

To thank me for the trip and to cement further the close relationship which was developing, the couple asked me to have lunch with them at the Vendome which of course is one of the most exclusive restaurants and one which I think I might just have heard of, but never thought I'd visit.

Since leaving the Navy I had sworn to myself that I would never possess a tie again and nor did I. So on this occasion arriving with shirt and light summer cardigan, my dress became the subject of the Maître D's much cringing apologies. Trying to explain that although of course it was with the utmost pleasure that the management welcomed his Lordship and party – *'Your usual table m'Lord?'* – he gave me an uneasy glance and explained in a deferential tone that it was not possible for me, as a guest, to go in without a tie. What followed, in defending me from this fatuous house-rule, was utterly incredible. Eddy just turned away with disdain, saying if this was the case he'd never step foot in the place again, but Marjorie, ignoring the grovelling pleas of the manager who had spotted trouble and said he could give me a tie, stood her ground and exploded into seething anger virtually spitting out her words at the top of her voice to the astonishment of the now riveted diners. They must have been aghast listening to her destroying the hapless manager. Time and time again she used *'fuck'* in the full flow of her aristocrat tirade, ending with the words *'you bloodstained little bastard'*. God Bless tough old Marjorie! I have never had a woman stand up for me with such venom and very much doubt if I ever will again! It endeared both Mamie and I to the couple for ever, and Marjorie was ever after referred to as *'Lady Bloodstain'*.

\*\*\*\*\*\*\*\*\*\*

My own circumstances remained unchanged. I was living a strange double life, with thoughts of Mamie uppermost in my mind I was constantly thinking of the day when she might finally leave her husband and we could live together somehow. Wherever I found myself – whether it was in the docks in Sunderland or rummaging in some Norfolk scrapyard I would always try to call her from a telephone box sometime during the day, hoping I would not have to press button B and there would be no answer, or worse still, have a man's voice answer the phone. My routine meant I spent most of the time away in my Peugeot travelling my mongrel mutt as companion. Then back to London, to my home – if you could call it that – in the damp cellar of an otherwise unoccupied house in Gloucester Terrace, just off Camden Town. Apart from Mamie, only Jack and Buddy, my two staunch friends, polishing away on my ships' lamps and copper pots and pans in the filthy workshop near the Brecknock, knew where I lived. I would have been mortified if by chance anyone I had known had called in to see me there. Whatever they would have made of it, I cannot imagine! No bathroom, just a single old brass tap over what had once been the kitchen sink and the smell of my paraffin stove. By contrast were my only too brief visits down to the coast to see Mamie and sometimes having to pretend my calling by was nothing more than a chance to catch up with her family news or to ask if there was any odd job to be done. Then back in London dealing with men and women who led civilised lives, the absolute opposite of my own, who spent weekends in the country, went to the theatre and galleries, kept up with fashion, took holidays and were part of a social scene I knew next to nothing about, except that now I was beginning to discover a sense of ease whenever I was with Mamie and any of her friends, now that I had tasted the first small fruits of success. Our relationship was accepted by them all; there were no disapproving glances. Even her husband with his air of resigned long suffering, still appeared to look upon me as some rather odd friend who helped Mamie out, kept the boys amused by taking them out on junk expeditions or gave them the odd French lesson. I didn't feel ashamed. They were strange days.

That Christmas was the oddest I can remember. I bought a tinned Christmas pudding to eat after some Fray Bentos steak pie and sat with my good friend Jack and his wife Mary in their top-floor flat in Cantelowes Square, just off Brecknock. The room was full of the smell of their two paraffin stoves, while my dog fell asleep, hopelessly overfed, beside one of the armchairs and I eventually did the same myself on their spare-room bed, covered by a slippery and rather foetid old eiderdown which had seen better days.

I was frustrated. I had no pretext to ring or call in to see my lover. Christmas was too private a time for that. It was time for families and even if I had plucked up courage to go down to Folkestone there would be nowhere I could stay. The back door to the old Admiral's house was shut for good and I could not impose myself on any of Mamie's friends on an off-chance of seeing her. I had rung my mother who sounded sad and said I would try to slip by early in the New Year.

At least one thing had cheered me up. I noticed with much delight that Harrods had their entire window display based around carousel animals and other items of fairground art which had been hired out by 'Trad'.

The New Year, however, brought its excitements. By luck, someone put me onto a small jobbing-builder who owned one of the old Georgian houses in George Street, just off Baker Street. The result was I became tenant, for I think £6 per week, of a light and airy semi-basement comprising one main room, nicely panelled, with a smaller room at the back, which I could use as an office, complete with phone, and also a coal bunker out in the area, which after a little work, could pass as a kitchen. I stripped the panelling, bought a fitted carpet and a Hoover and with much pride hung my first wall decorations – one simple watercolour of a harbour scene and an early 19th century flintlock with its copper powder flask. Things were decidedly looking up and I was making money, principally thanks to the fairground bonanza. And so, I decided the time had come to buy my first brand new car. I bought a lime-green Zephyr 4 of which I was immensely proud, equipped with a custom-made roof rack, sprayed to match!

Next I followed up the suggestion made by the smooth hotelier to whom I'd tried to sell the *Pequod*. I contacted his nephew, Mark, at Bass International.

His grand office was in an imposing building just off Piccadilly. We took to each other at once, the tall man himself being not much older than the 'general dealer' sitting opposite him and who had parked his awful-coloured car a little way down Regent Street! He told me he liked cricket and had played for the Sherborne First XI. He remembered my brother vaguely – *'School House, wasn't he?'*

He explained how the brewing trade was developing. The architects and designers were always on the look-out for artefacts that could be matched to a specific pub: nautical things for the 'Lord Nelson' or 'Trafalgar Tavern' for example (easy!), or, for pubs such as 'The Bull's Head' or 'Golden Fleece', old wagon wheels and Victorian farm implements or wooden bushel measures. Themed decor! And this was where I came in. I could see now how useful I might be to them. It was quickly decided it was worth my meeting with the various company architects and designers who were working at this elevated level on projects which were so important with plans and budgets, and a few months later I was to become a small but important cog in a large commercial machine.

By now anyway, most of the ship-breaking was going to Belgium or the Far East and the fishing industry closures were coming to an end, so I could spend more time trying to meet the demands of the architects and designers I was now in touch with. No more buckets seemed to be coming out of the dockyards. The big scrap firm in Rochester had completely cleared the naval base at Sheerness without result so far as I was concerned. The days of the *'Bucket Man'* had gone. No more Cypriots stitching in the evenings, but I had enjoyed a good run and sold well over 500 leather buckets and was constantly being asked if I had any more. The cannons which I was having cast in Folkestone were no longer a good proposition but I was still using my stalwart cabinet maker, David Richards, for repairs on the carousel animals and the odd piece of furniture.

Within a matter of months after my first flooding the London scene with fairground art, restaurants were being decorated with it, smart clothing stores in Regent Street would use it to promote some new line in menswear and the odd piece began appearing on TV, proving the props buyers had seen its potential also, all of which led to an ever-increasing demand for it, particularly from my friends Viscount and Lady Bangor. Even though at twenty-six I lived for the moment – no plans, no insurance, no thoughts of past friends or an almost forgotten family life, just vague hopes that circumstances would turn out to my advantage – I was well aware that all this too was not going to last for ever and that my meeting with Mark Maley was going to lead to the opening of exciting new doors and a gradual beginning of the end to scavenging trips to the shipyards or into the fading world of the country showmen.

**********

Bleak weather is not the time for long trips, so I redoubled my efforts to track down any travellers whose winter quarters were anywhere near London and I still had some amazing finds in the most unlikely places. On scrubland on the edge of London Airport, where to the drumming sound of an old Viscount on its first upward climb, I found the Beech family in their wagons and there I parted with a few quid, becoming the happy possessor of a wonderful contraption called a Peacock Spinner, made by Ortons. Even under the arches at Barnes Bridge there were more treasures to be found. Here a family of showmen kept a small permanent fair going through the summer months and their carousel was decorated with some of the finest and most delicate art nouveau paintings one could imagine, stored under one of the bridge's arches.

The winter weeks turned to months and slowly, sources of fairground art began to dry up and I now began to give more attention to the demand for anything to do with dying trades: old grocer's scales and decorated tea tins, sign-written fascia boards such as 'Purveyors of Finest Comestibles', 'Hatters & Hosiers to the gentry', even such amusing window signs as one which boldly stated 'Ladies undergarments made to measure'. The possible field was limitless – butcher's chopping blocks, outsize scissors from a tailor's or a 4ft hanging boot which once adorned the front of some superior boot-makers', and at this stage I began to have ideas that it might be possible to make these kind of things myself.

Any small village shop, or for that matter any kind of long-established business, town or country, might prove to be a source. The hunt was on for anything which could recall the golden days of the Victorian and Edwardian period. Shops like 'Trad' and 'Dodo' were the trendsetters and acted like magnets to young professionals setting up home as well as to other dealers. My earlier friendship with Chris Wray, when he bought a great number of my ships' lamps, was now beginning to bear further fruit as he was starting to use this kind of memorabilia and pop art to decorate his emporium in the King's Road.

The London trade was swinging; American and Continental buyers were pumping all the worthwhile businesses full of cash and times were good with buyers easy to find.

On one exploratory drive through the Medway Towns, I quite by chance happened to take a side-road through a village called Snodland. The place consisted of little more than several rows of shabby-looking council houses, a large pumping station for the Mid Kent Water Company, a garage and a defunct coal-yard beside the branch line which had fallen victim to the infamous Beeching. No shop, nothing. So I decided to head on to the ship-breakers, Lynch's in Rochester, where with luck I might find a few bits from the Chatham Dockyard in their surplus stores.

Turning towards the Medway and the road to Rochester, I saw, on the edge of what looked as if it had once been a decent-sized cherry orchard, a few lorries, sheds and two or three showmen's living wagons. A sign propped in the hedge said '*Body's Haulage*'. Some of the sheds were separated by a run of sheep netting and it looked as if it was a showman's depot because leaning on a tarpaulin which had been draped across one of the shed fronts, was a board garishly lined and lettered '*Wards Family Amusements.*'

Here began an unlikely adventure: the last but epic discovery of the oldest 'ride' in the country and the friendliest, saddest little travelling showman I ever met, whose fortunes had diminished over the years until nothing was left to him but the odd opportunity to set up at village fetes with a side-show or two and a set of swing-boats... '*Wards Family Amusements.*'

Freddy Ward could only have been around five foot two inches tall, wearing probably the most frayed and soup-stained black suit I'd ever seen, but oozing character, under a small porkpie hat, à la Frank Sinatra, jauntily tipped back on his head.

Without hesitation he called me up his wagon steps. The inside had seen better days. His equally small wife greeted me warmly, offering me the customary mug of tea.

From that day onward, Freddy became part of all my last deals involving travelling showmen. He knew them all, this side of London and beyond. He knew their rides and what they'd put away. He knew that not many miles away someone had the oldest shooting gallery in England with so many carved eagles on it you'd lose count, and a fascia board with so many coats of 22ct gold leaf on it, it would fetch a fortune. Yes, he would be pleased to help me out. To dear Freddy £10 was a fortune as he brokered a good dozen discoveries in the ensuing weeks.

But best of all, next door to Freddy lived his landlord, Old Man Body, now over eighty. His sons ran a haulage business and lived in one of the council houses further down the road. The old man owned the orchards on account of having made money at the fairs and he'd settled down and taken to growing hazel saplings, twisted to contorted shapes, which had been all the rage for walking sticks after the Great War. Back then he'd laid up his roundabout and concentrated on his hazel walking sticks and setting his sons up in the lorry business.

The story unfolded: the old man was known locally as Walking Stick Body and Freddy knew that somewhere in the sheds the sons had what remained of Body's 'Gallopers'. Apparently all the horses, with their barley-sugar rods, had been sold to Lord Montague of Beaulieu, together with most of the running machinery and Freddy had watched it being loaded, but he was sure there was still quite a bit remaining. What was more, he told me, there had been a big carved plaque with the lion and unicorn on it, given it was said, by Queen Victoria to the original owners on the Isle of White and from whom Walking Stick Body had bought it. One of Body's boys had told Freddy that this had been left behind. The ride, as Freddy called it, went back to the days when the first roundabouts had been brought over from Germany. He became more and more enthusiastic. Would I be interested? Would I!? Would I like him to go round to Body's and ask and maybe he would have a deal... what a difference another £10 or even £20 would make!

His small black-suited figure disappeared towards the lorry yard. He wasn't gone long and the smile on his face told me things had gone well. Walking Stick Body had let him into the sheds and sure enough he had found no less than eight eagles – German Eagles he described them as being – all 4ft high, all carved and some with the gold still on them. They had been part of what was known as the centre drum of the old roundabout. Instantly I knew that each would be worth hundreds, such was the demand in this new vogue. He'd also seen that the carved lion and unicorn plaque was still there. Needless to say I bought the lot and Freddy's face lit up when I peeled off the crisp pound notes for his commission. I'm sure he seriously believed I was being over-generous. I couldn't tell him that I was going to make over £1,000 on the deal for certain. Even to hint that it had been a one-in-a-thousand buy would have jeopardised any further deals he might arrange with the small-time showmen he knew.

The carved *'lion plaque'* as he called it was in fact early Victorian and I later persuaded Montague to buy it, but I never told him about the eagles as I rather thought he might have reckoned these should have been included in the purchase of all the horses together with all the old working machinery. So far as I know, it's still all down at Beaulieu.

The sale of those eagles was only rivalled by my selling what was to be one of my last great buys that year. From the derelict Pleasure Dome at Sutton Coldfield, which had been mentioned by Collins as an afterthought, I had dragged out a pair of 8ft figures from an organ front in the form of Atlas – supporting the world – known to the antique world as *'Caryatids'*, which I sold to David Hicks in Belgravia for a large sum. I recall wondering whether I had gone too far in asking almost double what I would ordinarily have done, but he seemed delighted with his buy and I remember his being very down-to-earth, even helping me to untie them from my roof rack, urging me to get in touch with him any time I thought I might have something which would suit him.

On the strength of these last two deals, when I was next in Kent, I bought a really fine 12-bore shotgun by Bland, from the last remaining gunsmith in Ashford. At the same time, I bought the last of his stock of wooden pigeon decoys, hoping some day to go rough shooting again – besides which, owning a good gun had always been something I had aspired to.

Just when I was thinking that all the wonderfully colourful, carved pieces of Fairground art were things of the past and I would never be hearing from little Freddy Ward again, I did. He rang me up to say he knew of something up at Eltham, which I really ought to buy. Someone there had what he called a *juvenile.'* He didn't think they'd ask much for it: they were now market traders. I asked what he meant and he told me it was a very small, hand-cranked roundabout mounted on a horse-drawn cart with small Andersons horses, Russian bears and miniature 1904 motor cars for the really daring children. It sounded too good to be true.

We got it back to Freddy's plot at Snodland on a low loader, where we tried to do some repairs. Sadly, a number of the horses were fairly badly broken and the entire ride was in need of some repair and repainting. If I was going to be able to offer it up in better condition, I knew it would cause a sensation, judging by Eddy and Marjorie's excited comments when I hinted that I might come up with a *juvenile'*. By this time they had become knowledgeable themselves about the old time travelling fairs, their machines and all aspects of the showmen's art and to get hold of a working *juvenile'* they knew would have been a stunning coup.

To maximise the potential I had to get the animals repaired. A broken leg is one thing, but to repair a carved head is another. Two of the heads were missing, likewise a number of legs. This presented a problem. David Richards knew of no one in Folkestone who was able to carve. I thought about the other towns in the area where some traces of the ancient crafts might still remain. The Cinque Ports, they had boat builders, so perhaps once there had been a figurehead maker. It hadn't been that long ago that sailing ships had put into Dover. I made enquiries and drew a blank in each case. Maybe Canterbury, I thought; somewhere there might be a traditional craftsman still working in some joiner's shop – an old man in a heavy twill apron who had a set of carving chisels still. I started at a firm of organ builders; they passed me on to a stone mason's yard, but no one was able to help. At the point of giving up, someone in an old-established builder's yard said he knew of a retired cooper, who'd once worked in Mackesons brewery down in Hythe and who now lived in Ash, on the way to Sandwich, who might just be the kind of person I was looking for. It had so far taken me all day going from one fruitless contact to another, but this did sound hopeful. Barrel-making did involve specialist tools and an expertise not far from carving.

Extraordinary things do happen – or at least they did to me – when you least expect them. I was almost out of petrol when I set off for Ash so I stopped in the village of Bridge where there was a single petrol pump outside a garage. Just before the man had replaced the nozzle in its housing, something made me ask if by any chance he knew of anyone in the area who might be able to do some carving for me. He smiled and after a pause he said that there was someone who still owed him some money for repairs to a motorbike and sidecar. This man had told him he could be relied on to settle up because he was working on Canterbury Cathedral for the Dean and Chapter repairing some of the stained-glass windows and armorial crests. He didn't know his name; all he knew was that he owed him £12 and lived somewhere out at a place called Lynsore Bottom. The man had never come back with the money although he should have been reliable as he was doing work for a bunch of clergymen over in Canterbury, or so he said. '*Maybe he could help you,*' the man suggested, clicking the rusty nozzle back into its housing. '*If by any chance you do find him, remind him he still owes me twelve quid from last year.*' Well, I thought, armorial crests must surely involve carved work, so I set off into the narrow lanes in the vague direction of where I thought this place called Lynsore Bottom might lie.

I eventually came to a crossroads in the middle of nowhere. There was a farm on the right and I could see a woman working in the yard. The house behind looked well-to-do. I got out of my Zephyr and called across asking if she knew anyone who worked for the Dean and Chapter and lived nearby. In fact I was in the right place; this was Lynsore Bottom and she owned the farm! She told me the man's name was Francis Boxall. Apparently he had arrived one day on a motorcycle and side-car, had lost some steady job and was penniless and was looking for any kind of work and somewhere to stay. He had told this kind and sympathetic woman that he had been working for a well-known sculptor by the name of Bainbridge Copnall who lived on the other side of Bridge, doing something called 'roughing out' but that had all come to an end. She had let him use one of the farm bungalows in exchange for helping out with the evening milking and doing the odd job. After a while he began going to the cathedral several days a week but usually made it back for the evening milking. She hadn't seen him for a day or two although that didn't mean too much as it was the cowman who always gave him a shout that things were ready and went up to the sheds with him. She had let him have the bungalow a little way down the road; there was a chance he might be in, but, she warned me, he had become something of a recluse and it was doubtful if he would answer to an odd caller on account of the police having come over on more than one occasion with an arrest warrant for unpaid maintenance for some woman he'd deserted in Lincolnshire and hence he was given to lying low. He sounded just my kind of man!

The bungalow windows were hung with sacking. In a bath outside the side door there must have been a year's supply of empty milk bottles and the ground was littered with every kind of household rubbish.

No sign of life whatever.

I bent to the letter box and pushed the flap, getting a whiff of a really stale smell. '*Don't worry*,' I called through the slit, '*I'm a friend. I have got some work for you.*' Still nothing. I stood back. Then I noticed the sacking in one of the windows fall back for a moment to be followed seconds later by a head suspiciously appearing round the half-open door. There stood the man who was about to become the first of the oddball, self-taught artist characters who were going to work for me full-time. I was soon to find out that he was whispered about in the village not far away, as being the '*man you sometimes saw up in the woods wearing ladies clothes, who sometimes had some kind of large bird on his arm - and him all bearded and that!*'

I soon learnt he had a Belgian goshawk which he flew illegally but I was never lucky enough myself to catch a glimpse of him in the woods although what I did see for myself not long after our first encounter was that he not only had a talented aptitude for carving, but that his sensitive imagination served him just as well when it came to painting and signwriting.

This furtive transvestite at Lynsore Bottom took a few weeks to put my horses from the '*juvenile*' to rights and the thing sold extremely well – bought needless to say by Lord and Lady Bangor.

Although it took a little time, I became a friend of my illegal hawker. He told me about his hunting, how he got his hawk from Belgium, how he'd made the bird's gesses from strips of leather cut from an old pair of farmer's gaiters and its hood from two pieces of different coloured leather from ladies' handbags and how he flew his bird in the woods belonging to the farm. He told me also he'd got a girl now, much younger than himself, who had run away from home to be with him. He said he'd once had one that slept in his sidecar with him. My mind boggled! He was that kind of person; a lost soul yet talented, coming over as a tough character but in truth weak and hopeless. I never ceased to be fascinated to watch the dexterity with which he handled his carving chisels and the deft expertise he showed whenever I asked him to copy some old shop sign. Old signs were now becoming *de rigeur* at 'Trad' and Eddy and Marjorie were constantly asking me to make copies of one sign or another they had bought. It seemed a good idea so I had a few rather crude ones of my own made up by my transvestite hawker in one or other of his two studios, either the dirty back room of the bungalow or just outside the kitchen door in the rubbish-strewn garden in Lynsore Bottom. I think the very first, done on a length of old floorboard was *'Rigden & Sons, Ships Chandlers'* with its varnish aged up with the touch of the blowlamp and finally covered with a little Hoover dust to look as if it had first been nailed up outside a Harbour Stores in the 1880s. The ideas were coming…!

In order to see how one of the London dealers would react to it, I asked Boxall to make me an oversize 5ft sextant, purporting to have been a chandler's shop sign. Second only in importance to the compass, these navigation instruments, I knew, held a particular fascination for the layman. Maybe it was on account of the vital part they had played over the centuries in helping seamen establish their position or perhaps it was because of their delicate and intriguing construction, which in the old days used ebony, brass and ivory. Either way I thought it was worth a try. Over the next few years I had quite a few made, some as large as six foot. One, I know, ended up *'not for sale'* – too rare to let go – in a Fine Instrument Dealers in the King's Road. Another, it was rumoured, had been bought by some American who donated it to the Smithsonian Institute in Washington!

I then asked Boxall if he would try a ship's figurehead, in the form of a turbaned corsair, the first really large thing I commissioned. I thought I might sell it to the Indian dealer in Portobello Road. If not to him, then maybe to 'Dodo'.'

A few weeks later, the job done, just as I was pulling up outside 'Dodo', thinking they might buy various other bits and pieces I'd rummaged up in the country even if they didn't buy my figurehead, who should I see but one-armed Knapp, coming down from the Portobello Road.

He knew my car and I knew only too well that he would be upset to see me offering things to 'Dodo' before at least letting him know I had some interesting things to sell – after all, he'd bought the whole of my scavengings many times in the past, right out on the pavement in front of the Westland Hotel and I could certainly not afford to upset him. But 'Dodo', if they bought, paid more. The proprietors of 'Dodo' might have seen a van pulling up and come out. It was either stop and risk upsetting both, or coast on past, pretending I hadn't seen George Knapp and lose an almost certain deal, or stop, just a little way past 'Dodo' and hope they didn't come out. It was the urgency of getting money back on the figurehead that forced the issue. I just couldn't miss the opportunity of two possible buyers right there and then. So just before George drew level, I stopped about twenty yards past the shop. At worst, if he didn't clear me out I could circle round a bit and then go back to 'Dodo' and then on up to the Indian in Portobello Road.

*'Lucky to find you here George,'* I said.

The first thing he did was what all the dealers do. No formalities, just a look in the car to see what you had. I opened the boot. There was the figurehead, very prominent with its garish colours, but looking quite old and faded with bits of damage here and there. There were the shop scales and their brass weights, a section of a marble cheese counter with its cutting wire; a couple of small glass-fronted cabinets and a few wooden measures and other old-fashioned paraphernalia all jumbled together with my six or seven fake sign-boards.

Knapp pulled the wooden figure with his one arm, turning it over... How much was that and the scales and their weights and the coffee grinder? He didn't like the baker's paddles and some of the other country pieces. The cheese slab was also pushed to one side. He hovered over the signs, but rejected them. I knew he always wanted a really hard deal, but he did pay in cash. The figurehead stood me in at £80 and a few hours of my own time. Heart in mouth, trying to appear casual, but firm, I said £260 the lot, knowing full well I would have taken anything over £180. His hand went down to his coat pocket and he took out the wad.

Such was my life in London, but I was beginning to understand all the varying aspects of 'the trade' and the possibilities it offered up and now that I had begun to diversify, I found myself spending more time in the country, near Folkestone (for obvious reasons...) and Canterbury, where my burgeoning interests lay. I invariably looked forward to days away from my room in London, except when a visit from my lady-love Mamie was in the air. No, life was definitely never hum-drum and what might lie round the next corner was never predictable. And a good example of this occurred about this time. Within the short span of ten days, I was involved in three of my most bizarre dealing episodes.

\*\*\*\*\*\*\*\*\*\*

It began by my thinking I would make another run down to Portsmouth, taking the smaller country roads once I had passed Guildford, because I knew from experience that by taking a cross-country route there was always the chance of catching sight of something of interest to someone with a sharp eye to the possibility of a deal, in any one of the villages or small towns you drove through. An old village grocer's, where dirty windows told you it was on its last legs and likely to close down, would be well worth a look. There, the reward for stopping might be a spare of old-fashioned brass scales, an enamelled tin sign advertising a long-forgotten brand of tea or a pair of wooden butter pats, or small painted drums for lentils or tapioca. Calling in at a long established chemists shop – some of which still had a gilded pestle and mortar as their trade sign – on the excuse of wanting to buy a tin of cough lozenges – might lead on to the chance of laying your hands on a few apothecary's jars. A builder's yard might well yield such things as a rusty old wrought-iron gate, a stained-glass window or even a weathervane. All this Victorian trade paraphernalia was highly saleable I had learned. The possibilities were endless, given a little luck. I was living by my wits and apart from a decent wad of one-pound notes in my hip pocket and I had by this time a healthy account at the National Westminster stashed away from the past years' successful dealings, and one can never be sure what may turn up, even in some sleepy village.

And so, alert to the least visual sign of any possibility, I thought I would follow the signs to Chichester, whereafter I would head along the main road to Portsmouth, where I knew it was as good as certain that I was sure to find something. Success in scavenging for things to buy and sell is subject to the law of averages and I felt I was due a little extra luck.

However, by the time I reached the outskirts of Chichester, I had had none whatever, with each town and village I passed through, showing every sign of early post-war affluence with all the well-established traditional businesses showing not the least signs of neglect, their fronts well painted and many with fine gilt lettering on their fascias. Clearly the local gentry had seen to it that all the local tradesmen were kept busy and nowhere seemed a likely source for a passing scavenger like me.

By now I was in the outskirts proper and it all looked suitably seedy, so perhaps I might see something before I got down to the dockyard area. Sure enough, my eye caught sight of an interesting-looking signboard beside the road, its peeling paint an almost certain indication that here might be a possibility. It read, 'Ornamental Stonemasons. Established 1910. Rumbold & Son.' Under that was a phone number of just three digits, none of which were legible any more. It struck me that the days of stone masonry were gone: that kind of work had become too labour intensive. There could well be something in the way of a garden ornament lying around – perhaps an old stone bird-bath or a sundial on a column; better still a marble figure or a few of those big stone mushroom things people call staddle stones some of which I had seen in a shop off Ladbroke Grove which sold garden stuff – all a bit out of my league! Anyway, it was worth a try.

I stopped, stuck the column gear change into reverse and backed up and turned into the entrance to the yard. Time and lack of business had clearly taken their toll: the whole place was overgrown, with big lumps of what looked like sandstone and granite half visible amongst the tall weeds. There was a shed, outside which stood a beaten-up old Morris truck with wooden sides. I could hear a whirring hiss of machinery coming from inside the building and the intermittent noise of some kind of grinding taking place. I looked in and saw an old man in a leather apron, working over a rusty metal bench, on which was a slab of stone, quite obviously a headstone for someone's grave.

*'I'm busy,'* he said without even looking up as he pushed the headstone this way and that, and the jet of water sprayed down onto his grinding tool.

*'I'm so sorry, I didn't mean to bother you,'* I replied, wondering how I could break the ice by making some carefully thought out, vague, enquiry as to the possibility of buying anything he might have for sale... mind you, there didn't look to be much chance, I was thinking to myself. I stood my ground, hoping for the best. Finally he did turn off his machine and the spray of water stopped and he stood back, looking me up and down.

*'Don't get many young gentlemen in here like you, that's for sure. Come for a job have you,'* he said with a hint of sarcasm in his voice, I thought, so I put on the hesitant stutter, which I had always found a good way of gaining sympathetic attention

*'No, no... it's just that I thought there might be something here I could buy to put outside in my garden, something which might go with an old place.'* Liar, I thought to myself, but that should do the trick, and sure enough the ploy appeared to have worked.

*''fraid not, my friend. Those days have finished: just look outside,'* he said in a voice which seemed to accept that the days of his kind of craftsmanship were over for good, now that it was a world of modernity and plastic embellishments. *'Pond things used to be my best*

line – *marble fountainheads, big stone geese and so on. And there were memorials with all the lettering cut in, angels over the top and that, but now its just the odd headstone. But it's a living: I'm closing down at the end of the year.'* I stood listening, trying to look suitably sympathetic, thinking it was best that I pressed on without delay. I said sorry to hear that he was giving it all up. *'It's a real shame that all the old crafts are dying out.'* Liar again, I thought to myself, because in truth, this is what I wanted them to do in a way, so that I could pick over their remains.

*'You're right there. Sorry I can't help you young man. At least you've given me a break from grinding off this headstone. I'll have to cut the letters into the bleeding thing tomorrow and then there's nothing coming along,'* he said resignedly, as he untied his leather apron and it was clear that he had had enough of stonemasonry. Then, just as I was on the point of leaving, he suddenly wagged his finger at me, as if to imply he was about to say something of importance, to me. *'It might just be worth your while going to see a friend of mine who's working for the Council, in Southsea, if you're going that way. His name is Albert. You'll find him working in the municipal cemetery: he'll be there today. You can't miss it if you're going in towards the city: it runs along beside the road just before you get to the turning to the Esplanade. Before the war, I did a lot of work on some of the memorials there, now he's told me a bye-law's come into force, which means all the old, unattended graves and the ones which had got overgrown, have got be cleared up and any of the old embellishment taken off, so they're left neat and tidy. He told me they've even been ordered to break up any of the old marble pots and that, in order to make chippings to put along the paths.'*

By now, more than a spark of interest had been aroused, even if it did seem a bit ghoulish and I began to think there might be something in it and worth a look.

*'God knows,'* he said in a tone of hopelessness, *'some of those plots from Victorian times, had ornaments all over 'em – things you'd never see today. Grieving relatives gave 'em whatever they could dream up, from angels, saints and cherubs, to lambs with haloes over'em, you name it and that's apart from all the cut-in lettering they used to do in those days. I used to do everything like that myself until the war came along. No one cares much nowadays.'*

'*It's a hell of a shame, I know,*' I said, turning towards the shed door, '*anyway, many thanks – it's Albert you say; any other name?*'

'*No. He's just Albert to everyone. Be sure to say George Fitt sent you along.*' And I smiled to myself thinking my friend the stonemason would probably ask this contact of his when he next saw him, if he'd sold anything to a posh kid during the week, hoping for something by way of thanks! Poor chap, he needed it; his days were finished I thought as I last saw him in my mirror, still standing by the shed door, as I turned out onto the road towards Portsmouth and into the city's suburbs of Southsea.

The municipal cemetery was easy to find. Its wall began in a quiet tree-lined road with few houses. At intervals along the line of the wall, groups of dreary yews had been planted, half obscuring the view across the city's huge necropolis. Perhaps some people even liked to watch what the undertakers refer to as an 'interment' taking place somewhere in the distance – the place was certainly big enough. I pulled the car up several hundred yards down the road opposite the heavy iron Victorian entrance gates, each appropriately adorned with a gilded ecclesiastical cross on a central panel of beaten metal. Above, in the middle of black wrought-iron scroll work, across the archway, were big metal letters gloomily stating the obvious – 'Municipal Cemetery 1902'. God alone knows how many people must have been buried there.

I had purposely stopped on the other side of the road so that I could get a good look in and assess the situation before going in to find my contact. It wasn't every day you have business in a municipal cemetery after all – especially when you're wearing a flower-patterned shirt and smoking a nice Players No 3., driving a decent car with a big roof rack. Now I was in Southsea, hoping to make a few quid with a council worker called Albert who worked somewhere amongst the acres of graves I was looking at. Life is really strange! I couldn't even see over to the far end of the place, as the consecrated ground (I suppose everything inside those forbidding gates, all the roads and paths inside are consecrated, as well as what they call the 'plots'?) rose a little and then appeared to dip away, as all I could see was the top half of the backs of houses which I presumed marked the far boundary of the gloomy place. To my left a row of barely separated houses backed right onto the cemetery, running the entire length of that part of the wall I could see. There was nobody in sight, except two figures in the far distance, bending over some grave or other – definitely not workmen.

A small building stood some way in at the far end of the entrance roadway, too big to be a mausoleum – more like what might be called a pavilion – from where I was it looked as if it might be octagonal. Dark-brown brick, with distinct Victorian features, small Gothic-shaped windows, and a large similarly shaped door strapped with enormous hinges, outside which stood a small flat-bed truck and two wheelbarrows. *That,* I thought, must be some kind of service building where they keep the grave-digging equipment and where the cemetery workmen could hide themselves whenever a hearse came along. Someone's got to be inside: they'll know where I can find Albert.

So, with a distinct feeling of unease that perhaps ordinary cars were not allowed inside the graveyard's gates, I did my best to drive slowly and reverently towards the parked flat-bed truck. Over the church-like door was a painted sign: 'Attendants Only'. I heard voices coming from inside. One of the barrows had a small sledge hammer in it and the other, two rakes and a shovel, marked along its handle as being the property of the borough council. I knocked gently, wondering what reason I could give for wanting to get hold of Albert. I couldn't just start with something like I'd been told he had got 'some things' which were a bit ornamental, in case anyone inside the little refuge building might not be in on whatever Albert was up to.

Three men in overalls were sitting on a bench facing the door and clearly they appeared surprised to see a young bloke in a flowery shirt standing in the open doorway. The stone floor was dirty and the place reeked of cigarette smoke. One of the men put a mug of something down on the floor beside a big Thermos flask and then looked up, saying somewhat gruffly, '*Well, mate, what can we do for you...?*'

I gave an oblique answer. '*Do you guys look after this whole place: it's huge!?*' I thought this sounded unbusinesslike enough to break the ice and to momentarily avoid giving the reason as to why I'd come. '*Someone called George out along the Chichester road told me I might find Albert here – have I come to the right place?*' I asked tentatively, flicking my eyes around the place in case I could see anything of interest.

'*That's me,*' said the one who'd put the mug down, '*what d'yer want.*' He sounded a fraction uneasy I detected. '*You haven't come along for the job that's been advertised in the Argus, have you?*' Well, of course I hadn't and I couldn't think of anything more soul-destroying than working in a municipal graveyard, summer and winter, digging graves, clearing weeds and watching the hearses come and go. '*No, actually I told George I was on the lookout for a couple of things to put in my cottage garden – to put them by the pond as ornaments... he just told me you may be able to help...*' I watched the reaction of the others as Albert began to smile. Something told me they were all in on whatever they'd got going and that I was very much in the right place!

'*All we've got, are some pots; the figures have all gone. I don't know if they'll do the trick. I'll show you.*' And at that he got up, pulled back some sacking that was draped over an opening in the brick wall and there, in the half-dark space behind, piled one on another, were stacked at least sixty or seventy marble urns! Fuck me! My luck really was in: stopping at the monumental masons on the way had really paid off. But having said I was only looking for a couple of things, how now, without giving away the fact that I was a dealer, was I going to be able tell him I would like a lot of what I had seen – if not all of them? If I did tell him, that would make him up the price, whatever it was going to be, and the whole deal might come to nothing – people very often become wary when they think you're going to make a profit out of something. So in order to act the naïve innocent, I gave an exaggerated gasp of amazement, followed by the words, *'my word, they **do** look something – wouldn't all my friends like a few of those!'* As if I knew a host of people with cottage gardens, all looking for nice urns, which were admittedly pretty hard to run across even in those days – 'desirable pieces' as those in the Trade would say! – and I had certainly learnt that they were highly saleable.

There were plenty of businesses which dealt in chi-chi garden ornaments of every kind, from fountains to cast-iron furniture, but I'd never come across much in the way of garden furniture myself, except for one old bird bath I had sold to a dealer in Crawford Street and that had been pretty badly chipped, so I knew condition didn't matter too much and here were all these things in pristine condition, perhaps a little on the small side, but nevertheless I was certain they were in the 'desirable' category! They were all that delicately proportioned, typical 18th century design, like – square base, slender stem with a tapering body, some of them elegantly fluted, all finishing in a wide top edged with a rim of egg and dart ornamentation. Some had a plain top rim. But even those, lacking the touch of early design, I knew would be easy to sell – or so I hoped! In amongst them I could see some squatter, somewhat bulbous looking urns, hardly elegant: more like 'pots' as Albert had described the lot in the first instance. These didn't look so good; most of them had metal flower holders inside the top and – horror of horrors – I could see some had inset lead lettering with dates and names and even worse some went further, saying *'To Beloved Mum'*, or *'Much missed, now with the angels.'* Those I could do without

Now it was time for the big question… *'How much are they – each I mean? I'd really like quite a few if they can be spared,'* I asked faltering a little as though whatever the price was, it might be too much if I wanted more than one or two. He rose to the bait…

*'Is three quid alright?'*

I could not believe it! My mind was racing with the no small excitement at the money I was going to make on this deal, especially if I could somehow squeeze a dozen or more out of the guy, because I was quite certain that I could knock each one of them out for at least £15 - £20 a time. I might even be able to sell some on the way back to London later in the day, rather than planning to do it the next time I was on my way to the coast. I knew of several smart dealers on the A31, if I went that way back, going up from Winchester to Farnham, and if I didn't have any luck with those, I could cut across to Reigate, where I knew from the *Antiques Yearbook*, there were likely places you could have a deal. That part of Surrey and West Kent were good antique areas, if you'd got the goods. As a last resort, there was a place in the Fulham Road I knew, or failing that, the man who'd had the bird bath in Crawford Street.

'*Any chance I could have fifteen of them,?*' I asked, all innocence. '*I'd really like more, I'm sure my friends will think they're super.*' What a load of crap you're giving the poor man I thought to myself. But it gets results, acting the innocent and pretending you don't know what you're doing!

'*You can have as many as you want, mate – cash of course – is that alright?*'

As I had a wad of just under £200 in notes in my hip pocket, I found it hard to conceal my eagerness to have a deal which was going to make me such a fantastic profit, especially that now I knew I was going to be able to get more than the fifteen I had hinted at as being my limit. Just how many I could get into the back of the car, I wasn't sure.

'*Your car outside is it?*' said Albert. '*We'll pass them out and help you load 'em on. You just tell us when to stop.*' And at that, he and the two other cemetery attendants began pulling the marble urns out of the storage alcove and I opened the car boot – when I had first bought the car, I had taken out the back seats to make it more like an estate, with plenty of room – and out they came! Some were slightly discoloured with lichen, while others were stark marble- white: some with fluted bodies while some had more slender bodies than others: some even had ornamental top rims while others were plain. Either

227

way, each and every one was the classical 18th century shape. Any dealer would be a fool not to get his hands on these, I thought to myself. But just as I was in the act of shoving about the twelfth into the boot, I saw one of the men coming out with one of the ugly squat urns I had noticed in the pile, with inset lettering on its side, saying, '*Dearest Mum. 1909-1952*'. And I realised instantaneously that to the men there was no differentiation between those of the classic shape and the ghastly modern ones! To them, one was as good as the next.

Just before he handed it to me, I said: '*You don't think I could have just the tall ones do you...? They do look a bit nicer,*' which was something of an understatement even to someone who wasn't a connoisseur of funeral urns! '*That's alright,*' came the answer as he took the few steps back inside the building and I heard him say, '*the geezer don't want any of the fat ones Bert.*' The reply I heard, much to my relief, was Albert's cheery voice saying that it didn't matter.

By now the car was beginning to sink back on its springs – the urns were not light. '*Well, that's your fifteen,*' said Albert, while inside the building I could see that the pile seemed to have hardly diminished at all. '*Want any more?*' he asked.

'*I'm a bit worried about the suspension – look at the springs!*' I replied. '*Perhaps another four or five: I can just about afford that.*' And so, one after another, out they came. But now I was nervous, not only about the sagging back of my car, but also on the realisation that anyone looking out of a back window of one of the houses, running along behind the cemetery wall to my left, would have witnessed what must have seemed a very unusual and suspicious scene taking place: a man in a flowery shirt beside an ordinary car, being helped to load marble urns into its boot. Anyone with half a jot of common sense would have known that whatever was happening, the men were up to something a bit fishy.

Just because a decent old stonemason like George had put me onto something that I knew could not be entirely honest didn't make matters any easier. Shadows of guilt lurked: cemetery attendants didn't go selling off old grave embellishments officially. This had to be a case of a 'little something' on the side. It's not an altogether unknown set of circumstances after all and one tries to convince oneself there's not much harm in it. Ill-bred totters might become involved in circumstances such as these, but not posh - speaking young men in flowery shirts! Just suppose the Municipal Superintendent, who I was quite sure knew nothing about all this, appeared unexpectedly at the cemetery gates? The best I could do, if indeed he was not in it for his cut as well, would be to try and bluff my way out of it – all innocence.

Sad to say, temptation and the sheer necessity of making a few quid, come as potent adversaries to strictly honest dealings to a young man making his way in a hard world and I was now beginning to feel more than just a little guilty and I began to sweat.

An even worse scenario flashed through my mind – some nosey occupant in one of the houses might think something fishy was going on and ring the police – I'd be finished. God forbid! I could imagine the headlines in some local Portsmouth rag… *'Public Schoolboy, or worse still, ex-naval officer found guilty of handling stolen goods: cemetery attendants involved in scandal…'*

Now all I wanted to do was to get out of the beastly place – fast. At number twenty-eight I told Albert I dare not put any more on and so, flushed with apprehension, I went back inside and as quickly as I could, peeled off eighty-four pound notes, saying I had to get to Winchester before three o'clock, by way of an excuse for being in such a hurry, shook Albert's hand with a deepening feeling of guilt, got into my car and headed slowly back along the roadway towards the cemetery gates. The last three hundred yards seemed interminable. Now I was starting to sweat. I was only too aware how odd my heavily-laden car must have appeared to anyone who saw it. I nervously looked in the rear view mirror. Nothing. Luckily, the couple I had seen earlier appeared to have had enough of remembrances and were gone and no new visitors were in sight. The empty tree-lined road awaited me the other side of the big iron gates and very relieved, I accelerated and was on my way.

Going to Winchester hadn't been all excuse, because I had decided that would be the best way back, up the A31, particularly as I recalled someone telling me there was a woman dealer in one of the villages along the route, in Itchen Abbas, by the name of Mrs. Hoare ; one of the banking family and a good buyer from all accounts, who dabbled in antiques and was said to have a soft spot for anyone starting out 'in the trade', so long as she made a little profit herself along the way. She was an exception. Most dealers I had learnt already, were a hard bunch, they might smile when it came to a good buy, but the majority were greedy and only too ready to beat you down, even if they knew you were selling something too cheaply. I felt my urns might just be the kind of thing she would like – you always have to try and convince yourself that whatever it is you sell, it's going to be desirable, as they say – anyway, she was worth a try and if I didn't strike lucky, then there were the other dealers along that route to Farnham, which was going to be my last chance to sell before I would have to head off back to London. Around Reigate would have to wait until another day.

Some forty minutes later I felt in high spirits as I entered the village of Itchen Abbas, with its timbered houses and air of gentility. So much better trying for a little business in a place like this, I thought, than finding some saleable oddment out in the London suburbs and selling it off to one of the few dealers with whom I had established some rapport with in those early days – for the most part, scruffy types, pretty low down the antiques dealing scale. I somehow always felt they took advantage of my ignorance in such matters as to what they went on about – the things age, and desirability and so on – all a load of crap – hoping they'd get whatever it was, just that little bit cheaper!

Hers was a large Tudor cottage; probably originally two, knocked into one. It sat well back from the road and a small oval sign, suspended from a post, read 'Antiques', in delicate Gothic lettering, just inside a short entrance driveway to the house. The lawns were well-kept and topiary bushes lent that additional touch of refined country living: all of which left me feeling uncomfortably out of place, with my Zephyr without its back seats, now filled with graveyard urns!

To cut a long story short, she turned out to be kind enough to ask me in for a cup of tea in her timbered drawing room after she had bought half of my entire load. Maybe she guessed where they might have come from, if she did she gave no hint of it. '*How charming; how well proportioned and in such good condition,*' was all she said before she asked me if I was sure I only wanted £18 a time for them.

'*They'd be just right for any small garden!*' she added as she turned away from my open boot and went indoors, beckoning me to follow. The best part was watching her go to a bureau, open one of the small drawers and take out an envelope, from which she extracted a little bundle of the old white, five-pound notes.

She paid me, smiling as she did so, even before she poured the tea, counting out the notes, one by one, while I sat, feeling somewhat awkward, beside one of the sofa tables onto which she delicately placed the money. A quarter of an hour later, it was '*goodbye*': she asked me to make sure I called in again if I had anything nice to sell, and I had a very good feeling, a sense of triumph, as I drew away, knowing that I was one hundred pounds up on the day already – less a little petrol money – and still with half my shady haul left to sell.

A hundred in those days was still good for a week's profit. Thinking about it made me remember once sitting in a high-backed booth in a greasy-spoon café just off the Portobello Road, overhearing two hard-bitten dealers talking about their week. One said he had cleared £27 on a deal down in Brighton and the other, in his raw Cockney voice, had replied, saying, '*Christ; I wish I'd had a week as good as that: that's for sure!*' So if I ever made more than £27 from a Monday to Friday, I really thought I had made it – as to £100, that was beyond my wildest dreams!

The day could not have had a better ending. I stopped in a lay-by to look and see what my trusty *Antiques Year Book* said about Mill House antiques, at Farnham, which I was thinking might be my next try. Although I had passed it before, I had never called in because, quite frankly it looked too grand, with its forecourt lined with statuary and garden furniture and the inevitable up-to-date Volvo estate parked outside. I tended to steer clear of places like that, fearing I'd get a humiliating put-down from some poncy dealer who thought himself superior, who after a desultory glance at what I had to sell, would simply say something like, '*No: it's not for me. I only deal in quality.*' The rough-and-ready world of Portobello Road was more my scene. It was only as a last resort that I tried my luck in places like that and then only after a careful look in the *Antiques Year Book*, in order to see if they were likely to deal in what I had to sell. Mill House Antiques, Farnham, had a substantial writeup which included a note stating the proprietor always gave good prices for, amongst other things, garden ornaments, large and small.

To my surprise, almost as soon as I crunched to a standstill on the gravel and got out, than a man of about forty appeared and came over to the car and said, '*Hello: I'm Don Collins. Let's hope you've got something tasty to sell me.*' It must have been obvious that I was not a buyer and I had the instant feeling he was a homosexual, the encounter beginning in the most friendly way, putting me at ease, as with a friendly smile he asked if he was wrong in thinking that he might have bumped into me before in the Portobello Road. It was quite likely that he might have done, but I was sure he said it just to be friendly.

'*I've got some garden urns* (hope he doesn't realise what they really are, I thought to myself…*), if you'd be interested,*' I began, going round to the back of the car to open the boot. He looked in. '*They look nice,*' he said. '*I like the ones with lichen on them. How much do you want for the lot? I can do with any number of these, at any time.*' Once again, I seemed to have hit the jackpot! I felt I could be a little more assertive than usual, taking into account his eagerness. *'For the lot'* I said, with a pensive pause, *'I'll take £300. There are fourteen of them.'* And no sooner than the words were out of my mouth, than he put out his hand to shake mine, at the same time saying, *'That's a deal, young man! Unload them later: for now, come in and have a drink. Let's hope we'll do more business in the future.'*

It had been a day I would remember for a long time. Throughout the tedious journey back through the suburbs to Putney and on via the West End to Camden town, I was on a high, hardly able to believe my luck and on the strength of my unbelievable success I decided that later that evening I would try out a Hungarian restaurant, just off the Edgware Road, on which I had cast an envious eye whenever I had passed it, wondering what it would be like to eat there. I had a thought that I might ask a dentist friend of mine along to share the meal. After all, I could certainly afford it! But on reflection I felt that perhaps he might be a little shocked at what I'd been up to earlier in the day. So in the event I decided to eat alone, thinking how I might fill in the remainder of the week.

I sat enjoying the new experience of Hungarian cuisine, thinking I had moved up yet another notch, having made a couple more civilised contacts such as Mrs. Hoare and Don Collins on my way back to London and even more to the point, I had made over £200 in a single day.

On Wednesday or Thursday I would head off back down to Portsmouth with my original intention of checking out the naval junk yards. Before that I might spend a day in the working-class districts of north east London which was the kind of place where one might expect to run across something saleable, going cheap, in a second-hand shop, or in what used to be called a 'marine stores' dealers – it always seemed the most odd name for the type of rag and-bone enterprise which they were, so many miles inland and nothing to do with the sea – generally set up in a ramshackle building which had some convenient opening which could pass as a shop window and invariably with a yard behind. Proprietors of such places took in anything from a bit of bent lead pipe to a broken tailor's dummy, either to sell or to pass on down the scrap chain – second-hand, scrap and junk, combined! Until not long ago, one such business existed in what is now an extremely up-market area in the Fulham Road, with its window filled with rubbish and on its glass, crudely written in white paint, were the words – *'Best prices given for copper, lead and brass'*. More often than not the owners were aged, filthy old crones, hanging on against the odds, defying the march of time, still dabbling in rubbish and thereby offering opportunities to passing 'traders' like myself or anyone else who could stoop as low as to rummage in the throw-outs.

Hackney, so I thought, presented a distinct opportunity, as I knew that the Hackney marshes had once been the centre of London's cooperage trade which supplied wooden barrels to the thriving brewery companies and all the many other industries handling liquids in bulk. The ancient crafts and methods of manufacture were fast fading out – in this case, it had become a world of aluminium casks and plastic containers. And that I deduced, meant there was not only a good chance I might find some old casks, but also there was the possibility that some of the specialist old tools with which they had traditionally been made, might just turn up in some junk shop or other. These were implements wonderfully made themselves, full of interest for their strange variations and intricate shapes, very often of boxwood, with brass bindings – these I just knew for certain would be much sought – after, falling as I had learnt they did, into the category of what dealers referred to as 'collectors pieces', rather grandly – added to which they were items of 'treen', which added an additional cachet. In those days I had barely even heard mention of the word 'treen', which was a description covering all very small antique items made of wood. One learns as one goes along.

What I had learnt already though, was that any decent old barrel, cut in half and varnished, with its hoops either painted up black or polished up to shiny steel, sold well. These I had seen outside smart mews houses and I knew of a shop in the King's Road on the corner of Glebe Place which sold them for £20 a time and a barrel out in a place like Hackney wasn't going to cost more than a quid or two.

Yes, I convinced myself, I would take my chances in Hackney: it might be just the place and on the way out there I could do what I always did – coast along any one of a thousand side streets, keeping my eyes open and my wits about me, looking for the ubiquitous junk or second-hand shop or any other kind of seedy-looking business premises which had clearly seen better days, and there, on some pretext, depending on what I was likely to find in such a place, it was always worth asking the owner if he had an old such-and-such which might have been thrown out, as you collected them.

Meanwhile that would have to wait until I had been to the National Westminster Bank in Notting Hill to deposit the small bundle of fivers I had taken off Mrs. Hoare and to make sure the cheque from Don Collins wasn't going to bounce.

As the day turned out, it was not a success. I was unfamiliar with that part of London, north and east of Camden Town and I had chosen my route at random. In Stoke Newington I drew a blank and as for the borough of Edmonton, my choice of hoping to find something there, proved fruitless. Its main thoroughfare turned out to be on the trolley bus route to the cheap dormitories of outer London and its side streets had the characterless look of somewhere which had been set up as an overspill for those of the working population of the East End who hoped to better themselves by going to live in long lines of council houses, put up in the twenties and thirties. Utilitarian shopfronts bore no sign of the skills of the signwriting of the early 1900s: no fascia boasted gilded wooden letters which would alert you to the fact that here was a business which had been established in Edwardian days. There was no old Liptons grocer's shop, on its last legs, where you might pick up wooden butter pats or old brass weights. Nor any ramshackle ironmongers, hung outside with pre-war enamel signs, advertising

Reckitt's Blue or Sunlight Soap. The place didn't even have a chemists with a traditional window full of coloured jars and bottles, which I would dearly like to lay my hands on – certainly no antique shop. No, present-day life had rendered drear Edmonton devoid of any chance of my finding anything to do with the long-established trades. Things did not improve once I got to Hackney either – admittedly, I did pass one second-hand shop, but that only appeared to be selling a variety of cheap-looking, out-of-date prams, along with clothes, all neatly displayed on hangers, each item with its paper label, headed *'Bargain, 2/6d., 3/11d'.*, and so on. On the window shelf a couple of pairs of ankle-strap shoes were being offered up beside a baby's papier-mache wartime bath – I knew that because my sister used to have one – In good condition. *'Clean. Only 2/-.'* What a stock! Still, as they say, *'Where there's muck there's money,'* but sadly not for me here, I thought to myself.

Hackney bore all the hallmarks of falling prey to the developers, with shops and houses boarded up, ready for demolition and any of the remaining businesses seemed unlikely to yield up a day's profit – down-at-heel bicycle shops, dry cleaners, newsagents and small corner shops, all interspersed with pubs that had seen better days. I did find one scrapyard, down a side street, along a track leading to a wasteland, which years ago must have been pasture on the edge of the River Lea, now in the shadow of numerous electricity pylons, in a no-man's land of broken wooden sheds and buildings which I took to have once been part of the barrel-making trade. Here in a strange wilderness of outer London, with the reed beds of the river clearly visible, the cockney scrapman made a living from the cast iron and steel coming in from the demolition of the first of the declining Thameside docks. At the back of the yard, two of his men were busy with oxyacetylene burners, dismembering a crane jib. Not much good to me and all more than a little depressing after my hopes of the evening before!

*'Before the war,'* the man had said, pointing vaguely out towards pylons on the skyline, *'the place was said to have been busy, day and night,*

*with fires lighting up the dark as the coopers went about their specialised work, heating up the bands and drying out the unfinished casks.'*

'*Sorry mate,*' he said. '*Can't help you: but the barrels, well, if you go further out along the track, you'll see some which have been left to rot. God knows who they belong to now – there's so many companies been buying bits of land out here.*'

At this, my spirits rose; oak barrels don't rot, they're made of oak and I'd find out who owned the land. Someone in the Town Hall would have the answer: that couldn't be more than fifteen minutes away and it was still afternoon… *Now* I was on the scent.

Grass grew between the two rutted edges of the track and my car bumped forward, seeming to be going nowhere but out into a surreal wasteland within distant sight of St. Paul's Cathedral and the buildings in the City with its hum-drum traffic on Commercial Road, bordering the docks. Who else might use it, I could only guess at: perhaps lovers out for a drive, urgently needing sex, who knew of this track, along which among the long grass and reeds, there seemed to be little chance of their being disturbed. That made sense. Or maybe those intent on dumping rubbish, out of sight, to avoid paying for its collection by the council. And then I saw it – a sight as unreal as that of my surroundings – a stack, bleached almost white by sun, following what must have been year upon year of winter frosts and wind: a heap, which must have been at least twenty feet in height, of *the* most exquisite little barrels, left to rot away.

For whatever purpose they had originally been made, I had no idea, nor indeed did I care. I looked at them with fascination. They were too small to have been made for the brewing trade as their capacity could have been no more than a few pints. Had there been just a few, what little knowledge I had of such things, might have led me to believe they had been made as apprentices' practice pieces, as was the tradition – but never in such a quantity as this. Had they been for transporting rare and unusual liquids used in some technical process, I wondered, liquids whose properties were best protected by the natural substance of the wood – who knows?

Something told me that perhaps they had been made during the war, for specialised use, never to be known about, some odd things were done in those days.

I stood in amazement, aghast with disbelief, gazing at this potentially golden find. This *was* turning into *the* most extraordinary week. To estimate just how many there might have been was quite impossible; hundred upon hundred for sure, maybe upwards of over a thousand *and* they looked perfect, with the exception of their tiny hoops which were red with rust and there were plenty of ways with coping with *that* – rust preventer and a wire brush usually did the trick. I could hardly contain myself, thinking of what I could make if I could buy the lot. In my mind I was already cleaning them up in the workshop – if you could call it that, just my own bench, covered in filth from the whirring mops, but it was a handy arrangement and Jack was a good chap and, I knew that he would let me store batches of the barrels there. Once I had them polished up, they would look terrific, in fact irresistible. I could imagine endless purposes for which they might be used. This was a jackpot; dealers would fall over themselves to buy them by the dozen! I would be the only dealer in the country to be selling 'treen' by the gross! I would call in and tell Jack about my coup, on the way back!

As I was stepping over the drooping, rusted barbed-wire which surrounded the patch of land on which my treasure trove lay waiting, I heard a flight of ducks taking off from the river beyond the reed beds, adding a final touch to the dreamlike moment as I walked through the grass and weeds to pick one up and it was when doing this that fate dealt me an excruciatingly cruel blow, because as my hands closed round the little cask to pluck it from the heap, it simply fell to pieces in my grasp – not only that, but by removing it, a small cascade was started, with several other barrels falling, disintegrating themselves, their staves and hoops rattling down the pile. I tried another; the same thing happened and I knew all my hopes were dashed. They had gone too far: the wooden staves had dried out and shrunk to the point at which the slightest movement caused the entire thing to fall to pieces. I knew my dreams of a thousand items of treen were shattered: the little casks were worthless: the entire mountain in front of me was nothing more than a mountain of wood and metal and was virtually worthless. I could hardly bring myself to turn away for thinking what *might* have been had I chanced on them a year or two before. It was now quite pointless trying to find out who they belonged to and I half wished I had never set out to try my luck in Hackney. I felt so deflated and distraught with disappointment, as I stood looking out across the marshes. I must have sighed heavily as I turned back towards the car, thinking, *'if only…'*

It goes with the territory, as they say: blighted hopes, false expectations and disillusionment – arriving too late, the thing's just been sold, or it was not what you'd expected, or was beyond repair and all that after some wild goose chase with most of the day gone, one's efforts fruitless. I had got used to it by now; it was no good going down the 'if only' path. There was always tomorrow, I told myself, which was bound to bring some small success and profit. Besides, I had already made more money in the last week in just one day than a metal polisher would hope to make in a month and it came to mind that I owed my friend metal polisher a few weeks rent for my workshop and now that I was flush, even if I hadn't made a hit this time out in Hackney, it was as good a time as any to drop by the workshop on my way back and settle up. I knew he'd be interested in hearing of my latest escapade: he knew what it was like to be self-employed, to go out looking for an opportunity, the only difference being that he had to go scratching round the edge of the metal sundries wholesalers like those in and around the Farringdon Road behind the City – businesses that sold anything which needed polishing, from the small brass rings which are inset into radio knobs, to aluminium kitchen utensils. And now, if things were really slack, since meeting me he had taken to calling at the antique shops in Highgate, Hampstead and along Chalk Farm Road, to see if they had anything which needed polishing. Sometimes another polisher would have got there first: on another, luckier occasion, he'd come smiling back with a contract which might mean good money for a few weeks. Over the years he taught me a thing or two about business. *'Don't you go for a quick profit every time,'* he'd once said when I proudly told him I had bought two copper oil lamps and sold them within the hour for £8 each. *'If you had 'em polished, you'd have got at least £12 each – bloody silly to let a bit of profit like that go begging, just because you're always in such a bloody hurry!'* It was like making an investment, he'd said, and I remembered this small piece of advice whenever I wasn't too pressed to turn things over right away. I had always been inclined to be impetuous, rather than weighing things up. Take the cemetery business for example – I could have really landed in trouble with that one, thinking back on it.

I could hear the whirr of the two horse power electric motors from outside his workshop and when I went in, there he was, in his leather apron, paper hat on his head, working at his spindle. A single 60 watt bulb hung from a dangling flex above the machine, haloed in the filth flung from the rotating mop-head as he pressed whatever he was polishing against it. I was used to the atmosphere of the windowless workshop – the place was hot and smelled of metal, mixed with the waxy odour of polishing compound, which men in that trade call soap. By then, I was well accustomed to the lingo used in the world of metal cleaning – 'dipping', 'scurfing', 'caustic bathes' and 'carborundum paste' for 'armour-brighting.'(that's the term for polishing steel). A wooden box of recently cast, dun coloured metal plates was on the home-made stand beside him, one of which he was pressing hard against the mop. In a matter of seconds it was immaculately transformed into a glistening sheet of brass.

He had become aware of my coming in and he turned round, black as the ace of spades from the hair on his head (or in this instance the paper hat.) to the cheap, metal toe-capped boots he wore. Apart from anything else, the man had a very good sense of humour and he smiled, showing a row of stained ivory teeth through the black mask of filth covering his face. *'We're not taking apprentices on today, so you can fuck off mate,'* he said with a grin. *'Although I could do with some help, I must say. You can see I am up to my eyes in it. I've got more than 400 finger-plates to do for Beardmores, by tomorrow morning and they've* asked me to do the knobs as well, so I can't really stop, if you'd got something you wanted me to polish up for you.'

'No, it's not that, Jack,' I replied as he tried to wipe the dirt from around his eyes. I could see a broken pair of goggles on the floor, by his feet. That was Jack all over, I thought. 'I've just called by to settle up for my rent. I have had the most extraordinary day.'

'It looks as if you did, or you certainly had a good week last week,' he replied, watching me peel off the notes from a wad that I had taken from my hip pocket and which must have appeared somewhat fatter than usual. 'Thanks Jim,' he said taking the money. 'But be quick with telling me about this extraordinary day of yours, because I've got to get on.'

So saying, he turned off the motor, drew a grime-encrusted chair without a back, from by the wall and sat expectantly waiting for some new revelation from the posh kid he'd let hire half his workshop. I knew he liked to hear about the kind of world in which I was struggling to make a living and I knew that he liked to think himself part of it now, somehow in a class above his own, where antiques meant something – gave you a little status – and were more than old things made of brass and copper which had to be polished. And I went on to tell him all about the stack of barrels which had been left to rot on the Hackney marshes.

'Phew: what a fucking shame – you're absolutely sure they really are too far gone? You could have made a fucking fortune on a lot like that!'

'Don't I know it,' I said, 'and you'd have had a good year polishing up the iron bands for me: any of the exporters I dare say would have taken the lot over time, but they had really had it. Win some, lose some; you know what it's like! But,' I went on without a pause, leaving him rooted to the filthy chair, 'it was a different story on Monday, when I'd gone down to Portsmouth to see if I could pick anything up in the way of dockyard surplus – you know, stuff like the lamps and old engine-room gauges, you've helped me polish – and what happened? I ended up in a cemetery of all places – didn't even get down to the dockyard.' And as I expounded on what had happened, I could see a look of disbelief and fascination spreading across his blackened face:

just how I had ended up in a municipal graveyard in Southsea and how Albert and his fellow gravediggers had loaded up my car in full view of anyone watching from the houses which bordered the cemetery, and me creeping out of the place with the car right down on its springs and how guilty I felt. Not that I thought Jack would have known much about urns, but he seemed really impressed that I had managed to sell off the whole lot, before I got back to London.

**My only dishonest 'scam', The *Earl Sondes* tobacco figure**

*'And you left half the bloody things behind – going back are you?'* he said with a hint of envy in his voice as he stood up and pressed the start button on his spindle. *'I would if I was you,'* he shouted over the noise of the motor, picking up another of the finger-plates he had to polish and as I went out I gave a rueful smile, knowing that what I had done had been a *one-off*, scavenging in a cemetery, having what could have only been described as a *shady deal* on the side, with a council employee whose sole business it was keep the graveyard tidy. I hadn't told Jack about the urns I had seen with the tear-jerkingly awful inscriptions on them to unknown members of some grieving Southsea family: people who had once been called Nan or Ethel,

leaving husbands who had names like Ted and Cyril and who had paid to have the sad lead lettering inlaid an age ago. I didn't even like to think about it; I think it was a class thing. I couldn't imagine anyone I knew having a cheap memorial like that, but I think it was possible that Jack's family might have done.

I had grown fond of the old metal polisher and I knew that he liked to think himself part of what I was doing at the time, as if it only went on in a class above his own, where antiques meant something other than brass and copper ornaments which he had to polish.

Two days later I was on my way back down to Portsmouth: this time heading for the Government Surplus dealers in the old part of town, where previously I had always had some luck, and the little shipbreaking yards, whose trade was scrap, along the creeks beyond the dockyard, as had been my original intention before I had stumbled on Albert and the urns. One of the dealers along Westbourne Grove, who shipped bulk containers to the States, where the market in those days seemed insatiable, had told me he would buy anything nautical, any time, *'Even ring me in the evening'* he'd said, *'if you've got anything good: I'm only in Cricklewood and you know I'll pay cash.'* That was always a good incentive!

As for the Government Surplus dealers who hung on in that part of Portsmouth which was due for demolition, where rents were cheap and little more than a derelict building might serve as a business premises, at these places you might find anything nautical. They existed on the continual supplies of obsolete naval stores, coming from the Admiralty's warehouses and from the Marine and Royal Navy establishments which were closing down. The world was changing, along with its tastes and the antique trade was keen to pick up what would nowadays be called memorabilia, from the country's once great Services. Things no longer had to be old in the antique sense, just so long as some self-styled dilettante decorator could persuade his client they were right for the scheme he had been commissioned to carry out in some smart kitchen or in one of the

243

many new trendy restaurants which were opening up. It was in places like the Government Surplus stores that amongst stacks of useless hospital bed ends, you were just as likely to find the odd navigational instrument to hang on a wall or a barrack room chest of drawers with nice brass corners, as you were to turn up some good quality officers' mess cutlery or china bearing the Admiralty crest, or, alternatively there might be nothing but a box of unused, Service issue, Arctic underwear! You could be sure of finding something on which to make a profit.

I was turning all hese possibilities over in my mind, as I found myself happily cruising down the Guildford by-pass, thinking of the money I had been lucky enough to make recently. I had made an early start and it was not yet eight o'clock, when the first seed of temptation made itself felt as I recalled Jack's last words before I had left him at his polishing wheel, the evening I had called in to settle up my rent, when just as I was leaving he'd said, *'not going back, are you – I would if I was you.'* It made me think of the pile of urns I'd left behind – money for old rope, if I dared go back. I'd told myself that I was not going to, but it was awfully tempting. It was still so early in the day that I could easily make it to Southsea, see Albert and his mates, have a quick deal – there'd be nobody about – and still have the whole morning to scavenge in Portsmouth and out along the creeks. Albert was bound to be at work early and be easy enough to find. I'd leave the car outside the gates at first and just stroll in, pretending to look at the odd grave so as not to appear suspicious, find Albert, do a deal – take not too many urns this time, so that there was still plenty of room for anything else I was likely to pick up. It was tempting to know that if I did this, and all went well, I would be starting the day at least £100 to the good. It was just a case of braving those foreboding cemetery gates one more time: I would still have most of the day in front of me: the whole thing would only take ten minutes or so. Why not, I thought to myself. Albert could stack the things just by the door, so that everything would be ready for a quick getaway, once I'd brought the car in along that foreboding little stretch of road leading to the maintenance building.

No, the idea was irresistible! After all it wasn't as bad as doing something like having a deal with a friendly undertaker, who just happened to have a stash of nice ornamental, bronze, coffin handles he had come by, from the crematorium! No, there were no real qualms in doing a little business with my friend Albert, I convinced myself even before I reached the end of the Guildford by-pass. With the decision made, the old A3 loomed up in front of me and I was well on my way to Portsmouth, and now, once again, the municipal graveyard in Southsea.

The temptation had been too strong to forego the opportunity of having a second deal. But even as I parked my car a short way past the cemetery gates, I was already beginning to feel uneasy, as a wave of guilt and apprehension swept over me. Maybe I shouldn't have come. But there was no one about, much to my relief and looking past the serried lines of graves towards the small red-brick maintenance building, I saw three men not far beyond, who appeared to be working, either sweeping or raking among the tombstones. Here we go, I thought, that must be Albert and his gang, and after my saunter of pretended interest along the edge of the consecrated plots, I was pleased to discover I had been right.

Albert looked up as I approached and when he saw who it was, he beamed, doubtless thinking he was onto an easy few quid again. He had guessed right! *'No car this time?'* he said, looking worried, *'can't do much without that.'* He paused, *'How many were you wanting anyway; we might be able to get 'em out last thing in the day, if you come back.'*

*'No, it's O.K., I left the car outside the gates: I just wanted to make sure everything was alright before I came in,'* I said as his mates walked over, having heard the conversation.

*'You just tell me how many you want and we'll get them ready quick, while you go and get the car. Today's payday and someone from the offices could be over*

*anytime with our wages.'* Perfect, I thought: he had even managed by chance to anticipate my plan for urgency.

*'Would twelve be O.K. – same price as last time?'* And at that I rather furtively handed him the required number of pound notes, based on the previous deal and he didn't even bother to count them before stuffing them into the pocket of his overalls.

'That's fine,' he replied, while the other two men just grinned and with no further ado, he leant his rake against the big wooden council barrow and set off towards his hoard in the cemetery outbuilding.

*'I'll bring the car down: give me a few minutes Albert,'* I said, setting off at a fairly brisk walk back towards the gates to get my car, quite oblivious to all the memorials of those buried on either side of me – after all, what did I care about them, they'd be none the wiser, urn or no urn on their grave – this was purely business and the sooner it was completed, the better. I just hoped no one was watching.

Quickening my pace, I was almost at the gates when to my dismay a couple appeared. At such an early hour this was an unwelcome surprise, no one, I had thought would be paying their respects to some departed loved one, as early as this, and at their sudden appearance, a wave of apprehension caused me to flush, thinking that they might hang about some grave near the maintenance building, which would mean delaying loading the urns, and if they loitered too long, there was a chance that someone from the council offices might be along, with Albert and the men's paypacket and catch us at it – shit, that *would* be the end, I thought. As it was, I passed them with a nod and a suitably subdued *'good morning'*, hoping to appear perfectly casual. In reality I was feeling distinctly tense and even more guilty than on the occasion of my first visit. I looked back, just before turning out of the cemetery gates, to see which way they were heading. To my horror, it looked as if they were going straight towards one of the plots close to where I had encountered Albert, when I had first arrived – not a stone's throw from the workers' outbuilding. The last thing I wanted at this stage was to be forced to give up my entire plan, now that I had paid for things which would give me a more than worthwhile profit, because every pound counts and needs must, when you're only twenty-six years old, buying and selling, who has only known what it's like to have a bank account for just over a year, with no one to turn to for advice.

By now I was beginning to fear the worst, but my luck held however, because just before I reached the car, by now in a state of indecision as to what to do, over the cemetery wall, between the yew trees, I saw the couple disappearing to the left, past the little building, out towards the far edge of the graveyard and almost out of sight from where I'd park up for loading. But I would have to be quick – it could not be long before they were back, however fond they might have been of some recently-departed soul, there was no time to be lost.

As much as I wanted to press down on the accelerator, I reverently crept slowly down the access road towards the outbuilding, half ashamed of myself for having been in such a predicament, fearing the worst that I might be caught red-handed, taking advantage of honest, humble workmen, intent on just doing a good day's work, all for the sake of a few quid. No, I told myself, I was never going to do this again. Anyway, the workmen were not all that honest, so what the hell, I wasn't totally to blame, what I was doing wasn't all that shameful. And then at last, after the excruciatingly slow crawl to where I was to load up my ill-gotten gains, I pulled up at an angle to the little building's door, to minimise the chance of being seen from the couple who were about their graveside business on the far side of the cemetery and leaving the engine running, I got out quickly and went to open the car boot, just as Albert emerged carrying the first of the urns.

*'I'll leave you to stick them in Albert; just be a bit careful. There are some bits of old sacking in the back, if you need it to stop them rubbing together and there's a blanket you can stick over them when they're all in. I'll get back in the car,'* I called back, thinking that I might look a little too conspicuous

and out of place, loading up in my flower-patterned shirt and cavalry twills. *'Just give me a shout when you're done.'*

I looked at my watch: all being well I would still be down by the dockyard before ten o'clock. Things were going like clockwork, thank God, but I hardly need say that any of my friends would have disowned me if they had known what I was up to!

*'That's three of them,'* I heard Albert shout eagerly as I wound down the window and looked anxiously out across the cemetery and back along the access road towards the gates. *'Do be quick Albert – just don't break any of the bloody things though,'* I thought to myself, as I heard thump after thump and felt the springs taking the extra weight. A bare two nervous minutes had passed before the happy voice of a newly enriched Albert announced: *'That's it, chief. All done,'* at which I tilted down my rear view mirror to make sure he had not forgotten to cover the contents of the boot with the blanket, as I'd asked, and as I did so I could see the three men standing, beaming by the door of their illicit emporium. Let's get out of here quick, I thought to myself!

*'Good stuff, Albert, many thanks. Maybe I'll see you another day,'* I called out of the window, knowing full well that this really was the last time I was going to see old Albert and his cronies, as I slipped the car into gear and pulled out onto the access road again, slowly and respectfully beginning my crawl back to the cemetery gates, outside which was the real world and the business of trying to scratch an honest to goodness living among the junk and surplus dealers of the naval town of Portsmouth.

Four o'clock that afternoon found me sitting, utterly dejected and bewildered, in the Hogs Back transport café at one of the oil-cloth covered tables, having a cup of coffee, trying unsuccessfully to enjoy an Eccles cake, while I mulled over the day's events and totted up the cost of my various finds and worked out a notionally hoped-for profit for each of the things I had bought. More often than not, it was a reassuring exercise, inasmuch that it showed my dealing

248

exploits were paying off quite handsomely. But in the last half hour something had gone terribly wrong.

I sat fiddling gloomily with my ballpoint, looking at the cigarette packet beside the coffee cup, on which I had made a list of my new stock. The list on the left-hand side began with: urns…£36. then came, signal flags…£3 (useful, I hoped for pub décor – hardly collectors items) followed by, Aldis lamp…£3.10 (looked interesting, made of steel, about twice the size of a baked beans tin, but that could be copper-plated, with a lens on the front and a small handle on the side you pushed up and down to make signals, from something like a lifeboat? You could never go wrong with marine stuff!) Next, 2 anchors…£2.10 (small. Always saleable.) 4 Guages (from an engine room on some frigate I had been told. Invariably made of brass, which gave them their appeal.) The best profit ratio, I thought, lay in the 6 Cruet sets…£12 (I was almost sure they were silver-plated, although the asking price, before I knocked the man down a quid on each, told me they were being sold as being made of chrome. They had come from the officers' mess at HMS *Excellent* – or so I was told when I found them in a jumble of discarded stores at the surplus dealers nearest to the dockyard gate. I couldn't go wrong on those: might even be worth taking them to a silver dealers, I knew one off Baker Street.)

The list on the right-hand side started with: 10 plates…£3. (gold-lined rims with a nice Admiralty anchor in an oval and they came from the same place as the cruets, if the man was to be believed, these would appeal to anyone.) Finishing the list of my new acquisitions was, Marlin spike…£1 (collectable tool used by sailmakers) and tin hat…5/- ( painted blue: the attraction of this was that it had the wording 'Gunnery Officer' stencilled across the front of it, which made it important and a certain 'seller'.) It wasn't exactly the stuff of Sotheby's or Christies, but you have to start somewhere and things were very different in the sixties. And it had only been an hour before, when I had set off from Portsmouth, more than pleased with my day's work, that I could see a profit in all the, let's call it junk, I'd bought – at least £20 and that had been without the

249

urns from bloody Albert. It had been my greed to have a go at them a second shame-filled time, that had meant things had seriously and most embarrassingly backfired on me! What had happened was this…

I had decided that I would get the best deal at the Mill House as far as the urns were concerned, where Don Collins had asked me in for a gin. He had been so keen to buy the lot on the previous occasion, paying more than £20 a go, and it was easy to cut across to Farnham on my way back, whereas I would have to make a diversion to call at Mrs. Hoare's again. And besides, however pleasant she had been, she was what a lot of dealers would have rather sneeringly referred to as a 'dabbler' and 'dabblers' were never to be relied on when it came to selling. Whether they knocked you down or not, real dealers like the ones who shipped all manner of junk off to the States, as did those off Westbourne Grove, were always anxious to buy and I could unload the remainder of my buys onto them in the morning. So it was off to Farnham, breezing happily along, eager to arrive at Mill House Antiques and looking forward to an Indian meal in my favoured restaurant off Praed Street, once I was back in London.

Full of confidence, now that I saw a pair of my *'garden'* urns standing outside amongst the white-painted metal garden seats, statuary, flower stands and the like, which lined the gravel forecourt of Mill House Antiques, I pulled up, thinking happily of the £100 profit that lay waiting for me – and maybe even another gin and tonic to cement this newly-established relationship with a dealer like Don Collins. For me, in those days, what with everything else, to make a new contact like this was an important step up the ladder. It meant I was really getting somewhere!

I was just moving the bits of junk off the blanket, to get at the urns, when the mill door opened and Collins came out. The crunching on the gravel had clearly alerted him to the fact that there was business to be had, if he was lucky.

*'You again; this is an unexpected surprise. It is nice to see you back –* James *– wasn't it?'* He said a little camply, as he came up to the back of the car to join me. *'More nice things for me this time I hope,'* and I could see him hopefully scanning the contents of my boot, with the customary dealer's eagle eye. I had pushed the metal stuff towards the front, meanwhile the open cardboard carton, half tipped over, containing the cruet sets and plates, remained firmly wedged on the blanket. He craned his neck under the raised boot lid *'Oh, I like the plates, James. Things like that are definitely for me – anything pretty and decorative.'* (Things *were* looking up for me... now I was even into porcelain!) He couldn't have missed seeing the metal junk and other bits, so when he queried, *'Anything else? The cruets aren't quite me, I think,'* I guessed he knew I had something hidden under the dirty piece of blanket.

*'I could do the plates for (slight pause) £25,'* I said, moving the carton aside, trying to sound authoritative and knowledgeable, as if I knew their value. In fact I had no idea of course! Then, folding back the blanket, I revealed the rows of urns, saying *'I could do this garden stuff a little cheaper than last time,'* hoping this offer might prove irresistible. But then alas, in one horrifying instant, came *the* most mortifying and embarrassing experience that had ever happened to me, as it registered just what that cretin Albert had done. Not only on top of the pile were several of the most appallingly unattractive, bulbous and virtually unsaleable 'pots', but even worse, nearly all of them had those awful, domed metal flower holders in them, just like ones you would expect to see in almost any undertakers' window or on the border of some crematorium's garden of remembrance. Albert had just grabbed the first that came to hand: he had, unluckily for me, stuck in a batch of complete duds. I had been at pains to explain that I only wanted the 'nice thin, tall ones' on my first visit: he had then forgotten and just loaded on those closest at hand. I flushed, knowing that it had been my fault for not checking – I had been too anxious keeping a lookout, to see what was being dumped into my boot. What an idiot I had been! Now I was completely in the shit!

Making matters even worse, on the very top one, the lead lettering glowered back at me, proclaiming '*Dearest Mum had passed away on October 17th 1948.*'

I can hardly blame Mr. Collins for visibly recoiling in disgust, throwing his arms up in an effeminate gesture of revulsion and disbelief. He must have been wondering how anyone in their right mind could be offering someone like him, a man of taste, such obnoxious articles. '*Call these garden urns…? Dear boy, these are simply too dreadful. Please take them away: I've seen enough. Don't tell me that the first ones I bought came from the same place as these? I thought they looked a bit small. This explains it: they've come from some funeral parlour. What on earth have you been up to?'* His words came gushing out and then he turned quickly away and went mincing back towards the mill house, calling out as he went, '*Forget about the plates!'*

**Figurehead for sale outside indian's shop in Portobello Road**

I tried to splutter some explanation, about a stonemason's yard and how I was sorry, but it was pointless. Just before going in, he turned, saying he would be very, very grateful if on another day I would be kind enough to return and buy back all the urns he had bought in the first place. *And* he would be prepared to take a loss. So would I please give him a ring. And at that the door closed behind him, leaving me standing, looking down on my stock, wondering what the hell I was to do.

The last thing in the world I was going to do was to buy back the first lot on top of what looked like a disastrous loss on this batch. At a stroke it had become anything *but* a successful day, because after stopping at the transport café, I looked to see exactly what I had paid for in the cemetery that morning... I had laid out £36 - a lot of money to me – for those twelve urns. Worse still was the fact that all save two were of the hideous, funereal shape with metal flower holders, and one of those was cracked, making it unsaleable. So I had just one traditional eighteenth century shaped one, for which I might get fifteen quid – perhaps a little more with luck. This meant I was heading for a disastrous loss of twenty quid and that was seriously depressing. Could I do *anything* I wondered, with all the others? Six of them had sad and repugnant inscriptions on them, making them abhorrent even to look at. The situation struck me as being strangely reminiscent of the business of a mummy's foot I'd bought, thinking someone was going to find it irresistible, only a short while go, which I came to loathe each time I looked at it lying on the seat beside me. I chucked it out eventually, unable to sell it, losing the eight quid it had cost me. And now here I was again, wishing that I hadn't even got these wretched things in my car. I did *not* want to go to bed dejected, thinking of what was in my car, to wake up facing a loss, to look and see how the dead were remembered, spelled out in Stygian letters of grey lead, onto what I had hoped would pass as garden urns – very profitable and seemingly, so easy to get rid of. However, it seemed that I had been taught something of a bitter lesson instead.

Sitting in my favourite Cypriot café at a road junction known as the Brecknock, at the back of Camden Town, I let the worst of the rush hour pass, before I called in at Jack's workshop, in order to drop off the metal bits for polishing.

*'What's up with you Jim?'* he said, clearly noticing my downhearted demeanour, as I dumped the signal lamps and other things on the filth-covered floor. *'This all looks pretty good stuff to me.'*

'Oh, it's not this,' I said, *'it's the bloody stuff I've got in the boot':* and I went on to tell him the sorry tale of what had happened that morning in the municipal graveyard and how, all through my own fault, I had ended up buying bits of funereal rubbish.

I had half expected him to be shocked, as I knew his wife Mary still went to church. But instead he laughed. *'Come on Jim,'* he said, *'let me have a look at them.'* And when I rather sheepishly drew the blanket back to reveal my mistake, he laughed again, paused, gave a nod and said, *'Oh, you'll flog this lot alright, knowing you. You've only got to pick out the lead letters and then grind them off as if there had been nothing there in the first place.'*

It was after midnight by the time we had finished. I gave Jack a fiver, but I must say, it had given me the nastiest of feelings, picking out those names and dates and memories with a screwdriver, before grinding off. But when the entire business had finished and the metal flower holders had been removed, I knew that one or other of the less discriminating junk exporters would probably be persuaded they were garden urns. And that was the way the somewhat bizarre episode ended.

It had been an interesting fortnight and I had learnt more than one lesson along the way. There was a moral somewhere in all this, I later thought. But once again, it *had* been profitable.

*********

Back once more to Kent and things were soon to change.

Demands from 'Trad' for making copies increased almost on a weekly basis and it was during that summer that my transvestite artist friend suddenly found his bungalow filled with stack upon stack of old penny slot machines I had run across in a scrapyard in Southend, which had been thrown out of one of the town's biggest Amusement Arcades.

In the same way showmen had never anticipated either the value or the intrinsic interest of their apparatus, nor did hundreds of seaside arcade operators, a sub-culture of the old travellers, appreciate just how interesting Edwardian penny slot machines were. Noone else had envisaged their potential to please the fun-loving sixties. I was constantly coming across them when I was scavenging about the seaside arcades. They could be bought for practically nothing now that the electronic age had arrived. Shiny steel balls whirled round chutes and disappeared. *'Score a hundred and win!'* For just one penny a garishly coloured disc went spinning and your fortune might be told depending on which segment the brass pointer had stopped at. For the daring, it was *'What the Butler Saw'* – the flipping pages as you turned the handle revealing skimpily-clad young ladies of the 1890s taking off their clothes until a fat Victorian bottom was revealed. These were at a premium. My suitably worded –enquiry to the management of the Blackpool Tower resulted in an entire lorry-load arriving at the unlikely destination of *'The Bungalow, Lynsore Bottom'* one late afternoon! Amongst the batch were several rare, very old machines in huge glass cases, portraying scenes such as divers rescuing treasure from a sunken wreck or the wondrous subterranean workings of an early coal mine, the entire scene coming to life on the injection of a single penny, to be accompanied by the tinkling of a music box. One of these I kept for a while and I know all the others were eventually sold for a great deal of money. My favourites remained the first-ever football machines, with the little metal figures of the footballers, each in his miniature knitted sweater, one leg jerking out whenever you pressed the handle, all legs flying on your opponent's side trying to stop the ball from tumbling into his goal-mouth. The whole lot would have gone for scrap, if, as the dealers say, I hadn't *had a go*, without knowing I was starting yet another craze.

Although the odd one still turned up, the sources quickly dried up and none of the trend-setting shops around Portobello could get any more and the craze fizzled out after a few months.

\*\*\*\*\*\*\*\*\*\*

Whoever it was in the late spring of 1962 had casually mentioned to Mamie that they had vaguely heard something about an 18th century Manor House standing empty in an idyllic valley a few miles from Canterbury was unwittingly going to change more than a few people's lives – mine amongst them.

With the least sense of practicality in mind she had rushed to see it. It had sounded like a dream and not even as yet in agents' hands – sitting in an estate of 600 acres mostly made up of hop gardens still being farmed along pre-war lines. It had been allowed to run down now that the owners, who were two delightful, bluff if somewhat eccentric, yeomen farmers both now getting on and neither with heirs, had thought it best to let someone else take the old place on with its brown-painted skirting boards its over-painted Georgian fire-surrounds, its sculleries and all the dark, heavy Anaglipta paper which covered most of the walls. Mamie was ecstatic about it. The farmers had clearly taken to my vivacious lover, her charm and good looks had worked their magic and she was asked if she thought a rent of £3 a week would be fair for the old house on a seven-year lease. Even her husband lost some of his long-suffering gloom realising that by selling their verandered villa overlooking the sea it would realise some useful capital and enable him to buy a partnership in some business; at the same time it might finally placate Mamie's ever-increasing bohemian whims and moods which he used to say were ruining him.

Her irrepressible need for some new and exciting adventure had won the day and what was more, the best part of it was that it was agreed that in exchange for helping do up the place I could have one of the former maid's rooms at the top of the house. After all, I had proved myself pretty useful up to then.

Turning off a small lane which ran from the valley's side towards the nearby village, what was to become my new home for the next four years was reached by a long drive, fenced with traditional old wrought-iron railings which had seen better days but was now rusted and buckled here and there. The drive ended with a row of well-tended tithe cottages inhabited by workers' families, before turning towards the big three-cowl oast and the adjoining yards which had grown up around the big old house two centuries before. Little wonder Mamie had been so captivated when she first saw it.

Swardcote Manor was a classic, brick-built, three-storied, mid-Georgian country house, with its front entrance facing north, giving onto lawns which had seen better days. The front door with its Georgian pediment and columns was seldom to be used except on special occasions when Mamie and her husband had some special guest over to dinner for the first time. The farmyard-side back door, with its long defunct Edwardian bell, was the entrance all of us were to use. A single tall copper beach half shaded the yard outside, beneath which were two large, long since uninhabited kennels for the poor dogs which were forbidden entry to the house in years gone by. Abutting the house, along one side of the yard, ran the unused sculleries and pantry of a long-departed lifestyle, where I was to have my storage space together with a small workshop. The rear of the house faced south, looking across a walled vegetable garden overtaken by weeds and an old tennis court, beyond which were wooded banks of oak, beach and hornbeam, and further on twenty minutes walk away, lay the village of Swardcote.

Settling into life at the manor was hugely satisfying and exciting, if for one reason only, and that was that I knew whenever I was going to be there, Mamie would not be far away. She was in raptures over her new home and as happy as I had ever seen her and her mood was contagious. In those early summer months of 1962, I spent my spare time painting all of the manor's 42 windows, stripping off old wallpaper, restoring the old fire surrounds, clearing brambles and trying to get the big lawns back into shape. It gave me infinite pleasure to walk with Mamie and her ageing lurcher together with the little mongrel travelling companion she had given me at the start of our relationship, through the long meadow, where in one winter's flood a stream had run and an otter had once been spotted. Now that I had my small workshop and space for storing things, actually in the manor house, life could not have been better. Perhaps best of all, I could use my Bland 12 bore, rough shooting along the Downs at the weekends. I could wake up to the sound of the rooks in the tall beeches and listen to the clank of farm machinery being made ready for the day's work in the hop gardens. It would have been impossible to ask for more. It was what one might call a perfectly marvellous state of affairs.

I suppose it was as a subconscious protest against conformity that I had vowed I would never work on a Monday, like everyone else, now that my destiny was firmly in my own hands. Years later, I admit I did, but by then circumstances had changed. In any week my routine was to leave for London last thing on Monday having drunk in every last drop of pleasure from my new surroundings. I spent a night in my flat in George Street before a pre-dawn start on the empty roads, away to my scavenging grounds, which more often than not lay up north. All being well, I would return to that enchanted valley on Friday, tired after days of unremitting pressure, trying to find things to buy in the old industrial towns north of Darlington and along the River Tyne. If I had had a particularly good week, before leaving London, I would call at Fortnum & Masons so that I could surprise everyone with some extravagant delights on my arrival back at Swardcote, to be eaten around the oval Regency table in the dining room with its stripped pine floor – Mamie's favourite room which she had so beautifully redecorated with delicate curtains from Colefax Fowler and the best paper from Coles in Mortimer Street. Times had certainly changed.

The necessity of making long trips was slowly diminishing. In London, I was spending more and more time in my back-room office in George Street, ringing dealers, hoping to set up some deal with my latest acquisitions. And now that I was becoming known, I would get calls from dealers themselves, asking what I had got, or from the shipping offices which were handling antique shipments to the States. George Knapp and others were still hard at it with their container loads, stripping the country of its heritage.

I was discovering by now that I had the bare bones of a proper little business. I had my new letter-heading printed up discreetly on the best Spicers calligraphers' paper in sepia, right across the top, in shaded Roman. It looked impressive with my new country address, "Swardcote Manor, Swardcote, Near Canterbury, Kent" and the London contact number in George Street.

Excursions, sometimes with Mamie, to villages and towns across the Weald yielded up more treasures from small village stores, bakers and the old-style family butchers. Every village had its general stores, the bigger towns their Provision Merchants, now all modernising and glad to have more shelf-room with the disposal of all the Victorian and Edwardian paraphernalia of shop keeping – the numbered tea tins, some even with Chinese decoration, the brass beam scales with their weights, butter pats and wooden scoops for barrelled lentils and the like – it was all going, as were all the enamelled signs advertising long-forgotten products.

From chemists came patent medicine pots for strange ointments and coloured apothecary jars and sometimes even those in beautiful Bristol-blue glass which had found their way to the cellar, never to be used again. I found small nests of drawers, each drawer-front labelled with its black and gold swag. There were few things that couldn't be rooted out with luck for very modest sums, now that modern regulations made the old way of things impossible to keep up.

In haberdashers you would find small cabinets for buttons and reels of thread – in butchers, old chopping blocks and shoulder trugs for delivering the meat – in gunsmiths there might be showcases for every type of shot and cartridge, perhaps some old wooden decoy or an old brass fishing reel. Dust-covered cottage oil lamps and strange old tools for forgotten crafts, lay waiting to be discovered in the ironmongers' cellars. If my luck was in, there'd be an old business sign done by the local signwriter, or some enamelled advertising panel. Just about anything could turn up to yield a profit on the day's work. Work? It was fun!

And what fun it all was throughout those magical Swardcote days. The more so for Mamie, whose romantic notions and appreciation of almost any situation the least theatrical, were enhanced by the fact that her eldest son had managed to latch onto the local repertory theatre, in the hopes of being taken on – not that he had the least idea of treading the boards himself, but because he was desperate to fulfil his childhood dreams of getting into the film industry, and this meant getting an ACCT union card. Acceptance by the theatre, in any capacity, such as the most junior ASM (assistant stage manager, little more than a dogsbody) would hopefully lead to this taking place. Happily for him and to the delight of his mother, he managed to gain employment at the Marlowe Theatre in Canterbury, which was well-known in the profession as being a stepping stone to the London stage. The result of this was that for some months, doubtless tempted by the prospect of a good meal and some enjoyment out of town, at a manor house, far removed from the customary actor's impecunious digs in the fume-filled city, Mamie found herself playing hostess to a variety of characters, both male and female, who were struggling to make their mark in the theatrical profession. At Swardcote they were welcomed with open arms. Given half a chance Mamie would have been one of them herself.

Enjoying a snack lunch in the kitchen, or on a fine day, out on the big front lawn, might see the then unknown actor Nigel Hawthorn (later to become the star of *Yes Minister*) charming and as unassuming as ever, swapping amusing anecdotes with Toni Palmer, whose sumptuous breasts, were, a little while later, to be in all their glory in episodes of *Coronation Street*. Most weekends one was likely to find Mamie in her element, as yet more theatre-friends of friends began descending, having heard of her charm and hospitality – actors amongst whom were Victor Spinelli of *Oh, what a Lovely War* fame, Rio Fanning, who played in *Z Cars* and even Ian Ogilvy, smooth and ludicrously handsome, who was later to star in the series *The Saint!* And many of the same ilk came fleetingly, talking endlessly, exchanging anecdotes, to the delight of their hostess, all on account of the irresistible allure of Swardcote.

During this time, I genuinely felt sorry for Mamie's somewhat bewildered husband, who uninterested in the Theatre and frivolous antics of its London set, had to accept his lot as provider for all the good times enjoyed by his rapturously happy wife, now that she found herself in new circumstances and in such idyllic surroundings. Whilst I was trying to make my mark by any means I could, just as those aspiring Thespians who traipsed in and out of life at the Manor were trying to make theirs, I remained something of an onlooker as I ploughed on with my 'work'. Indeed, my horrid-coloured lime-green Zephyr with its roof rack, standing in the yard outside by my scullery workshop, told a very different story. I had other things to do than to listen to throwaway lines, hoping to impress, such as , how *'Marlene' still looked so very young and was such a good friend of 'dear Victor and Graham..'* I knew that Victor was Victor Spinetti, who had joined us for more than one evening after playing at the Marlowe; Graham was his *friend* with whom he shared a flat in Marylebone, not far from where Marlene Dietrich lived and with whom they were bosom *chums*...just to think that only a stone's throw away, my time in London was spent in a one-and-a-half-roomed semi-basement, without a bath, underneath a builder's office, just off Baker Street, made me smile, thinking about it!... *'And darling, simply everyone is buying their shirts now at Deborah & Claire's in Beauchamp Place'.* I confess my ears pricked up on hearing this and I went by the chic little shop not long afterwards, having had some successful deal and ordered several floral shirts of the most fashionable kind to go with my long hair and flared trousers, which were *'simply de rigeur, darling'*, for anyone on the way up!

Whatever either of those two disarmingly outdated farmers must have thought of all the goings-on in their erstwhile family home, I cannot imagine. They were just as likely to see Mamie offering a cup of tea through her kitchen window to some tramp who had drifted into the yard, in the hopes of picking up some casual work for a day or two, as they were to witness the comings and goings of the more outlandish characters who disappeared inside the back door with its dysfunctional bell. Added to which, the farm tractor driver's wife, who helped Mamie in the house, let slip there was talk in the village of life as it was now, up at the manor, with all the folks from London, coming. Worst of all, there was a rumour of a 'fancy man', living in from time to time, who bought and sold antiques! To which *I* would have replied, innocently wide-eyed had I heard it, in the favourite words of one of the old farmers, whenever confronted with the unusual – *'well, bugger my soul!'*

'Such were the great days at Swardcote!'

More seriously, Mark Maley at Bass International had asked me if there was any chance of finding them an old Hansom Cab for a project they were doing in London. I said I would see what could be done. After a few enquiries it became clear that although at one time Hansoms had been the most common form of city carriage, virtually none had survived. They had now become the rarest of all old horse-drawn vehicles. The only option was to have one made.

The budget that had been mentioned seemed to me enormous, so I asked David Richards as to the feasibility of making one. Always the consummate craftsman, he said that only the wheels might pose a problem as long as I could get a few good photographs for him to work from. I knew of a long-established wheelwrights firm in Ashford, which did work for the Royal Mews, so the problem of the wheels posed no difficulty.

By this time I was keeping him busy enough almost to warrant working for me full time. Would he take the plunge or would I in fact take the responsibility this involved? He had already told me that he knew somewhere that a workshop could be set up if I wanted it.

Everything seemed to be falling into place. I took the plunge, buying a wartime pre-fab as a workshop, re-erecting it on the patch of land, which happened to be inside a dogs' quarantine pound on the hills behind Folkestone.

I made David Richards a partner in this, the very smallest of manufacturing businesses and I told him it could be called D. W. Richards. I have always harboured a predilection for staying quietly in the background.

Splendidly coach-lined and the interior sumptuously upholstered in leather by a business friend of David Richards, the finished cab finally went up to London, to be installed in a large pub in the North End Road – at the opening, the Bass directors were delighted. I think they thought I had been able to find one. It made a great impression and there was even a mention of it in the *Evening Standard* gossip column. I believe the cab is still there to this day.

Now that I had cabinet-makers working for me, business was a more serious challenge. I was stretched, particularly as I had to spend time looking for the source of all the old timber we were using.

Christopher Wray's Lighting Emporium in the King's Road had now become my preferred selling point for any lamps I had. Chris, who I came to know very well over the years, as his business grew and mine became more diverse, had a great sense of humour, was eminently civilised and we both enjoyed the pavement deals we had standing there outside his shop while the traffic worked its way along towards Sloane Square or out to Putney.

But I had begun to feel that my visits to the breakers' yards up north were soon going to be over for good. I found myself saying,

*'Just one last try'* – but then, if I did have some success, it would be once again: *'One more try!'*

On one of these 'last tries' I came across a tiny harbour on the Firth of Forth. Apparently back in the 1870s it had been a privately-owned, coaling port, with a row of workers' cottages by what had once been the loading dock, with the owner's house and stable block, some little way back, facing the harbour mouth. The broken-down jetty was stacked with the usual heaps of metal, crates and other breakers' rubbish. I ended up buying one of these crates, in which, still wrapped in their soiled brown paper wrappings, were no less than 20 copper and brass, standard-pattern, naval divers' helmets, today worth around £1,000 each. Even in those days, each one was worth the equivalent of a good week's takings. One helmet was put into the scales, the needle touching 32lbs – copper; at the time was 2/6d per pound – incredible! They were £4, but if I took the lot, I could have them at £3.15! And that meant I would not have to go up north again for one more try – or so I thought.

Oddly enough, it was not that deal which made the visit to that tiny harbour so memorable; it was the sight of what must have been the smallest lighthouse in the British Isles. A quite exquisite little building, the whole affair standing only some twelve feet high, lantern long gone, but its Gothic windows still intact below the lichen-covered dome. I was only able to walk halfway along the harbour arm as it had started to collapse. I would dearly have liked to have had a closer look and seen inside the small entrance door.

That such a relic still existed amazes me to this day. I discovered later that this was the oldest lighthouse of its type in existence, built in 1802. Today, it would have been removed carefully and re-erected in some nautical museum. I was going to remember it – one day.

For all the excitement of these small adventures in odd corners of the country, nothing could compare to the tranquillity of life in the countryside at the Manor. The long meadow lay shrouded in early morning mists, most autumn days. Hop picking was almost over. From the house you could smell the sulphur from the hop-drying ovens in the oast. The corrugated huts along the valley were crammed with the last pickers from Bow and Stepney and a dozen wagons were drawn up along the meadow's edge. One or two of the Romanies' ponies grazed, while their lurchers ambled from wagon to wagon, hoping for some scrap of food. At twilight in particular, the scene was remarkable, out of time and if the participants had been wearing peasants' clothing, it could well have been a scene from a painting by Breughel, dimly lit by twenty or thirty camp fires.

By now I was beginning to lose touch with the world of metal polishing and plating and the amusing days of lunch-breaks in Gino's Italian café at the Brecknock, with dear old Jack and his sidekick, young Buddy, from down the Mews. The connections were fading, even then, in London... there was time for 'one last try' to make a quid or two... this time along the Thames.

Blackwall, in the closing days of the great spread which was London's docklands, still boasted one or two repair yards hanging onto a tenuous business. It was here in one such dock that Trinity House annually repaired and repainted all the buoys and lightships from our coastal waters and also stored all the necessary equipment and spares for launches, tenders and lighthouses in commission around the British Isles.

Along one side of a dry dock, were a row of thirty early 19th century cannons, all well tarred, barrels some three feet long, touch-holes clear – each one numbered on the side of the carriage. It was a scene reminiscent of the *Pequod*, only this time, the guns were real. They had originally been our naval fleet's secondary armament, post Trafalgar, and had been retained for use as signal guns, issued to various lighthouses and shore stations for use in fog conditions whenever a foghorn was not in working order or not in place.

Back in Kent, using my new Olympia typewriter, and on my best Spicers headed paper with the Manor address, I wrote to the Honourable Members of the Board of Elder Brethren at Trinity House, saying, as an ex-serving officer, how deeply grateful I would be if they could see fit to release just one redundant signal gun from their depot at Blackwall – adding that it would be marvellous if two could be spared as then one could stand at each end of our garden terrace. I hoped my letter would give the impression of some well-to-do old mariner finally retired to his family's country retreat and who now wanted them as reminders of his career and perhaps more particularly those of his forebears.

It seemed that it must have struck the right note. Permission was given for me to remove two guns for the princely sum of just £5 each. The old boy network ploy had worked. It seemed too easy.

On the collectors' market, a pair of cannons like this would be worth a minimum of £500, but as ever, keen on a quick turnover, I sold them on the day my hired van collected them, to a dealer in Crawford Street who obviously had someone in mind as a buyer from the moment he saw them. So for the sake of a tenner and the cost of van hire, I netted sufficient to give myself several extra days of relaxation throughout the coming months, in which to enjoy the delights of Fortnum's goodies and time with my paramour.

On the strength of my first letter, I thought there was no harm in trying for another two. So after a couple of weeks I wrote again, thanking the Elder Brethren, saying just how marvellous the old guns had looked – hoping none of the board had a country estate in Kent and might call… but how much grander it would be if I could balance the display with another two guns, if they could be spared and just how grateful I would be and as a mark of appreciation I would make a donation to their distressed seamen's fund. I think old grandfather Babb would have turned in his grave, but it wasn't going to stop his grandson from behaving in a duplicitous manner, even if he had thought of the consequences. My request was granted!

Again I had a truck collect the pair – still at £5 each together with my promise of a suitable donation – all somewhat nebulous I confess. This time I had a different idea. I was going to try to sell them to a collector and maximise my find!

Over time, if you knock about the trade for long enough, making a mental note of this or that, it is almost certain that you'll pick up the name of some specialised collector. I had already gathered that collectors are, in fact, dealers themselves, buying and selling as the mood takes them, whenever they become bored with parts of their collection, principally dealing with other collectors and sometimes with small private museums abroad – and there were plenty of these in America I had heard. But unless you were in the swim, there was no ordinary way of being able to profit from men like this.

It so happened that I had once bought what at the time I had thought a very rare 19th century type of gentleman's pistol, something called a *'pepper-pot'* with six barrels which revolved, each fired by a separate percussion cap. I had bought it at a shop in Salisbury and almost immediately afterwards regretted it, thinking I had been rash in the first place and had more than likely paid far too much for it. I tried to sell it in Winchester on my way back to London, but the dealer declined, saying it was, as I thought it would be, too pricey for him, but going on to say that it might be worth my while to contact a collector he knew, should I come this way again, as the man lived not far away, on his estate, near Warminster, by the grand name of Bishopstrowe.

His story is worth telling.

Born into affluence at Bishopstrowe House, the young Keith Neal went through the accepted public-school system and gaining a degree in humanities at Oxford, opted for a life in the art world. Quite by chance, one of his first tasks in the world's foremost auction house of the day was to inspect and catalogue fine paintings and the collection of armour in Blairgowrie Castle in Scotland. He very quickly decided he was more interested in the intricacies of the manufacture and use of arms and armour, than he was in the more ponderous researches needed whenever dealing with the authentication of Old Masters.

Soon after joining the auction house, he became head of the department dealing with antique firearms, armour and ancient European weapons and at the outset of the Second World War was given the job, on the instructions of Whitehall, of acquiring any available collection or single pieces, throughout the country for shipment to America in order to raise much-needed dollars to support the war effort. The owners of many of the great country houses were persuaded to part with all or part of their collections.

This scheme reaped huge rewards for the wartime government and although more than comfortably off already, it made Keith Neal richer and much revered in the world of antique firearms, accredited with being possibly the world's foremost expert. He had capitalised on his position by buying for himself a large number of the many thousands of weapons that had been offered towards raising funds for the war effort.

By the time the war was over he was in possession of the finest private collection of antique firearms in the country.

When I finally did go to see him, I was shown in past Corinthian columns each side of the front door and into a large marbled hall, each side lined with plinths topped with Roman busts. In the middle stood the very finest example of an 18th century bronze cannon, in perfect condition, every fitting on its teak carriage also bronze. Room after room in that grand house was arrayed with serried lines of firearms of every conceivable type. Above these, on the walls, arranged in geometric patterns, were smaller weapons by the dozen. With pride, the man showed me cabinets housing the finest and rarest cased sets of pistols and mahogany plush lined boxes containing the finest makers examples of officers side-arms from every era of warfare from the 15th century to the present day. I saw it all. Personalised Winchester repeaters from the American West and the first of the famous Colt revolvers were all part of the man's amazing collection.

My turning up with an insignificant little pepperpot was almost laughable, but Keith Neal was more than affable, seemingly showing a genuine interest in what I had brought him and what else I dealt in and the likelihood that I might find something else for him. Sadly not a very good pepperpot, he'd said, but certainly worth £20 – and so I made a profit after all.

Just before leaving he walked me across to the stables where he housed his cannons, each with blocks and tackles suspended from the stable roof above for hoisting them should the need arise and then the workshops where restoration to any of the carriages was carried out. I was shown superb examples in brass and bronze mounted on teak carriages of every size and shape; stubby bronze mortars used on Clive's campaigns in India and variations of huge 2-ton howitzers and all the varied types of breach loaders from the 1600s up to those from the Crimean campaign.

I learnt that he was in fact the one man to whom Scotland Yard turned in the event of a murder being carried out with some outdated weapon. He was very proud of that. It was an experience well worth the small profit of the £4 I had made when I sold him my pepperpot and when eventually my last pair of cannons from Blackwall were taken down to Bishopstrowe that little profit of £4 turned into one of almost £600!

*********

The entire field of reproduction was by now burgeoning and my friend the Indian's small metal workshop at Ruislip was now a fully-fledged fifteen-man factory in Suffolk, manufacturing brass items together with smaller types of brass lamps, ships' clocks and even telescopes that were partially made up by the last of the nautical opticians in Clerkenwell. He had foreseen the demand, not only for the American market, but also to a lesser extent, for the Continental dealers. The most voracious market of all was the east coast of the States. I was told there were no fewer than 12,000 restaurants in the greater Boston area, each one potentially interested in nautical decor.

There were more dealers in New England than there were in the whole of the U.K.

It was always possible to sneak a look at one of the shippers' labels in the Indian's emporium to see where the goods were destined for, and for whom, which was more important. His goods were stacked against the walls, on shelves or already wrapped in brown corrugated paper ready for the shipper's lorry to collect and this acted as a great incentive for anyone to buy, seeing the volume of what had already been obviously sold. No dealer liked to be outdone. And this of course was good for me.

Because I was being pressed from all sides with orders now that I had ventured into new selling fields, calling at shops in and around Sloane Street, the King's Road and along Pimlico towards World's End and Fulham, it was not long before I had the carpenter's shop of a small, family-run, builders' firm, knocking up my first rather crude, but convincing, trade signs, which were now in vogue. I had had the idea to make the signs which incorporated, initially rather simple, relief objects such as a 19th century coffee canister, or perhaps a half-cheese for a purveyor of groceries & comestibles which needed the expertise of a good carpenter. Nautical signs were always received well: a sextant in relief, for example, is easy to make, similarly an anchor or a ship's lamp. Signs with these on could be headed *'Ships' Chandlers'* or *'Marine Stores'* and so on. None of this warranted the attention of a carver, just a decent carpenter with a little imagination. It was, in fact, almost *de rigueur* to incorporate a decorative sign in any trendy scheme. For example, a nicely-painted bull's head, shaded lettering across the top saying *'Butchers and Gamedealers by appointment since 1836'* might find a good home in any smart kitchen in Kensington. Or, an old-fashioned dairy sign, depicting a grazing cow beside an old milk churn – or a dairymaid's bucket – lettered *'Eames & Sons, Dairymen of Repute – Daily deliveries by handcart: hotels supplied.'* The variations were endless and signs like this had never been seen before because in reality they had never existed. I had quite by chance struck into a very rich vein!

Nowadays you see attempts at cheap copies everywhere worldwide, in pubs and restaurants, generally cast in one piece made of fibre glass with screen-printed lettering, made in Taiwan or Indonesia.

An amusing incident occurred soon after I became involved with the builders' firm that had begun making up signs for me. The proprietor's son was running the concern and had been to a half decent school, but he was something of a *'spiv'*, who was doing very well from local brewery contracts, as he was discreetly able to manipulate the latter's architects to his advantage *'with preferential treatment.'* He also ruthlessly squeezed the last drop of effort out of his workforce that included very useful signwriters, who lettered pub fascias and hanging signs for the local brewery and some of whom were to be employed exclusively by me as time went by.

In this particular instance I had an order for one or two different ships' chandlers signs – old floorboards cut out to length, edged with some kind of ready-made moulding, on the front a sextant or some other object in relief and lettered in a bold 19th century trade type face *'Ships Stores. All manner of chandlery supplied'* and as an alternative perhaps, *'Chandlers and nautical instrument dealers. Whalers requisites supplied at short notice.'* It was easy to conjure up one of a thousand possibilities. As for the whaling supplies, all of New England was obsessed with anything connected with the whaling industry and there was no reason why some odd relic might not have turned up in, say Aberdeen, the home of our own whaling fleet... finally finding its way to the Portobello Road.

Being pretty sharp, the builder, knowing that I was not going to leave him with anything to dispose of, by way of one or two having been overproduced, certainly now that he knew about the eventual destination of the majority of signs he was making up for me, instead of making just the two I had asked for, when I went to collect them, he presented me with no less than 8, on the excuse that it was the only economical way to turn them out. It was small time blackmail, but I obviously had to take the lot.

Quite naturally, the Indian was reluctant to take the lot as they were an initial try-out, but after a drop in price, we did a deal.

The following week when I was delivering my latest batch of country artefacts to 'Trad' next door, I just happened to go into the Indian's shop, to find him smoothly moving an American buyer towards the back of the shop where he had the eight chandlery signs stacked. The American moved one aside, looking interested, then saw another which he turned over to reveal yet one more... I heard him say *'Gee Frank, where the hell did you get all these. They can't be real old ones, these eight!?'* I listened in disbelief as the Indian explained that they had come from the largest chandlers up in Aberdeen, whose warehouse occupied the biggest single building on the waterfront. He said each side of the building had two signs on it. I could hardly believe the American dealer's reply when I heard him say *'Is that so? I'll take the lot!'*

It was just as well that I was making things to order, perhaps some new line, which of course all the dealers knew wasn't old, but just looked convincing: this meant I wasn't having to use guile, deceit, or tell a lie when I sold it to the dealer. On the odd occasion when a new contact queried the authenticity, I did not find it difficult to skirt the question and reply in a knowledgeable tone that it does certainly have age: *'It certainly appears to have some age, don't you think?.' – perhaps as much as a week or so!"*

There weren't comparable items on the market in those days and anyway the expertise of the buyer was not about to be put into question by his having a close look at something which he badly wanted to believe was old. There must have been more than a few lingering doubts, but you have to weigh this up against the disappointment it would bring if the complete truth had been exposed.

Week by week, I was exploring fresh possibilities of selling as the demand grew, which made it necessary to take on a motley band of part-time outworkers, who had an aptitude for the easier kind of quasi artwork which had up to then been exclusively carried out at

Lynsore Bottom. It was extraordinary what talent lay undiscovered in the most unlikely places, a smallholder's wife who had been though art school in the fifties, the ubiquitous odd-jobber who's never very far away in any country village who could do some varnishing and painting – even a garage mechanic who had a surprisingly good feel for primitively shaped and carved items such as decoy ducks.

Sadly my transvestite friend had told me he couldn't take the pressures I was now exerting on him and he was soon to be away to Lincolnshire to work in a bird sanctuary. Which he did, taking my beloved Bland shotgun with him which he had borrowed one weekend and I never heard from him again. He had turned out to be such a sad, but highly-talented individual, but so weak that I couldn't bring myself to do anything about the gun, as I reckoned he had paid his debt through all the remarkable work he had done up to the time he disappeared into the Fenlands. He even gave me the name of someone else he knew who could carve, should I ever need a carver again.

But before this requirement became an absolute necessity, more than a year later, I became the first person to see the virtually never-ending potential in bringing to the market a type of ship model known as a '*half-block*', or simply a '*half-model.*'

Any kind of ship's model was highly desirable and always sold well. I had in fact already bought one, months before, without really knowing what it was because it had been mounted on a board and embellished with simple detail and I thought it was just the end result of some seaman's time off watch, spent making something to take home after the voyage.

Now, however, I knew better.

Every vessel whose hull had been made of riveted metal plates, from the early part of the 19th century, starts its design life in the ship-builder's drawing office. Working from plans, the model maker goes to work, making a section of half the hull, usually in knotless

273

yellow pine, which is the perfect carving and shaping timber. The model will be precise, generally to the scale of 1:150 and then on this model the position of the various metal plates are marked onto the complex curves of the hull. This is then passed on to the moulding loft – generally a long wide shed on ground level and here scaling up from the lines on the model, templates of the small model's plates are then expanded to the full size. From these templates, the iron or steel plates are cut, ready for riveting into place on the skeleton of the growing ship, as her hull takes shape in the yard.

This was all explained to me in the most unlikely place: in the then somewhat seedy small town of Faversham, inland, but standing on a muddy creek, an insignificant tributary of the river Medway. Its only claim to fame being the explosion in a munitions workshop in the Great War which had killed almost one thousand of the town's inhabitants and the fact it was the home of England's oldest brewers, 'Shepherd Neame'. Now by-passed by the main road it was the last place you would expect to find a shipyard.

But in fact, if you had ever been lucky enough to go up the Amazon, the chances were that you would have continued your passage to the upper reaches beyond Manaos on a riverboat built by Messrs. Pollock & Co. of Faversham. I only heard about the yard because I used to pass old man Pollock's country house whenever I was on my way to or from Lynsore Bottom. It was going to seed like the whole of the shipbuilding industry. I gathered the old man was terminally ill and his motor-yacht was parked by the stable yard on its long commercial sixteen-wheeled trailer, gathering sprigs from the overhanging yew trees. I understood the yard in Faversham was doomed to extinction. It was an interesting little yard. They knew their business, launching vessels up to the size of large tugs, sideways into the creek at an appropriate high tide. You thought it was going to turn right over when the ship hit the water in a roaring cascade of spume. In reality there was never any need to worry; the drawing office had designed its hull to perfection through the use of the half-block model system.

It was customary for a yard to keep the model in the drawing office for a year or two in case the vessel sustained any damage serious enough to warrant repairs to her plates and after that it would be dumped in any convenient back store, or the older ones, simply thrown away.

I struck up an immediate rapport with the yard manager who was more than helpful in allowing me to take almost anything I wanted as he knew the days of the yard were numbered. The yard specialised in the construction of pretty little riverboats which were shipped away in parts and rebuilt on the banks of great lakes and rivers across the world.

I gathered that on average the yard had produced two to three vessels a year. Multiply that by fifty and you get some idea as to the number of models tucked away in odd corners. It does not take much imagination to think of the number which might well have been in existence in all the ship builders' yards in the country.

Nobody had thought of this before.

Admittedly, in their crude drawing office state, un-mounted, criss-crossed with technical lines showing the various curves and plate positions, they did not look inspiring as a piece of nautical decoration but, mounted on a length of nine-inch demolition floorboard, painted a washed-out bluey-green with the hull lined, with a name, date and tonnage (albeit in most cases quickly invented), all sign-written in a neat Roman script, they became instantly desirable.

I cleared the yard at Pollocks.

Working from the shipping industry publication, *Ship Builders, Owners & Repair Yards 1963*, I carefully typed out individual letters to every one of them founded prior to the 1920s.

I had a more than 80% affirmative response. Replies came from the smallest yards on the creeks and rivers of the south, to the largest yards in the north which had historically built our great clippers in ports like Sunderland, Aberdeen and along the Clyde.

Usually I could get fifty or sixty models of varying sizes into my Zephyr. As to price, in most cases, I was just asked how much they were worth to me. If I paused slightly as if to assess the question, I might be asked if 10 shillings each would be too much...! Many were simply given to me. In one yard in Goole, I was shown into a moulding loft where, fixed on every crossbeam, bow to stern, were models of every ship the yard had built since the 1870s. Yet again it was the stuff dreams are made of. In all maybe one hundred and fifty or more; all for shillings with the casual question as to just how many I had taken when I went to pay at the office before leaving.

I called at the yard three or four times and I was worried that someone in the offices might start wondering what I was doing with such large numbers of these models, as my original request had been for some *'several'*. No one appeared to care.

Sweeping the yards took almost eighteen months. I was selling often in batches of ten, twenty, thirty, or more at a time once I had cleaned them up a bit and mounted them on backboards.

It seemed fitting that the last batch arrived one afternoon in the Manor yard, stacked on the back of a flatbed B.R.S. truck on its last delivery of the day, all the way from Aberdeen, Hall & Co., who had built some of our finest old clippers, and who in response to my request had sent down all they had without charge. I suppose they looked on it simply as an exercise in customer relation!

I guessed similarly there might be models in cases in shipping companies' offices. Again my guess proved to be correct. I often went into the sad, decaying premises of some erstwhile proud trading company, to find on offer for a few pounds, the most exquisite models of some of their merchant ships, which had once steamed the world's trade routes, and I came out with treasures.

It was onto the roof rack for these, three or four at a time, from almost every trading port in the country – Cardiff, Hartlepool,

Bristol, Liverpool and the City of London! Nowadays, such models fetch thousands of pounds. Even then, before there had been no recognised market for them, I was able to ask up to £200. Petrol for the round trip, maybe £5, mugs of tea somewhere and a smelly eiderdown in a guest house £1.10 shillings, with an outlay for the actual goods of no more than £30, meant I wasn't doing badly! Results had exceeded my expectations and Fortnum's did particularly well out of it and for a while I kept a fine collection of these and other models on the walls of the backstairs at the Manor.

**My delicious M, camera-shy in Morrocco**

Signs and half-hull models now became the backbone of the business. Since the last of the old ones had come and been quickly absorbed into the trade, with endless requests for more, I had been testing the feasibility of making a good copy. The first one I had laboriously done myself, reckoning that a skilled craftsman like David Richards with all the tools at his disposal would be able to produce one in less than half the time it had taken me. It was only the compound curves around the stern which posed any problem, but after a few trial runs with a good eye and working from one of

277

the original clipper hulls I had held back, Richards was able to turn out between twenty and thirty hulls a day. It was then up to me, in the scullery workshop, to paint the upper part black sometimes with a row of white gun-ports and the finishing touch of some delicate scrollwork on the bows, before fixing them to their backboards and gluing on the stumps of masts. The entire operation was viable and the profit ratio far more than I had hoped for.

Orders for these became prolific. The Indian took them on a regular basis, very often forty at a time or more. 'Trad', although Eddy and Marjorie liked to think of themselves as above dealing in commercial export lines, were ordering them in similar numbers.

A rapacious demand was now springing up from all quarters, primarily from America, where by now I had discovered who most of the buyers were. Orders came in from dealers in San Francisco who wanted them, as they did from New Bedford Massachusetts. They were in demand in Europe from Madrid to Oslo and some orders came from as far afield as Argentina. Their appeal appeared to be irresistible – half the world seemed hooked on a nautical theme for decoration.

In order to keep abreast of the demand, three more individuals joined the band of outworkers, exclusively making half-models. One a clever young builder/carpenter in a nearby village: the second an experienced joiner who had been apprenticed in the naval yard at Chatham. Each of these was given different hulls to work from, ocean-going tugs, trawlers and coasters: all quite different from the standard classic clipper hulls which were being turned out in the new works. It is surprising what the promise of extra cash for a weekend on the home bench will achieve and it was all a success.

The third hull maker was my father! Just how that came about, I shall explain a little later.

*********

It was soon after this that I fulfilled one of my ambitions: to buy a big American car. I was put onto a dealer called Ouveroff. He advertised in the *Sunday Times* He had one station wagon to offer. He sounded incredibly smooth. A deal was arranged on a Chevrolet Impala, 3-litre, left-hand drive, which he'd bring up from Ascot for me if I could meet him in Town. He'd give me a couple of hundred for my Zephyr, sight unseen. The greatest excitement awaited me in the Manor yard when I arrived the following weekend. Mamie's boys, past prep school by now, thought the car was terrific, even if it did have plastic seats. It was American, big, sleek and powerful.

Change was in the air. The farm, including the Manor, was to be sold.

My first workshop, in the pre-fab on the hills behind Folkestone, had now been left to the mercy of the poor rabid dogs, and thanks to some additional funding – which wasn't actually necessary – by way of a sleeping partnership with some of Mamie's friends who had moved down from Hampstead and taken the largest of all the houses in the valley – I established a proper little factory on the edge of Folkestone, employing eight or nine men who predominantly made military furniture, while David Richards was involved with the half hulls and all the special items which had begun to be ordered by the various pub and restaurant designers, now that word had spread from that initial contact with my friend Mark Maley at Bass.

The offer of money, from Mamie's Hampstead friends, came as an amusing insight into human nature. Liberal-minded, rich and given to spur of the moment involvements in interesting situations, particularly as they were well aware of Mamie's predicament, with her lover in the world of muck and money and a sad melancholic husband, they found all my activities most amusing, especially as they got a lot of pleasure from summoning up names for the new range of secretaires and chests I was making for the John Lewis group such as the *'Corunna'*, the *'Sebastapol'*, the *'Raffles'*. I found it all a little embarrassing sometimes, but additional funding was always useful and it cemented a friendship.

Amusing to look back on, but worrying at the time, was a Sunday morning when I was out in the yard. On hearing the low sputter of a Velocette motor cycle, I looked up to see the village constable draw up in full police uniform. I knew him well and I had once played nine holes of golf with him. He was of the old school, softly spoken, deliberate and always friendly. On this occasion however, he had a certain air of seriousness about him. Getting off his machine and removing his helmet, he came over to me, looking somewhat embarrassed and asked if I would mind going down to the police house in the village because he had few things to ask me. A nasty feeling in the pit of my stomach took hold – what on earth could this be about? Not again…

Thirty minutes later it had all become clear. For the second time, my infamous criminal record had reared its head – the man of dog tracks, boxing booths, scars and larceny was being brought in! The constable asked me if I ever dealt in jewellery, did I sell any pictures, had I sold anything to anyone from the States? Well, yes, I did sell lamps and things to Americans up in London and from time to time, a ship painting to a dealer in New Bedford, called Kranzler, but nothing else, certainly nothing like jewellery. He seemed satisfied with my answers, but gently refused to tell me why I was being questioned.

In fact the answer was that for the past twelve months there had been a spate of unresolved cases of antique and fine art thefts, revolving around the *'open'* market at Bermondsey, where of course the goods could be taken down to Long Lane, a street away, wrapped, packed and crated for containers which could then be loaded by the end of the day. The police were trawling through the records on their computers to collate any known criminals who were currently involved with the antiques trade…!

*********

With the sale of the estate looming and looking to the future, now that I had a healthy bank account, I asked our landlord about the possibility of being able to buy one of the old farm cottages, before the estate sale; in fact one of the oldest, listed in Hasted's historical records of early Kent, built on the foundations of an Anchorite chapel dating from the 11th century. Now in a tumbledown state, almost overgrown, some quarter of a mile from the 'big house'. With it went a small field and several disused hoppers' huts and a collapsed flint cook house. I knew I had enough money to restore it. He agreed a price of £1,160 and the field £200 extra!

Allaying my delight and excitement at the thought that buying the cottage might mean that Mamie could come and live with me, came news of my mother's death. She, so far as I knew, was alone in knowing my address at the time and it took me by surprise to be given the news by Mamie one evening when I had returned from a day with the outworkers. My father must somehow have traced the number.

It was with some trepidation that I thought of the funeral to come. I knew it would be brief and simple as my father had a loathing for all matters connected with the clergy. I remember him berating the Archbishop of Canterbury whenever his name came up in the news. I knew my brother would be there, most probably in uniform and my sister over from France and I was certain that all the various naval uncles would be coming along.

The gathering was quite alien to me. The aunt of the dark flat off the Finchley Road was there. My brother asked me if I would have lunch with him one day on board his destroyer which was refitting in Portsmouth. Standing rather aimlessly, as one does after cremations, outside by the dry rose bushes, I avoided any questions about what I was doing now and was pleased to leave them all in ignorance, as I drew out of the car park in the Chevrolet station wagon. I liked to think that I had lived up to my poor mother's expectations. She hadn't enjoyed much in her last few years and I hoped what I had achieved would have made her happy.

**Paradise: The re-built Spanish finca which looked across to Tangiers**

But now that we had finally met again at my mother's funeral, I had a tentative rapprochement with my father. In return he began to take a bewildered interest in what I was doing and my craze for half-models. He never asked me where I was living, or in the broader sense just what I was doing, which was a relief to me. He never came to my works and I am glad he never did, as given half a chance to express an opinion, he would have told me just how to run it and what mistakes I was making. Anyway, rather pathetically, he asked me if he could try to make a hull or two over the weekend. It was sad thinking about it, poor man, with not much going for him, I presumed he was still pedalling away to his office by the station, lonely, with time heavy on his hands alone in the old Admiral's house. Not surprisingly, as he was in fact inordinately clever, his tugs were really good and I ended up paying him £4 for each one every time I picked them up.

He went away after a few months to teach in a prep school up north and I didn't see him after that for several years. He had had to leave the house on account of its having been willed to my brother, sister and myself by the worthy old Admiral.

*********

There was a month to go before the move. We had been in the Manor for two years and now, jubilation! Once again I was asked to go with Mamie and the family. I think she must have been at her most persuasive even in the face of her worsening relationship with her husband. The new house was once again to be rented. Now that Mamie and her husband were well-known to the social set in the area, another large 18th century house had been offered only nine miles away and was certainly large enough to accommodate a lodger who could help out with the lawns and garden and who might arrive back with goodies from Fortnum's.

Euphoric at the thought of the coming move, to make things even better, I decided the time had come when I could afford to buy the American station wagon I had been lusting for ever since I had seen it for sale in the Sloane Square showroom of Lindrum and Hartman – a brand new 4-litre, white Rambler, complete with whitewall tyres, with a price tag of a little over £4,000. I gave it its first run down to Portsmouth with the idea of showing it off to my brother, to have lunch on board his Battle Class destroyer and at the same time it would give me the opportunity to look around the naval surplus stores and scrapyards.

It felt very strange indeed, re-entering the dockyard gates after so long: a feeling of suspended reality, smelling the old smells and the sight of everything I had longed to leave behind me. As in some weird waking dream, I walked up the ship's gangplank and stepped onto the quarterdeck. In the officer's mess, the sight of the Admiralty china I'd known so well and the silent shuffling of the stewards round the table drew me back and I wanted to be away; if I stayed I felt I might never escape again.

The move came at last and life settled down once more to its daily routine in the new surroundings, with a view out to the marshes and the Isle of Sheppey. My usefulness was fully appreciated by Mamie's husband at the time of the move, as apart from one small load in a rented van, I had managed to take everything the nine miles to the new house with four trips in my Rambler. Mamie herself was very excited at the thought of making new friends and I was happy enough, setting up a very small workshop in one of the sculleries.

Happy too with Mamie, even more deliciously attractive, now that she was in her fourties and looking as lovely as when I had first met her. Jarvis, my faithful old mutt, had by now settled into his new existence living as a country dog, under Mamie's wing whenever I was away, sharing life in the house with a young badger she had rescued and a pet rook which lived in the kitchen. I often wondered whether Jarvis remembered those innumerable journeys he had made in my Bedford vans and the nights spent in cheap B & B's, curled up at the foot of my bed, with his travelling water bowl beside him. It was to be another few years before I had to lay his little dead body into a grave, marked by a headstone made by one of my carvers and wrapped in my favourite old bridgecoat.

I was spending less and less time in London now that the works van took the furniture up on a weekly basis.

I also had my cottage to finish, which was absorbing every spare hour of every day.

Now that the arts department among the milk bottles at Lynsore Bottom had gone, I had to rely on lettering and artwork being done by my dubious builder friend's signwriters or by a would-be guitarist, who had worked for him. Stewart, the guitarist, was an ex art student, who lived in one room with his girlfriend and their baby, in a back street in Whitstable. One of the builder's men had mentioned discreetly that he knew someone else who might be useful to me. In essence that was the way my workforce was being put together, someone knowing someone else.

For carving, I was now relying on a local coal miner I'd heard about, whose name was George and who had a name *'for a bit of carved work'* which he did part time. Apparently, this aptitude is not altogether unknown in miners, due it is said, to their working and shaping the coalface, with what amounts to chiselling tools. And what is more, he had a brother who also *'did a little'*, should the need ever arise. The Kentish miners were well-known for their belligerence and strikes were common and I very soon learnt that George was not an easy man. He was, however, amazingly talented and was very soon to become a mainstay of the business, the main carver with, to a lesser extent, his brother Frank.

As a test piece, I had given him a picture of an American eagle, with wings outspread, one foot on a shield bearing the Stars and Stripes. I had decided it would look good as a ship's stern board, mounted on a curved board with a heavily-carved rope edge. In reality there would have been no ship's stern board as small as 5 foot 3 inches, but this did not alter the fact it turned out to be an exemplary piece of work, good enough, many months later, to be shown on the frontispiece of the publication *American Antiques* as being part of the Ayres Collection in the American Museum at Bath – described as an *'Eagle from the stern of an American ship, nineteenth century, painted in gilt "fir".'*

Although nautical signs were the most popular, traditional pub signs were also beginning to find their place in the current decor vogue. Easily shaped or cut-out wooden relief, such as *'The Cross Keys'*, *'Three Tuns Tavern'*, *'The Plough Inn'* or *'The Anchor'* were all easy subjects for any carpenter and became steady sellers. The use of Dutch metal leaf which cost a fiftieth of the price of 22ct gold, but looked just as good to the unpractised eye and the relief with a dark background, gave pieces a look of class and authenticity.

A useful discovery was the fact that Butcher & Co., the transfer makers who had supplied me with all the Royal Warrant transfers for my leather buckets, had in their range, fairly large pictorial transfers which covered the entire spectrum of the now dying traditional trades: butchers, grocers, dairymen, bakers and a host of others. All of these had originally been painted by commercial artists of the highest calibre. Under varnish they became undetectable from original artwork, which of course not only looked good, but commanded a considerably higher price.

Stewart, the hippie guitarist, had the most exquisite touch for lettering – never too precise, and with a very good eye for the shading and double-shading in the style of the Victorian signwriters which was so vital in giving the right appearance. With all the work I was able to give him, he began to prosper for the first time.

Much of what I was dreaming up was tongue-in-cheek, some probably almost authentic, more by guesswork than anything else, but a great deal totally fictitious and very often with an amusing secondary interpretation – *'Good Lodgings for Seamen to be had. Apply Dolly Lambert, 3 Dock Street'* or *'Rooms by the hour. 1/- …With attendant female staff, 1/6!'*

Varying in shape and all small enough to be packed in a suitcase were what was known as *'little sundry'* signs, which would be bought by way of a souvenir of a visit to Portobello Road. The signwriters pumped them out – *'Alice Cockwell Laundress. Good service provided.' 'Thomas Ball & Sons, Kensal Rise, all erections demolished'* – to name but a few. For the more trendy kitchen, there were *'Pies and Faggots 2d, 6d & 9d'* and *'Tarts, any filling 1d a time.* The whole idea was a huge success and only got better over time.

To begin with I had a very small portfolio of photographs to show my clients: pictures of the odd trade sign, perhaps a naïve painting or two and some of the first pieces turned out by the carvers. You would have called it a portfolio, those dozen or so loose photographs I used to pull out with pride. That was at the beginning. Not many years later I could turn the pages of the firm's so-called catalogue, showing over a thousand items. By the time I sold the business and the market had begun to be flooded with copies, the business offered one thousand six hundred different items, most of which were trade, pub and professional signs. Most important of all was the fact that I had no competition. I was alone in this expanding market.

One of the biggest problems was to find sufficient supply of old floorboards with which to make the signboards and the backing for the steady flow of half-models. Edging you could buy new, because once painted it didn't show, but it was vital that the backs had the same weathered appearance as the fronts. Hundreds of feet were needed on a weekly basis. The only source was demolition, which drew me back into the world of scavenging and dirt. More yards, piled high this time with bricks and beams, old front doors and stained sinks – not exactly enticing, but essential.

My friend Mark Maley had joined a new and even more thrusting company designing and building English-style pubs for 'expats' in the Gulf States and money was obviously flowing. I was not only his company's preferred supplier, having won my spurs with the Hansom Cab, but word had spread and approaches were coming from all quarters now that the commercial world had woken up to the fact that interesting and decorative interiors were going to pull in more punters and mean more business for the restaurants, hotels and any good *'Olde English'* alehouse!

**********

Although I was starting to re-emerge into everyday society, after the early years of Bella Vista and lone existence in semi-basements, it was Mamie who made the friends. I was too wrapped up in business. It was all too much for her husband, ever oblivious to the fact there is more to life than what it costs.

As a relief from the often sad and frustrated atmosphere in the house, there were interesting and amusing neighbours to be visited, who made the two years in the new house another very different and memorable experience.

Almost opposite, in a small thatched gatehouse to the park of Earl Sondes estate, lived a stage-designer, Michael Trangmar, who taught at the Central School in London and who was then involved in designing sets for the stage show '*Man of Magic*' on Broadway. He was a gentle, self-effacing queen of immense talent and someone very much after Mamie's heart. His best friend was Peter Cook, son of the stage celebrity Jeanetta Cochran, who lived in another of the Sondes Estate cottages on the other side of the park. He was in fact a Master Silversmith, but penniless, eking out a livelihood through small commissions. A true eccentric – couch grass grew up through the tiles of his drawing-room floor, creeping up the back of his sofa; hot water for his rare baths was achieved by sprinkling coal-dust over twists of rolled-up newspaper in the bottom of his ancient boiler. In addition to this it was not unusual to find him in his rudimentary, brick-floored kitchen, his horse inside, standing beside the wooden draining board, the smells of unwashed pots and congealed fat mingling with the warm scent of horse dung! It was said that he had slept in his mother's bed until he was in his thirties.

About a mile away lived the writer, Alan Neame, who had in fact grown up in the house that Mamie and her husband were renting. The epitome of camp waspishness, novelist, poet, ecclesiastical scholar and former lecturer at the University of Baghdad, he was outrageously gay, genial, and the possessor of a rather studied but brilliant sense of humour.

Just down the hill from Alan was another, much younger writer, John Goldsmith. He had been educated at Winchester, had published his first novel at the age of 21, had broken into screen writing, but was now working part-time in London as an editor in a publishing house, while awaiting inspiration for his second novel. Although I felt that academically and socially he was on a higher plane than I was ever likely to aspire to, we hit it off at once. His clarity of thought, common sense and interest in every aspect of human behaviour was well beyond my grasp, to say nothing of the fact that his father was the Queen's eye surgeon, Sir Allen Goldsmith. I was therefore flattered but bewildered when he hinted that he would like to work with me for a year or two. I had taken him on my rounds of the outworkers a couple of times and he said that I badly needed organising. I suspect he had seen me making notes on my Players No.3 packets. He was right of course.

It so happened that John's rented cottage lay on the once huge estate of a nobleman, Earl Sondes, whose fortunes had seen better times, and it was thanks to John introducing me to the estate's land agent, that now even the drink-raddled Earl himself, living in just a few rooms of his great mansion, Lees Court, was unwittingly to play a cameo role in influencing future events.

His land agent who we knew socially had already given me a discreet tour of part of the almost empty mansion and suggested that if I were to call one morning before the drink had taken hold, there might be something I could buy. The old man was not averse to making a few pounds on the side.

Accordingly, I called one day. The door was opened by the great man himself, in a soup-stained cardigan. I mentioned the name of his agent, saying rather hesitantly I was looking for some old things to use as decoration. He nodded me into his study-cum-office- come living quarters. There were signs of past grandeur, the odd portrait, crooked, a fine long case clock by Tompion I noted, shelves filled with leather-bound volumes, a Regency sideboard and two leather armchairs.

Gruffly, slurring his words, he asked me what it was I wanted exactly. Who was I anyway? I explained that I lived nearby. *'Ah there,'* he said. *'That used to be another house of mine. Want to look around here now do you – the old family bungalow?'*

*'Well, I would like to, but it's not exactly that,'* I replied and choosing my words carefully went on: *'Your land agent told me that after the sale*

*Christies had left behind a few old things which weren't wanted any more, I would really like to buy something if I could.'*

*'Like what? It's all gone – all the stuff's been sold.'* But then, much to my delight, he pushed himself out of his chair and lurched towards the door, saying he thought he might just have time to show me a few rooms of this vast ancestral home. This will be interesting, I thought to myself, as throwing his arms about expansively, he led me through one great half-shuttered room to another, slurring on about shooting-parties and how grand the ballroom had been in the old days. Dust-sheets lay about, the odd remains of a broken piece of gilded furniture and enormous curtains hanging in shreds were the only things I found myself looking at – nothing I could use. By now I knew he was just showing off; it had become a joke. He was amusing himself at my expense, laughing as the booze took hold, talking about his 'bungalow' and just how splendid it used to be. Finally, we reached a corridor, smelling of mould that led to the pantries and the dairy block. I knew it was a lost cause. I just wanted to get out.

Pushing open yet another door, the Earl muttered something about the butter having been made there; the best butter you'd find anywhere, the Estate butter. There in the corner was an interesting jumble of stuff which looked promising; I saw a standard lamp, chased ormolu, a wooden butter churn, and some birds, a fish and a stuffed squirrel in glass-fronted cases. This was more like it! And then I saw the blackamoor. An 18th century carved wooden Indian figure. God knows how it had ended up in the old dairy building. *'Nothing here,'* he said, waving me out.

As he tottered back to his room he was unaware that I was now carrying the small carved figure. Then he noticed it and asked what it was. I attempted to explain that it was something tobacconists used to have years ago, standing on the shop counter. Suddenly it turned into a pantomime. He wouldn't let me go before I had acted the part of the tobacconist and shown him just what would have happened in the shop if I was a customer wanting some Virginia tobacco.

So I put the figure down, and pointing to the row of books, pretending they were drawers, I attempted to come out with some period sales patter, like *'No finer plugs nor flavours more exquisite than these tobaccos m'Lord – absolutely no finer in all Virginia's fields.'* Absurd! Grown men playing at a lord, rag-and-bone man and tobacconist, but that's the way you sometimes have to play it if you're going to win. In any case my act appeared to have been good enough to warrant permission to leave, because after a healthy swig, the Earl stood up abruptly saying he'd had enough of it all and now he must get on – (with what, I wondered?) I could take the wretched thing if I liked, he'd enjoyed the show. No mention of any payment!

\*\*\*\*\*\*\*\*\*\*

Mamie finally walked out, after one of those rows which began with some trivial complaint her husband drearily moaned on about - the behaviour of one of 'her' boys and how much it was costing to keep the dogs, the pet badger and a rook – all ending with a furious and irreconcilable clash. While I could hear all this going on, I slid away into my workshop. The next morning, Mamie packed her suitcase; looking tired, but as lovely as ever, and left, to stay with friends in Suffolk.

Rather pathetically, on the evening after her departure, her bewildered husband asked me what I thought had got into her and what I was going to do now that the house would be closed down with her gone. For the first time, I told him a lie because I knew full well just why she had gone and I knew where she was going to stay before coming back to live with me, now she knew my cottage was ready. I said I hadn't any idea and I felt guilty as I cleared up my workshop and closed the door of my room for the last time the following morning.

\*\*\*\*\*\*\*\*\*\*

Those early days in the cottage saw life as good as it gets. Mid-thirties, the best years, brimming with confidence, gloriously sex-filled and happy with an abundance of small successes, engrossed in the exhilaration of creativity and when no obstacle seems insurmountable and one feels immortal. Days when I could not wait to get up soon after dawn to face the challenge of another day, to be enjoyed to the full, whatever small taxing problems might be lying in wait. In between visiting the various artists I found time to rebuild an old brick and flint building that lay in semi-ruins in one corner of my field. It had once served as a cook-house for hop-pickers and was now to become my new private office where John Goldsmith would later join me. Before this, my primary concern was to organise the hotchpotch of outworkers into a working unit. It was all such incredible fun.

I had now all but lost touch with dear old Jack up in Camden Mews, black as ever, I imagined, still in his folded paper hat. When times had been good for him his conviviality with the world in general had led him into something of a drink problem and that was the last time I heard of him, until he died a few years later due to his lungs becoming clogged with greasy dust from his Cannings mops. That coupled with having been on one too many benders to celebrate Islington Council's permission for him to remove all the old copper street lamps in the borough (he had learnt a bit in the years of our association, but sadly never quite enough) and in trying to get a lift back up the Caledonian Road from his favourite pub, singing happily, legs swinging from the back tailboard of a mate's lorry, he had fallen off. Apparently, still quite happy, he lay in the road until a passing nurse, seeing the emergency, cut open his flies to the amazement of the passers by, to relieve the pressure of one of his testicles which had swollen inside his trousers to the size of a small melon. Sadly, in hospital, he went downhill fast. I think that just about summed up Jack's life!

*********

My sleeping partners, Mamie's close friends, who had bought the big house just down the valley, had said I could use their stable yard, quite free of charge, should I want to get all the outworkers together under one roof, so to speak. The separate stalls would make good workshops and I knew it would provide them with a certain amount of amusing interests to watch as I tried to make my little fortune.

This was an offer I would later take up.

I already had the loose co-operation of my tricky builder friend. Barry was his name, friendly, but always just skirting the edge of petty blackmail. I had already seen the odd thing that he had made along the lines of mine, poor imitations, just altered slightly, in one of the shops near Portobello Road and that said it all.

The carver, George, was fully committed now that I could keep him in constant work. I had the aspiring guitarist in Whitstable. I had a garage mechanic in Hawkhurst, who made our primitive decoy ducks and other bizarre and misshapen pieces that always seemed to go down very well in places like New England. The half-models just went on and on and I enjoyed adding the finishing touches to them, inventing their names, fixing them to the painted backboards made from old flooring and then giving them the final dusting from the Hoover bag!

It must have been through something more than just pure chance, that walking up the track one day, came a couple, the wife pushing what was obviously a very second-hand pram. The man was carrying a sketchpad. The path was a bridle-way, leading to the woods that ran along the valley's southern edge above the cottage. Level with the house the woman shouted in a broad Yorkshire accent, *'Just going wooding.'* Mamie, of course, immediately responded by asking if they'd like to come in for a cup of tea. This was typical of Mamie – I was not so sure I wanted a pointless interruption.

The husband, Kenneth, was an artist. It was clear that they were pushed for money. They had managed to scrape up enough to buy a small house on the edge of Canterbury. They had no car and no means of support other than the infrequent sale of one of Kenneth's paintings. I imagined his work was nothing special. In fact, he was a protégé of Sir Gerald Kelly, head of the Royal Academy, and had been destined to become an R.A. himself. However, he had recently caused a rumpus at an exhibition in London when he overheard some mildly derogatory remark about one of his paintings and had flown into a tantrum and stormed out. When at last I did see his work, I recognised it as masterly. He deserved to be an R.A., but it was not to be, he upset too many people along the way and if the art-world requires nothing else, it does require a good deal of back scratching, not petulance. He understood all the techniques of the old masters; the layering of paints, the subtleties achievable by every differing brush stroke, but he was also a Yorkshireman and not given to humility and difficult to handle when it came to it.

And come to it, it did – eventually.

That afternoon, after a cup of tea, without the least suggestion that I knew it would be as useful for him as it would be profitable for me, I very tentatively suggested he might consider doing a trial painting for me, such as a portrait of Lord Nelson, copying one of the famous portraits in the Maritime Museum or the National Portrait Gallery. I would make up a board, about the size of a pub sign and we would see if it was worthwhile, if he could do it, say, for £30 or so. I think at this stage, the poorly executed pictorial pub signs Barry was turning out for me, were selling around the £50-£60 mark.

He said he'd let me know. When he rang later and said rather hesitantly he was prepared to give it a try, I was sure his wife, Eleanor, had pressed him to take it on as I felt he considered it rather beneath him.

When I saw the result a week or so later, it left me speechless. In every way it was as perfect as the original he had worked from. It was an object of fine art. I knew I had a gem. Portraits, naval battle scenes, military engagements, all were highly desirable at the time and were very soon to be meticulously copied from famous originals hanging in the great galleries and museums. Henry VIII, by Holbein, was one of the most sought-after of Kenneth Newton's paintings, followed by William IV for the 'Regency Tavern'; 'The Kings Head' was a painting of Richard III. Any 'Admiral's Head' was easy. A copy of a Stubbs made for a 'Newmarket Tavern'; for the 'Waterloo Tavern' or 'Duke's Head', the famous portrait of Wellington by Goya, perhaps superimposed on the battlefield at Waterloo and so on...

The one I personally liked the best, was his copy of the 16th century painting in the Louvre, depicting the top half of two unclothed lesbians, one delicately holding the other's nipple between forefinger and thumb. This made the sign for an imagined pub called 'The Two Friends'! I think there must have been at least fifty pubs or restaurants across the world that had that sign as part of their decoration. All Kenneth's paintings gave a supreme edge of quality to the business that it had lacked. Eddy Bangor in 'Trad' took virtually the entire output for the next two years, except for some I sold to Burge in Sloane Street. In the end, I had a stupid, puerile row with Kenneth over the size of a head-and-shoulders portrait of Henry VIII, that he had been asked to paint on a smaller board than usual. Not bothering to take time to re-work a scaled-down template to accommodate head and shoulders on this smaller board, Kenneth simply used his original template of just the head which by itself filled the entire board, thus making it look ridiculous. Needless to say, the client, who was in fact Eddy Bangor, rejected it out of hand and when Kenneth heard of this he took umbrage and refused to do any further work. He cut off his nose to spite his face and however hard I tried to pacify him, he never painted another thing for me. He had no other income and it was a sad end. The Academy had turned its back on him and he was reduced to animal portraiture for local country folk, which was pathetic given his talent. After that I was not going to be able to meet the demand which his work had created for some time, but what it had done was to bring me into closer contact with a lot of smarter dealers specialising in interior decoration.

All the while Kenneth was, if somewhat begrudgingly, turning out his fine portraits, Eleanor, his wife, was becoming impatient to do something herself which might add to the family's meagre income. Hints were made. With a look of north-country steeliness she told me she had also been through art school; couldn't she do anything? Have a try at painting herself? She had watched how Kenneth did it. I really didn't want to disappoint her, though I knew only too well by now that art school meant next to nothing. Talent and ability were all that mattered. You either had it, or you didn't, and the chances were stacked heavily towards the negative. But she was persistent.

There was a fairly constant supply of Victorian and Edwardian chests of drawers coming in. It had always struck me as a great shame simply to break them down for the old mahogany and pine. I decided to give Eleanor one to paint as an experiment. Most of the chests were of no great quality, pine, with wood knob handles and worth about a fiver at the time.

I sketched out a design by way of decoration, a nautical theme on a bluey-green background, involving drawers bordered by painted rope, crossed flags and anchors and the entire front of one drawer a seascape with a clipper-ship as the main feature. I thought it might be appropriate to have the signwriter add some kind of seaman's motto, such as *'England for Ever'* , date it in the mid 19th century and for the final touch, have the seaman's name on either end. The idea paid off! Naïve undoubtedly it was, but that was its charm. It struck a chord and no one had seen anything quite like it before. It started a worldwide craze for furniture and accessories painted in this type of nautical style. This first chest of drawers was bought without a moment's hesitation by Liberty's and appeared on the front cover of *House & Garden* as part of their winter display that November.

The bandwagon was beginning to roll.

From assiduously watching her husband's various techniques, Eleanor later went on to become an accomplished naïve artist, bursting with character – half Beryl Cook, half Lowry: lopsided birds and animals, street scenes of remarkable detail with every shop front filled with wares, usually completely out of proportion, working painstakingly for hours until satisfied with the smallest detail of a drayman's cap and boots or the apron of a grocer standing outside his shop as the wagon passes. Sometimes she would work late into the night to satisfy the demand which had now become incessant. The insatiable American market had for a long time prized naïve art, discovering it had also existed in England, to a lesser extent, for the past hundred years or more, but up until now had gone unnoticed.

So the business now had acquired an artist whose work ethic was unsurpassable and whose only wish was to be asked for more. She was so keen, now that she felt a little bonanza was coming into view, that I had to cool her aspirations down by saying that by all means make the most of it for the present; it would probably last for a year or maybe two. As I write this, however, more than thirty years on, she is still sitting at her paint-clogged easel!

Now there was a sense that palmy days had arrived, even from his miner's cottage, George's brother Frank, transmitted offers of willingness to become involved part-time, but as I had already had several approaches for *'artistic help'* which had all turned out to be a waste of time, I was not keen and tried to put the idea to rest as gently as I could by testing him with an almost impossible task. Perhaps unkind, but necessary.

I gave him an old print depicting an Austrian military officer in full regalia, mounted on a Lipitsana trotting horse, cockade hat and all. I felt a bit cruel, suggesting he might carve horse and rider, in profile, about four feet long and three feet high. I really did not want to take on anyone else, have the responsibility of keeping them going, although the time-consuming craft of carving did mean that supply could not keep up with the constant demand I was experiencing – anyway, I was sure nothing would come of it.

He rang me three weeks later. He said he had worked odd evenings – could I go over and see what he had done? Rather sheepishly he carried the carving out of his shed and laid it on the patch of grass behind his semi-detached house.

The features of the folds in the uniform, the over-pronounced spindly legs of the horse, the too squat figure seated on it, but with every last bit of detail sculpted in, told me at once I had yet another naïve prodigy.

The last, but in a way the most important member of my cobbled-together workforce, fell into my lap in the most unexpected circumstances.

During the time that Swardcote had been her home, Mamie in her inimitably broadminded way, had struck up a close friendship with a cultured couple who lived in some style, not far away, gardening and rearing pigs for slaughter. The older of the two was Cambridge educated and decidedly of independent means. As time went on and Mamie left her old life to come and live with me, the relationship blossomed into one of an even closer relationship which was of particular interest to me, as I not only liked them a great deal, but because, on the side, as dilettantes, they took up dealing in antiques. Outings to nurseries to buy plants, interspersed with happy and amusing dinner parties had by now become enjoyable events. We even talked of the possibility of taking holidays together. I refer to Mamie's broadmindedness, as to those of us who had been brought up before the war, even to talk of two men living together was something of a taboo subject and as to forming any kind of relationship with them it was virtually unthinkable – certainly in middle class English society…

Anyway, on that particular evening, when Mamie and I were settling down to dinner in the cottage, with this couple, from outside came the noise of tyres on gravel and through the window I saw a rusty, old, green Ford Thames van pull up.

Out of the van stepped the man who was to become my *'ager'*, right-hand man and general *'fixer'* – the one whose imaginative little deceits added the final touch of authenticity to virtually everything that was turned out over the next few years.

He was dressed in a manner quite out of keeping with the Ford Thames: a loud, but well-cut, dogtooth check sports jacket, suede shoes, neat white shirt, complete with tie and cavalry twill trousers. He had a ruddy country look but with a certain bearing, tall and with long dark hair he brushed back as he came towards the cottage door. He looked about forty.

His accent did not quite match the image of the van either, smooth, with just the slightest country brogue. He apologised for disturbing us and asked if a Mr. Croft was at home.

He said he had some interesting things to sell. He had heard in the village that I liked antiques; for a moment his eyes drifted to my station wagon and our friends' XK120. So with the supper left warming on the stove, we all trooped out, intrigued, to have a look. Our new friends were themselves dabblers in antiques and on the fringe of the interior decoration trade in London, where they had a number of friends in the business.

The unusual new caller then started to pull the most extraordinary things from the back of his van: a full-length overcoat made from lion's skin; a regency candle clock in the shape of a lyre; picture after picture, none with frames but all on ancient-looking canvas, all certainly early 19th century.

This was too good to be true. I didn't deal in things like this, but of course I knew they were unusual and probably valuable. The odd thing about them was that almost everything had signs of having been in, or close to, a fire – strange singe marks and discolourations, presumably from smoke. The quite obviously doubtful source of this hoard – the man, his Ford Thames, his very plausibility – did not deter our friends from being the first to ask just how much he wanted for the lot, at the same time asking me if I wanted to buy any of it. They must surely have guessed it had all been stolen, but in a strange way, the man's demeanour was too relaxed for this to have been the case. Odd.

He came in to have drink. His name was Dave Smith; his brother was foreman up in the apple-storage sheds in the village. He was living *'away'* he said, looking after Lady Tyrwhitt-Drake, widow of Kent's last High Sheriff. There had been a fire, out in the stables, or so he said, but I wondered – and he had been told to clear away the lot. Either she was too old to know what was going on or had no idea of what her husband, who had been a great collector, had stored away. It all seemed a bit hot to me.

Our friends however arranged for him to call on them the next day, by which time they would have the cash. It was quite a coup and I was certain that I would have some cut in the deal, but thought it unseemly to mention it over the rack of lamb.

Somehow I had the feeling I would see Dave Smith again. I knew he thought I might be useful to him. He had that almost pure gypsy charm, edged with guile, but quite at ease with his social superiors, to the point of chattiness, and well-dressed enough to fit in anywhere. Later I found out he was indeed half gypsy – a *'wrong side of blanket'* job during a hop-picking.

It had been clear he knew everything that was going on in the area. He even knew there had been someone who had worked for me at Lynsore Bottom. All this I found slightly unnerving.

He did return, but as before I had a feeling that it was too dangerous to buy anything and thought it best to ring our friends and pass him on to them – how naïve I was not to have realised that he had already called there, of course, and this time even they had declined to buy it all it seemed, although they must have been sorely tempted. They had, however, bought all the very choicest pieces.

I soon discovered that Dave Smith was almost openly dishonest, brimful of duplicity, smiling benignly with every devious circumstance he contrived, but clever, of that I was left in no doubt, with an appreciative eye for the better things, their looks, their age, their feel and their value and how best to exploit the entire caboodle. I somehow knew what I was letting myself in for but nevertheless I took him on as my general help and *'ager.'*

The first thing he did was help to install those of the outworkers who had elected to come and work in the stables, which Mamie's friends had offered me – banging up benches, looking in the demolition yards for timber, fetching and carrying, painting and varnishing and trying out new techniques for ageing, not averse to adding a few wormholes with his own 4:10 shotgun. He revelled in it all and I rarely had to tell him anything more than once, which took a weight from my own shoulders at the time.

The only trouble was, soon after he came to work on a regular daily basis, he brought along an odd little Irishman called Johnny O'Brien, who he went to some lengths to explain was still on the run from the authorities, having deserted during the war. It became clear from intermittent absences that the two were not only drinking partners, but into skulduggery which one could only imagine. Johnny, often speaking in irritating riddles, had always parked his own three-wheeler van, some way away from the entrance to the stable yard, usually behind bushes and I came to the conclusion that the story of his desertion was in fact true. He gave no address, shied away from giving any details as to his past and on no account would he accompany Dave whenever he had to go into town. I found it all rather unsettling and I could have done without him although in a small way he was useful and his wages minimal.

*********

When I did get up to London, I still enjoyed a pavement deal for the odd speculative piece I'd found, or had made, which was surplus to any order I might have. In an unintended way, I was becoming established, and dealers who hitherto I might just have referred to as being good buyers, were becoming clients, regularly on the phone. There were some foreign dealers you bumped into, a cut above the rest, who seemed not to fancy bargain hunting in Portobello Road, preferring to frequent the smarter shops of Knightsbridge, Pimlico and Chelsea. On account of this, I never failed to call on Burge in Sloane Street with anything new.

I was now becoming well-known as something of an odd shadowy figure who was supplying the trade with altogether new and imaginative items for decoration. I knew that most of it was being sold on as genuinely old and this in itself amused me. Half-gypsy Dave and his gnome-like deserter friend, Irish Jimmy, were making such a marvellous job in the ageing department.

It can't be said that I set out to deceive in order to take in those in the trade I was selling to – the hardened dealers who were always out for a good bargain, who always knew their wads would tempt one into selling cheap. That was the challenge: to outwit them, never with a direct lie, but like so many politicians, a little economy with the truth. Pretty well everything is fair game in the trade. Whether dealers acknowledge it or not, it is a fact – certainly when buying and selling amongst themselves. I never sold anything directly to the public. Perhaps, in fact, I didn't take in those dealers, I just thought I had: perhaps they saw me as a profit potential regardless and I was sure most of them, whether they knew it or not, were selling on to the antique hunters in the street, all the things I was turning out, on the strength of their visible antiquity. Mine had very quickly become a straightforward 'manufacturing' business based on my assimilation of the feel and looks of all the old rubbish, which had so fascinated me when I was growing up in Somerset in the early 1940s. I simply had a feel for anything old and loved experimenting in processes which gave things the appearance of age. With my own imagination, a little creativity coupled with the skills of the artists and odd-jobbers who worked for me, I was producing art for a mass market and at the end of the day this was going to give a great deal of pleasure to numerous buyers worldwide. On my part there was no deception or so I would like to think. The dealers gave me orders – they knew what they were buying. I was proud of the fact that the feel and look I was giving to everything that was being turned out seemed good enough to stand up to scrutiny and bear comparison to authentic artefacts of a much earlier period.

English dealers were now shipping out 'junk' in containers themselves. Bermondsey market was awash with bulk buyers. Portobello Road was drawing numerous American and Continental dealers, especially now that Germany was thriving. The turnover of goods was astronomic.

Quite a number of the big American retail stores in New York, like *Bergdorf Goodman* and *Bloomingdales*, were trying to source my naval and military painted furniture, through their London agencies. After Eleanor's success I now had more than two or three painters who had got the knack and by degrees the London agents were making direct contact with me. Similarly, so were some of the stores in Dallas, Atlanta and San Francisco and I was becoming almost overwhelmed with orders and I was finding it hard to cope.

It was on a trip to London that I had a chance encounter that was destined to bring the next excitement and a wholly unexpected widening of my horizons. This meeting happened in 'Trad', my favourite place to linger once I had done my business elsewhere and had time to spare. I had always liked to assess the stock and see the buyers come and go and to wonder at the way his Lordship handled them. Sometimes it could be an education. I liked to see how much of the stock had come from me, what had sold and what had not. Among the rows of old tea tins and brass grocers' scales, I saw some decoy ducks of mine, with strange long beaks, each feather painted by Eleanor, made by the garage mechanic in Hawkhurst. Eddy called them *'cocky-olly'* birds and he was always good for a dozen. Besides these, a gilded bull's head, doubtless from some French butcher's shop, vied for supremacy with a carved military dragoon's head made by George. On this occasion as I stood musing, I became aware of two men coming into the shop. One I was sure I had seen before in 'Trad', carrying an old sign of some sort out to his car, as I was going in. His was quite some car, I remembered, a beautiful cream-coloured Mercedes drop-head.

The man's name was Douglas Fisher, the first person to import the new Italian coffee machines, owner, designer and decorator of London's first coffee houses, the 'El Cubano', followed by the 'Mocambo', in Knightsbridge, very much the *'in'* places in the late fifties.

He smiled on seeing me, as if he knew me already. Looking vaguely in the direction of the military bust, he said: *'Very good stuff, yours, my friend.'* At this, the other man, possessing something of the same air as Fisher, but somehow reminding me of Mr. Toad, with his sallow skin and flicking, greedy eyes, turned to me and said quite matter-of-factly, *'Douggie's told me about you.'*

My encounter with them had been on a Friday. The following Sunday morning, I was working in the garden, when up the drive came a black Mini Cooper and to my utter astonishment, out stepped Mr. Toad.

With smooth, easy charm he introduced himself as Rubin Farbey, proprietor of the largest television and film prop-hire company in the country. He was a serious collector of Roman statuary and a would-be restaurateur planning to set up a chain of eating houses, that he was going to call 'O'Rourkes'. His idea was to be financed by a small unquoted company called Rameses Investments Ltd., of which he was one of the directors. The company itself, a small offshoot of the Bass Charrington brewing empire.

It was difficult not to fall under his spell. He had something of the eastern Mediterranean about him, the silken friendliness, calling me *'Cock'* all the time, overplaying the common touch, but he was deadly serious when he put his proposed deal to me, there, out on the grass, as Mamie went into the kitchen to make us both coffee.

Mamie overheard everything that was being said and told me afterwards that she knew it must have been very flattering to me, but that she didn't take to him one little bit and that I should be careful.

His proposal was that I should supply him, or rather Rameses Investments Ltd., with all the decorative artefacts, old fittings and embellishments that were going to feature as the main appeal of the new restaurant chain. It all sounded just the same as Fisher must have done with his coffee houses and, later, with his two restaurants in South Kensington, which were still very much in vogue, one of which I'd been to – '*The Contented Sole*'. Rubin must have seen the possibilities, had a direct line to someone on the Charrington Board and so the plot had been hatched and it now seemed that I was to be part of it.

He said I'd just have to come up to town as soon as possible and make myself known to one other of the directors in the company offices opposite the Garden House Hotel, so that they knew I was bona fide. He added that I would also be expected to help the Rameses designers in getting the best results from the artefacts I would be supplying, by looking over the proposed sites beforehand seeing what would best fit where, and so on. That all seemed to make good sense.

There was no room for delay, he said, in making up a stockpile of decorative pieces of the widest diversity I could come up with, ready for his scheme's launch in six to seven months' time. Monthly invoices would be settled, on presentation, by Rameses – he would see to that personally. But now, the smallest condition, Cock... fifteen percent of my invoiced charges had to be paid, in cash, to Rubin Farbey. A kickback! I could not believe it. Was this what went on in business at this kind of level...? Querying whether this meant over and above what would have been my normal invoiced prices, he could see I was on the point of baulking at this irregularity and quickly went on to suggest that, as a sweetener, I might hold back some of the very best things, as he was thinking of buying a small shop in Holbein Place, where WE could sell them, splitting any

305

profits fifty-fifty and I would also have part of any proceeds if he sold the shop. He'd get one of his Chelsea women to run it: zebra skin sofas, Benin chairs, ivories mounted on silver, shell and horn ornaments, everything the rage, along with the most bizarre and unusual carvings I could produce. *'You know old cock, you've got the greatest imagination – just get going, carte blanche.'*

Of course I knew Mamie was probably right, but I couldn't help but admire the man – so smooth, so adept in his ability to seduce and make the proposition irresistible.

I knew that whatever I did, I couldn't put all my eggs in one basket. The floodgates were going to be near bursting point, and John still wasn't yet ready to join me. I was going to need more carvers and although I didn't know it then, I was going to lose Kenneth Newton. By now, luckily, my tricky builder had been deserted by his commercial artist – he had finally screwed him down to breaking point and now the artist asked me whether I had any work he could do.

His name was Jim. He was the most down-to-earth of all those who came to work for me at the time and became adept at painting all the decorated furniture, apart from being a portrait painter of considerable talent.

The last of the artist outworkers I had taken on at this stage was the set designer, Michael Trangmar, whose swansong had been designing the set for the 'The Man of Magic', on Broadway and later doing the same for the show's run in London. After this he had had enough of the rat race and teaching at the Central School of Art and took to part-time painting for me, in his tiny gatehouse.

For carving, there was George's brother, Frank, who had so amazed me with his Lipitsana horse. He duly left the mines and went to London to buy his chisels at Terranti's.

By now the stable yard had become a hive of activity, with the noise of saws and chipping at demolition timber mingled with the ribald shouts of Dave, the finisher, asking if anything was ready for him and Irish Johnny, in their varnish stall. By now, Dave's trousers, he would boast, would stand up by themselves, being so stiff, on account of being so spattered with the Gedges varnish. The outworking signwriters would sometimes come to the yard for a day or two, rather than working at home, which was something I liked as I could gently guide them towards the subtleties of 19th century style and show them examples in the various reference books I had. *Early Advertising Art*, an American publication, was particularly relevant, as was *Art & Ephemera*, published in England, showing the more decorative aspects of 19th century advertising art.

It struck me as ironic, thinking about it, that I was finding my time in the Navy had not been wasted in this new venture of mine. First of all, I had learnt about the problems of casting, which I put to good use in producing my cannons. My time in the technical drawings office had taught me how to follow plans, which had been of paramount importance when my cabinet maker had constructed the Hansom Cab from scratch. Most importantly of all, my Dartmouth time spent in the engineering workshops had given me a good knowledge of metals – how to braze and solder, weld and rivet and when necessary, cut with oxyacetyline. You may well ask when knowledge of this kind came in useful, working primarily with wooden artefacts. Principally, it became invaluable when it came to making up old iron hanging brackets for three-dimensional signs which had supposed to have started life hanging outside some ancient business. The odd fake repair, using a patch of weathered copper, attached by well-rusted nails, was also a good ruse to achieve the look of authentic age (as time went on this became something of a trade mark, which could hardly have gone unnoticed by 'the Trade', selling these *apparently* authentic-looking pieces). At other times I might use rusted tin sheet, or the easiest of all to hammer into the crevices that had been carefully gouged out, where rot was supposed to have been, was lead, from any scrapyard, which had presumably come from some conveniently sited roof within the reach of the thieving hands of the odd passing gypo! It was lucky that I could talk the same language as the metalworkers in the nearby blacksmith's forge, when discussing the different problems of using all the varying old pieces of metal we used – the difficulties in using wrought iron, as opposed to cast, which was far more difficult to work. How best to fix this or that to something we had made, either to weld or braze, or bind up with ancient strands of copper wire and so on

My 'fixer' and 'ager', gypo Dave, and myself, were also constantly on the lookout in the scrap and demolition yards, for parts of old ornamental gates and railings, from which authentic-looking hanging-brackets could be knocked up.

All the various difficulties of conjoined work involving part wood, part metal, came to the fore when I was asked if I could cut a small horse-drawn omnibus once belonging to a railway company, into two halves. I had unearthed the thing in a barn outside a nearby village, which, years ago, had been a train 'halt' on one of this, the oldest lines in the country – the Whitstable to Canterbury to Elham line, whose old track is now marked by nothing more than the last remains of a bridge or cutting and a straight line of trees and bushes which had once bordered the sides of its track. An imaginative nightclub owner wanted the two halves, sideways on and suitably restored, complete with wheels and axles, one half to be mounted on a wall to serve as a bar and the other half to form the entrance to the cloakrooms – exciting and typical of the expansive way in which decoration had begun to evolve in the seventies. My part of the job completed, the two restored halves were duly delivered to London, to an address in Mayfair, and I never saw the end result. Nightclubs weren't exactly my scene.

By now I was gaining confidence with each new challenging commission, and that, coupled with my creative imagination, gave me the assurance I could produce virtually anything, using the skills of my carvers, cabinet makers and painters, coupled perhaps with a first cursory glance at one or other of my reference books which, when looking at some original and well-executed work, might help spark off some altogether new idea. Artefacts of absurd peculiarity, as well as those of a more conservative nature – but often enormously oversize – were commonplace. Take for example, a 19ft. long double-sided codfish - so heavy it had to be made in two halves and lifted with a mechanical hoist – suitably aged to look as though it had been made sometime in the early 1900s, or before, been 'lost' and 're-discovered' behind a shed, covered in brambles, not far from Whitstable harbour. The client who ordered it, asked I have it photographed by a local press photographer, so that he in turn could show the photograph to *his* client, where it had been discovered. In this particular incidence, the latter had been involved in the development of the new Boston Waterfront and was looking for something really eye-catching apparently!

Another wildly unlikely commission was to make an outsized, carved, wooden head of a Grenadier, complete with mutton chop moustaches and helmet, hollow at the back, with sufficient space for a 'doorman' to take shelter in, as it was to stand at the entrance gateway of a Thameside country club, near Maidenhead. The owner must have had more money than common sense, as it wasn't going to be long before the wood would dry out, the glued sections shrink and the whole amazing, eye-catching whim of some military nut, was going to disintegrate. The client loved it however.

Or have a reclining camel, 6ft 6ins long, completely gilded, the humps of which hinge open to reveal cocktail cabinets! Things like this were *de rigeur* if you were out to impress in the 60s and 70s, and the craze led to my producing hundreds of outsized fishes, cows, bulls, sheep and strangely weird birds and animals, supposedly once to have been old trade signs, or simply the work of some long-forgotten carver, who had perhaps in one instance, made an enormous penguin and then inserted an old railway station clock into its belly! Nothing was impossible, or too outrageous and I did my best to take every opportunity to astound, by producing the most bizarre items of decoration I could conceive, should, as often was the case, I was given carte blanche.

One day a woman called Rosemary appeared in the stable yard, which was the centre of activity in those days. She and her husband ran a smallholding – eight cows, sixteen sheep and a clutch of laying hens – on adjacent land belonging to 'The Hall', as the big house was called. She asked me if I had any carving work: she had been to art school, but for the moment she had had to put her chisels away. Her husband, she said, could make up a bench for her in one of the disused cowsheds.

With Rubin's shop that he was going to call *Naïve*, due to open in Holbein Place in less than six weeks' time, as well as everything else that was going on, I thought there would be no harm in applying the *'Frank test'*, to see if she could really produce anything which might be useful to the business. At least it would get rid of any further pestering if it all turned out to be a waste of time. She said she knew a lot about Chippendale and Sheraton, egg-and-dart borders and all the other classic stuff, but I said I wasn't into that and hoped she would be able to lower her sights somewhat and carve me a straightforward copy of a horse, maybe along the lines of a Stubbs, about six feet long perhaps. I gave her a photocopy of a print I had in one of my reference books and told her she could take some of the old joists which had come from a demolition yard which were used as carving wood. She said she would try and I then forgot about it. I did see her a few days later, talking to Frank and George, my principal carvers, and I noticed she took away some glue, which I imagined was to glue up some of the timber which I said she could take. So maybe there would be a finished article after all, but more likely I thought, it was going to be an attempt that would fail.

About a fortnight later she rather coyly asked me to go and look at what she had done. Down to the cowsheds I went, somewhat begrudging my time on what I knew would be a wasted exploit. When I finally got to look at what she'd done, it was pathetic – completely hopeless. Yes, there was a horse with knees all knobbly, the nose hopelessly too long with a thin and pointed head with its ears slightly out of place. But almost forcing myself to look at it, lost for words, it began to dawn on me that it did have something. The more I looked at her effort, the more I liked it. It was quite simply, utterly primitive!

But thinking the horse might simply look absurd to most people if I had it naturistically painted, I decided to have it gilded in 'Dutch Metal, the substitute for gold leaf – and then off the top of my head, I thought of the idea of having the words *'The Golden Reaper, Stallion, winner of three consecutive races, Barham Downs 1803,'* written across its belly. I then partially rubbed the words away with wire wool, so that it was only with difficulty that one could decipher what it said. It looked what you might call *'interesting!'*

In due course it went up to the *Naïve'* gallery as part of the initial stock and I thought no more about it. Apparently it was sold within a couple of weeks or so of the opening. To whom, or to where it went, I had no idea. The smallholder's wife who had carved it only asked me, if she could do one more thing, smaller this time and perhaps more classical. She did some head or other, which was a failure. The whole business seemed to be beneath her, and that was that.

Nobody had seen anything quite like the *Naïve* gallery and it became well-known.

Frank had carved a naïve hanging fleece, which Rubin hung outside as the shop sign. Now, some of the most bizarre and to be quite honest, ridiculous pieces of art that my imagination was capable of dreaming up, were going to be displayed before, hopefully, the astonished and receptive inhabitants of one of the most exclusive residential areas in the world. With this in mind and the world in an altogether new mood, Rubin reckoned he would be on to a winner – for my part I was not so sure, but with the promise of a 50/50 split on any profit and costs paid on each delivery, there was no holding back. There was just a creeping suspicion that he might not keep his word, but this proved to be quite wrong – at first.

By the time the shop had been filled, zebra-skin sofas and all, with the most chic woman that Rubin could conjure up to run it, he decided it would help if he went down to the gallery, as he called it, to do some selling himself. There, he really laid on the selling spiel, with techniques any market trader would have been proud of, except that he did it in his inimitably silken way, with more than a slight economy of the truth.

A typical city gent came in one day when I happened to be there and said his wife had been in earlier and seen the most amusing old painting of a couple of courtesans, so he believed, which she would like to give him as a present should he like it. It was, of course, one of Kenneth Newton's *Two Friends* – copied from the original in the Louvre. The man seemed very interested and when he queried its price and age, I heard Rubin say it was very probably a mid-18th century copy, and the price was £650. Without a murmur the man asked that it be sent round to his flat in Drayton Gardens as soon as possible! I suppose my production costs would have been perhaps no more than £60!

Not everything sold as well, but there seemed to be a market for anything, however extraordinary, from an enormous Blackamoor's head with mouth open wide, to reveal a wall clock, to a couple of strange greyhounds with elongated necks made by the garage mechanic, who had been asked if he could manage a pair of pharaoh dogs. He had managed to attach rather splendid collars made of scrap brass and they next turned up on a television set of a play being shot in Ireland. Everything sells in the end.

The property market was in full swing and it was soon clear that Rubin now had every intention of selling the place, but in the meantime while the property prices were still rising, he took full advantage of making what he could out of my work, all the time knowing that the hold he had on me was the fact that I was wholly committed to the production of all the Rameses items. That still excited me. The little gallery had become well-known by now and was in fact highly profitable most of the time and it did introduce me to an interesting section of society which otherwise I would never have known. Smooth city men who Rubin knew and smart women who lived in Eaton Square and Drayton Gardons who had time on their hands and more money than common sense. These, apart from other eastern Mediterranean-type cronies and property men to whom Rubin referred to as *'useful contacts.'*

By the time it did finally come to be sold there had certainly been no diminishing in the friendliness of our association, especially as I was deep into stockpiling for his restaurant project. But suddenly there was a distinct lack of any mention of the sale proceeds being split, even when I knew the sale had gone through without a hitch. As the weeks went by and it became clear just what sort of person whose protégé I had become, Mamie said she had known all along he was the type who would have happily taken the pennies from his dead mother's eyes and suddenly I realised that I was not going to see one penny from the sale myself.

I was not in the habit of taking things lying down and I decided I would ring Rubin's solicitors and with all the subtlety I could master, gently suggest that it would be best if they jogged his memory as to our understanding, as there were certain *'complications'* in our relationship which could well become direly embarrassing if they were to surface. They obviously knew the intimate details of some of the nefarious dealings undertaken by Rubin over the years. It is impossible for anyone as devious as Rubin, in the restaurant and property *'game'*, as he called it, not to become enmeshed in scratching the odd council official's back from time to time, leaving them a little richer and probably more besides... not to mention the means by which he had come by one or two of his most valuable television props. I knew a lot and however amicable my conversation was with those solicitors up in Hanover Square, they knew it was loaded with threat. I got paid.

I suppose you could rate the 'Naïve Gallery' a success, but I knew it was based on one person's whim and his wish to squeeze the most money possible from my small business in the country in any way he could, always with that smooth charm, endlessly laying on compliments to his collaborator, *'Cock.'*

In the final analysis, the success of my business, however, would depend on the type of work which was coming through from people like Mark Maley, who had moved on to Ayala Designs Ltd., a firm operating worldwide, building pubs and eating houses, and work commissioned by architects associated with the large hotel groups, who apart from their call for décor, were going to keep Richards busy in Folkestone with a variety of bar, lobby and restaurant fittings. I knew it would not be long before I turned my back on the production of the military furniture and was already quietly casting about for a possible buyer who would take on the business, allowing me to take David Richards to continue in a workshop I would provide, making the half-models and all specialist items. Neither I nor my sleeping partners had reaped much benefit from the operation, except in my case it had provided an entrée to some of the good London stores.

As to the gilded stallion, my 'Golden Reaper', made in the cow sheds, it was to be more than ten years later that I heard something of its new life. I was talking to one of the Pimlico dealers who knew most of the interior decorators and he asked me if I knew where it had ended up, to which I replied I had no idea. He said it had been bought by Inchbald, doyen of all decorators and principal of the Inchbald School of Design, who had introduced it as the centrepiece for a scheme he had been commissioned to carry out in the Tattersall's banqueting suite in the New Berkeley Hotel – perhaps the most prestigious London hotel of the day. He had heard it was still there.

On the pretext of having friends who were coming over from Kentucky, who had asked me where they should stay, I wrote to the Berkeley saying that I had been told 'by a racing chum' that a remarkable carving to do with horse racing had been acquired by the hotel and how very interested my friends would be if they could see it if they stayed there during the time they were in London.

A week later I had a reply. The second paragraph of the hotel's public relations department ends with the sentence … *'As you know, there is half of a wonderful brass horse mounted on the wall, the other half being owned by an American.'* It had now become brass! As to being owned by an American, even I cannot for the life of me understand this flight of fancy.

The letter ended with an invitation, at my convenience, to visit the hotel to be shown the so-called brass horse. They hoped my friends from Kentucky would find the enclosed photograph of the dining suite of interest and yes, I could bring my own camera and take a picture from another angle. So I went, complete with Polaroid, met an obsequious under-manager, who escorted me along the plush carpeted corridors to the finest Burmese teak doors of the Tattersall suite which he reverently unlocked and there it was! Mounted on a wall of dark brown suede and underneath it, an engraved brass plaque, over a foot wide, on which were written the words, *'The Golden Reaper, Stallion, winner of three consecutive races, Barham Downs, 1803,'* just in case anyone had difficulty in deciphering the faded writing on the horse's body.

While I took a quick photograph, the manager told me that only recently the suite had been the venue for Lord Anson's wedding party at which the principal guest had been Her Majesty the Queen. And she, sitting directly below the carving had been heard in heated discussion with others at her table, remarking what an astonishing feat it must have been for such a delicately proportioned stallion – three races in one afternoon – quite extraordinary! But the story doesn't end there. It seems the animal has become immortal … by some bizarre fertility procedure, the equine specialists in Newmarket must have produced a clone of this famous stallion – now seen grazing on an 18th century landscape. I must explain.

Very recently I was sitting making out a cheque for a young artist friend who had done some woodwork for me and having applied my signature, sat back and looked up at a collage of odd pictures, scraps of reference, bills etc, pinned to the wall above his desk. And there to my utter amazement was the Golden Reaper. An outsize photograph on a page cut from *The Guardian* newspaper, dated 6th October 2004, mounted now on a background painting of a typical 18th century landscape with our champion jockey Frankie Dettori sitting in the foreground, being interviewed.

The article does not mention where the interview was taking place. I was keen to learn more: was it still in the Tattersall suite or had it been reborn somewhere else…? Someone said it might be in the Jockey Club.

At first glance the 'Golden Reaper's' surroundings seemed unfamiliar, but after a close comparison with my old pictures taken at the Berkeley, I could see that although the furnishings were not the same, the position of the pillars and the wall lights were identical – the only difference being that the suede had been removed and the background had been painted as an early landscape. It was the same animal.

I was intrigued. I had an architect friend of mine write discreetly to the Berkeley on the pretext that many years ago he had been to a function there, seen the remarkable carved horse and had been impressed. Now that he had seen it again in *The Guardian*, he was even more impressed, realising that it must be one of the world of horse racing's most treasured relics … could they tell him anything about its history?

Again the reply was some time in coming. When it did, it was incredible. *'The horse was purchased at an auction by a designer in 1972. It had been originally covered in horse hair, but that had been removed some years ago and the wood beneath it polished up to its current finish.'* The letter ends, *'I regret that I do not have any further information about the carving, which is, as you know quite astonishing.'*

My work was acquiring some notoriety in the trade by now and some of the country dealers in the area were attempting to emulate what we were doing. I saw poor copies, mostly of the painted furniture, but I also noticed crude carvings in some of the export wholesalers. It had no effect, except that it was becoming more difficult to get hold of the chests and boxes and the other types of furniture which lent themselves to conversion to nautical and military pieces. By the end of the 1970s I knew of eleven small, homespun, two- or three-man outfits not far from Canterbury who were at it. I saw nothing they were making which had our look of authenticity.

On the subject of authenticity, I am still ashamed to say that there was one instance of total deception. It was to be worked on my good friend, Mr. William Kranzler of New Bedford, Massachusetts. He was a small rosy-cheeked man with crinkly hair, who had a shop in Johnny Cake Hill, New Bedford. He said it was a shop for purists, with nothing reproduction, specialising in things nautical, although from time to time he did like to buy quality glass and china and other select *'smalls.'*

He always rang me whenever he was in England. That was certainly a compliment from someone who was an official appraiser for the State of Massachusetts and had been in the business all his life. The one thing he had always wanted to buy was the small tobacco figure that I had acquired from Earl Sondes. Before I had decided to keep it, I had taken it to my semi-basement in George Street, intending to get it valued. This was where Kranzler first saw it. It was seldom that the prospect of a good, quick profit failed to sway my decision as to whether to sell or not, but in this instance he left George Street, disappointed. I had decided I liked it too much, particularly when I thought of the way in which I had come to own it. So when I moved into my new home, it took pride of place, on a huge oak lintel over an unused fireplace, just inside the entrance.

Kranzler came over two or three times a year to buy. Although I did like the man, I tried to put him off coming down to Kent, as I was certain that I had nothing for him. The lamps and nautical pieces had come to an end, I wasn't scavenging the ports any more. Tea tins and old shop scales or enamel signs and butchers' wooden trugs would hardly appeal to him and as for signs and carvings and my painted furniture, all this he would class as reproduction. But he insisted.

I picked him up at the East Station. I took him to the stable yard and showed him the first of the restaurant stockpile – the outsize hands holding gilded boars' heads on simulated pewter dishes, made of wood, covered in cheap silver leaf, huge game pies surmounted by carved and coloured pheasants, lettered with some provision merchant's name in Melton Mowbray. He was bemused. He said some of the Boston restaurants had now taken to using artefacts like these for decoration, but they were *'real genuine,'* he thought. So it was now spreading across the world.

Over a cup of tea back in the cottage, I watched his eyes wandering and assessing each little piece of decoration, every ornament and bibelot in the drawing room. He hinted, none too subtly, how nice the Battersea snuff boxes were and how hard it was to come by early porcelain now, looking enviously at the cabinet in which Mamie had some exquisite pieces of Blore Derby. Finally he couldn't help blurting out he would really like to buy something from the house. Although I said I sympathised, I told him quite firmly that nothing in the house was for sale – everything was a very personal possession of either Mamie or myself and was part of our new home.

Tea over, pausing at the door on leaving, he looked at the tobacco figure, saying he would give a very good price for it. Wouldn't I just let that one thing go – for a really good price?

I heard from him four months later saying he'd be coming over again and that as usual, he would be staying at the Cumberland Hotel.

I happened to be in London for the day soon after his arrival and I went to the Cumberland to meet him. He wanted to come down to Kent again. Inside the hotel I was pleased to see that the dining room walls had been hung with a series of amusing, rural country scenes I had recently supplied to a Hampstead architect.

The coffee-shop also had some of our artefacts and I recognised two different signs of long-forgotten city coffee-houses, which I had conveniently *'found'* in the East End and which Eddy had bought from me.

When I had heard he was coming over, I knew it was going to be a repeat of the previous visit. I knew I had nothing for him, except for one thing. I had asked George to make an exact replica of my little Blackamoor, its slightly bulbous nose, the large hand-cut, rusted nail which held the one moving arm, the colours of the head-dress and the feathered skirt; it had to be perfect, so that even side by side, the detail would be a perfect match. One was to be indistinguishable from the other. The final touches I would work on myself. For his visit, the one I had had made was to be the one which stood inside the cottage entrance. It went exactly as I had thought it would. He had the same look of disappointment when I gently reminded him that nothing in the house was for sale. So with the fruitless visit over it was time to go back to the station for the early evening train to London.

I don't think Mamie would have liked me to do it, if I had told her, but I could not resist the temptation, for sure enough as she called goodbye from the drawing room and he was just going out of the door, he paused, looked at me and gently took the figure down, most carefully. *'James,'* he said, *'please can't I change your mind, I've come all this way...?'*

It was too easy: it struck me like some schoolboy prank and I began to laugh, Kranzler looked bewildered, mortified. He must have guessed, surely. We both stood there and he turned it in his hands, feeling it ... *'Won't you?'* he said imploringly. *'Why is it so funny that I want this piece? They're not even English you know – these things used to come from Virginia with the tobacco which your Bristol merchants brought in.'*

Now acting as if I had finally been defeated, with the falsest of sighs, I said, *'Oh well, to tell the truth, it's just so amusing that you doggedly keep on trying to get me to sell it and now I think finally you've worn me down and I suppose it's only right you should take it home to where it belongs. You've persevered enough!'* He beamed as he held it for one last loving inspection before asking for newspaper to wrap it in for the journey back to London.

Still highly amused, I asked what the 'real good price' was he said he'd pay... Remember!? *'Well, let me see, this little fellow must be worth two hundred and fifty pounds ...'*

*'Oh dear,'* I replied, 'I thought it was going to be a lot more than that.' I was only too aware that I had paid George £48 for the carving and I had done the rest. I replied I thought at least five hundred. *'It is quite rare you know,'* I said with shades of Rubin creeping into my little act at this stage. To be quite candid, I did not feel ashamed, doing deals like this could easily become compulsive.

I drove back from the station still laughing to myself, through the shabby streets of outer Canterbury, with the last of the small shopkeepers and the odd old crone sweeping her steps, while I was thinking of the wider world out there and how odd life was. How could I have played a trick like that on someone I really liked? I had begrudgingly agreed to take £350 pretending it was a bad deal ... with all that work of finding the old cut nail, the clever mixture of the emulsion paint, after all that had made the whole exercise pretty costly. I did feel guilt when I took the old earl's original out of the cupboard and put it back in its pride of place just inside the door. The awful thing was that one day at Wingate & Johnsons, where I had gone to collect some buying agency's cheque, I learnt that poor William Kranzler had died of a sudden heart attack whilst unpacking that last consignment they had shipped to Johnny Cake Hill and I was left wondering whether perhaps in some way the figure had been damaged in transit, to reveal the fresh demolition timber or a flake of emulsion paint, which would have given the game away. Perhaps it was this, and the shock of the discovery, that had proved too much. I will never know. Many, many years later, my house was broken into and most of my treasured small belongings were stolen. Luckily, not my tobacco man who was always much admired. Later on, after yet another quite aimless robbery when my office things and television were taken away in a roll of carpet, I imagined it would only be a matter of time before the Blackamoor would go. I had another made, with the idea of hiding the old one away.

I was robbed again and this time the figure did go, but by now I could not remember which one had actually been standing on its little bracket in the drawing room. Thoroughly dispirited I sent the remaining one away to be sold at Christies and made an insurance claim for my original. But had I got it right…? I'll never know about that either. The one at Christies sold for £1,200.

*********

The Rameses business, which involved all my various men and women artists, outlasted my involvement with Rubin's own private brainchild 'Naïve' by several months. The shop in Holbein Place was sold. I had learnt how conveniently forgetful Rubin could be whenever he owed what he referred to as 'serious bread, Cock!' But notwithstanding this, on went Rameses, the cheques kept coming in and Rubin took his monthly rake-off.

One day he asked me to go to London and sit in on an important board meeting. The first two O'Rourkes were scheduled to open within a couple of months – one in Walthamstow and the other in Dover Street. There was also the likelihood that the company would be buying a large railway building in Manchester, which was going to be turned into a 200-seater eating house to cater for the boom times, now being experienced in the North Midlands. If it came off it was certainly going to be a big project, with the kind of budget that exceeded my own annual turnover and more. If he could get me involved in that, then the fifteen percent I was certain he would expect was going to be very tasty for him indeed.

The board meeting was a revelation. The room was thick with cigar smoke. There were glasses on the table and the cloth was blue baize I remember. There were bottles of gin, whisky and Martini on the side and jotting-paper in front of each chair. Four or five men were already seated when Rubin took me in. There were introductions – names like Benlian, Zhilka, Saluman and Badasolio. From their looks, they might well have first sat in on meetings like this in any back room from Tangier to Beirut, the sallow skins and heavy gold signet rings all combining to give the place a distinct whiff of something ominous – of business danger. Jackets off, it was down to business. It all went over my head: talk of vast sums of money, of some new club, trying to get a gaming licence, how pressure could be applied. I don't think I would have liked to cross them.

The board came to the Manchester project. Rubin, to my embarrassment, pushed my involvement and stressed my somewhat dubious credentials – I'd done this and that – been around – America – clever – and been in the decorating and design business for some time! He made it sound as if I was far more than just a general dealer who had drifted into this kind of situation by chance. I tried to look serious. They obviously reckoned Farbey's acumen and his choice of me as his representative on site to see the place through to opening, as there were nods of approval and someone said: *'Well that's the Great Northern Eating House dealt with then.'*

The meeting broke up shortly after that. One or two stood around with Rubin, while up to me came a Mr. Hacker, the company accountant. Rather sheepishly he said he had all my invoices on file and for a moment I thought he was going to say he thought they were rather high, but no, he paused and not quite knowing where to look, in a very low voice he asked if all the stock which they referred to: *'Was it still there? Available to the company? In store? It hadn't got mislaid?'* When I said it was still there, his relief was tangible.

The inference was unmistakable. There had been one or two unexplained phone calls coming down from the Rameses offices of late, asking if some of the items in stock – in one instance a large number of very fine stuffed game trophies I had bought – could be taken to a private address out at Hendon. I'd imagined it was something special Rubin had arranged and had thought no more about it at the time. But there had been another occurrence when an expensive chandelier had been sent down for me to store and that had also eventually been delivered to a large house in Highgate. All a bit odd. Mr. Hacker had presumably seen all this before and had probably been forced into making adjustments to the books, as things quietly disappeared – write-offs with no explanation given. Oh my God, now was I being used as a useful conduit, for private side dealings of the directors and was poor Bass Charrington the sucker of the piece?

I did go to Manchester once. I went with a pleasant, in-house architect. He had done the drawings and we exchanged ideas for the design sketches. He knew I had no experience but he *'knew the score'* and was extremely helpful and fell in with most of my ideas – booths like the interior of Victorian first-class carriages, both bars to look like the old booking offices, with fretted station canopies and for the *'piece de resistance'* – accepted finally by a somewhat sceptical board, but swayed by Rubin - the Pay Desk, the reconstituted 1802 lighthouse I had seen two years earlier at the end of the harbour arm of the old coaling port on the Clyde – I'd have it taken down carefully and brought down by lorry – *'Sheer brilliance Cock,'* had been Rubin's reaction to the idea … *'I knew you'd come up with something spectacular.'*

As it was, the whole idea of spectacularly decorated Eating Houses collapsed, the directors realising that Rubin's intention to try to open a new one every month was quite impractical (I could have told them that, but it was always a case *of 'more gear Cock: we need more gear.'* He couldn't have been thinking of the 15%, I don't suppose!?) Times had suddenly become difficult, the property market was falling, the money supply drying up and the Yom Kippur War was on the horizon.

I had, in fact, rung the scrapyard on the Clyde, to be told that the old wooden lighthouse had been destroyed the year before, so the scheme would never have turned out as planned, but it had been an interesting challenge and had it gone ahead I would have relished it for sure. No one could accuse me of a lack of confidence in those days.

At least I was fully paid up for the huge amount of items I had made for Rameses, now stored away in one of the stable lofts. They had agreed to pay for storage. Someone in Farbey's office rang me just once, suggesting I might like to buy it back – at cost. It struck me as just a shade suspicious I thought. I could hardly believe that sophisticated home owners would like a three foot high, gilded padlock, lettered: 'The Very Reverend Stott's Patent "Eversure" Chastity Fitment Co.,' or six foot long naïvely carved cows with oversized udders! O.K. as 'gear', but not for your man in the street.

The cessation of the Rameses' contract and my contact with Bass Charrington came without any warning and as I had fifteen men working for me at that time – sometimes more – with all of them depending on me to provide a livelihood it was critical I find alternative markets. Their output was too large to be absorbed by my normal trade customers, most of whom were in London, except for a few who were the embryo of an export side to the business. This was a dire challenge and had to be faced without delay: Friday pay-days, cashflow, where was the money going to come from now that Hacker's cheques were finished?

The first thing I did was to close down the Folkestone furniture works. It had become unprofitable. As luck would have it, a local entrepreneur, who ran a very successful mineral water company, was looking for an opportunity to move into the furniture business which apparently was the prime interest of one of his sons.

What the bottler didn't know, was that once he had taken the business over he was not going to be able to take advantage of Dave Richards' skills for very long because in something of a devious pre-arranged move by myself, within three weeks, David Richards told him, with much regret of course, that he was unable to carry on working under the new ownership and he was going to have to set up in his home workshop relying on private work coming in. But in fact, this was so that he could continue making all the speciality pieces for me.

The rent cheques, signed by Hacker, came dribbling through religiously, month after month, for almost another two years. Meanwhile rats and rain through a leaking roof did their work. Things split, the paint began peeling off and anything that had been gilded, turned black with damp. There it lay, stacked, jumbled into piles, a sorry sight and an eerie reminder of the Rameses adventure. Deterioration soon meant that all this decorative stock became useless. Amongst it had been a rare collection of animal trophy heads which Farbey had asked me to store on the company's behalf. Matters had not been improved by the fact that the conniving pair of Irish Johnny and Dave Smith had been given the job of moving the stock from one loft to another on a day I happened to be in London. It does not stretch the imagination to guess what they had got up to. A rough evaluation of the stock I was supposed to hold added up to some £40,000.

Rameses and Bass Charrington might never have existed. The lines were dead. No one from the company contacted me. As months passed by, I should of course have rung Hacker and made a clean breast of what had happened to the goods they had paid for, but I didn't and as time went on, I was haunted by the possibility that I might be sued for the entire amount of £40,000. Luckily that didn't happen!

Meanwhile somewhere up in London, one of Bass Charrington's auditors, running through the Rameses accounts had finally discovered an unaccounted for amount of some £40,000 and reported it to one of the Board. Consequently, one late Saturday morning in summer, an impassive and distinctly upper-class man arrived on my doorstep with his son, introducing himself as one of Charrington's directors and apologising for the intrusion over a weekend. He had just happened to be in the area, he said, taking his son out for half-term and thought it might be a good opportunity to check out the position of the stock, which appeared in the Rameses' accounts since he had seen my address on the invoices.

He was holding a sheaf of papers in his hand. The moment of my undoing had come, I thought. So, nervously beginning to sweat, expecting the worst possible outcome, I took the man with his little boy in tow, over to the sheds where the stock had finally been put away after my friends sold The Hall. Lying in the half dark of the old sheep-shearing sheds, lay the pitiful remains of barely recognisable signs and artefacts, which I had once been so proud of, jumbled higgledy-piggledy together with what was left of a once spectacular collection of stuffed animal heads, one of the company directors had asked me to put into store. The rats had got at these. There was barely a shred left. The poor man stood transfixed. I remember the boy picked up the tusk from a half-eaten warthog's head and asked his father if he could keep it. His father didn't answer him but instead he looked at me and just said, *'Is this it? Is this all of it?' 'Yes,'* I replied apologetically, explaining that no one had come to collect it and I had forgotten it was there. Dumbstruck, he folded the papers, which I suppose must have been the lists of stock, put them into his jacket pocket and that was it. I half expected a letter in the days to follow, but no one came and I think that perhaps Hacker had prepared him for something like this.

All the while Dave Smith had been working himself into a position of some importance. Not only was he invaluable as a finisher and 'ager' – and he was well aware of it – but he was also the transport man. His old transit with its roof rack was ideal and it suited me not to have to buy a new van and he knew that too. He had done the runs between Folkestone and the stable yard, and was doing a bit of dealing on the side, often turning up with chests and other useful pieces of furniture for painting. All this gave him leverage when it came to getting paid and he could make the point that he'd gone out of his way to get some very useful furniture and had taken extra time in collecting board from the demolition men. From time to time there were inexplicable absences. He and Irish Johnny in the transit, sometimes would disappear for a whole day. I had suspicions that all was not quite right, but because I was completely dependent on Dave's expert finishing and ageing, I didn't raise the subject.

It was going to be some time before the full extent of his nefarious exploits were to be revealed. In the meantime I was pleased to buy any additional furniture from him for painting in our trademark style, marine or military.

**********

Now it was vital to find the new markets urgently. Germany was booming I knew. France was trickier. I'd go to Germany taking my photographs. I flew to Dusseldorf and had a little luck – what I had to offer dealers seemed to surprise them.

As for France, I had already made a connection with an important dealer in the Rue Jacob, to whom I was supplying mostly nautical signs and ship models, so I decided I would try Switzerland. I knew the Indian next to 'Trad' in Portobello Road had Swiss clients: I had seen his shippers' labels. I did try the decorators' shops up in the old town in Geneva, where my photographs once again proved to be productive. On the strength of my success, Mamie flew out and we stayed at Hotel Angleterre beside the lake and luxuriating in warm recollections of the previous night's lovemaking, watched the *'jets d'eau'* on the lake fountaining up into the morning sky.

It was on that visit that my lifelong enjoyment of Havana cigars began. I visited Davidoff's and was forever after hooked. The aroma of the huge humidor room under the shop, the perfectly rolled Perfectos No. 2s, with the white bands, a smaller variety of the cigars smoked by Castro, and the beautiful artwork on the boxes of Bolivar's and Rey del Mondo's captivated me. It is still the same today, exquisite examples of ephemeral art which is what I was striving to emulate – the quality and interest of an age gone by.

Back at business it struck me that pattern-making by the carvers, followed by casting, had to be the answer to producing the relief elements for my new type of signs. It would be a quick process and the reliefs could be turned out in quantity. Individual carving took too long. If I could cast in aluminium – later it was to become fibreglass – I could easily cover the entire range of trade and professional signs without having to wait for the carvers.

None of the carvers liked the idea. Short-sightedly, they thought their livelihoods might be threatened. There were mutterings of *'Royalties'* – after all, they'd made the patterns. In fact what it did was simply make the business better for everyone.

Trade in London was good. The dealers were busy and demand for everything my assortment of artists were turning out was reflected by the increasing number of phone calls I was getting, sitting in my flint-built office in the field.

I took on one more signwriter, who had the touch I needed, and who had a feeling for the varied styles of 19th century lettering as well. I also found another cabinet-maker who had worked his apprenticeship in Chatham Dockyard. Amongst other things, he quickly mastered the making of our half hull ship models. This all led to a surplus of production from time to time, which stifled cash flow, making it imperative I find ways to have this surplus absorbed without pushing our exclusive line into new outlets in competition with the established market.

The ability to supply relief signs in quantity soon became important, owing to an introduction by one of the principal London buying agents to the Horchow Company of Dallas, who wanted to incorporate into their bi-annual catalogue a range of relief signs aimed at the professional class, which could be personalised with the buyer's name on it, covering doctors, surgeons, architects, accountants, stockbrokers and dentists – even vets and people in the oil business. With some amusing slogan, which in the case of the doctor might be *'discreet nightly visits arranged'*, beside a small Gladstone bag in relief, or in the case of the dentist, beside a tooth gripped in the jaws of a pair of ancient dental pliers, the slogan *'all extractions guaranteed painless by the inhalation of modern gases.* The vet's sign presented a momentary problem, thinking of what relief might be applicable and in the end I asked George to carve an eight-inch long retriever holding up a bandaged paw. All these became a great success and every six months, through the London agent, Horchow generally ordered upwards of one hundred and fifty of these small *'professional'* signs, which was good business by any standards.

They must have struck the right chord in a big way, because a couple of years later, when the Horchow scheme had run its course, I was on one of the first Delta Airline flights to Atlanta, idly looking through the in-flight magazine, when I was astonished to see in the special offers section, a set of cocktail glasses, each emblazoned with a miniaturised picture of the range of professional signs we had produced for Horchow. I felt it was difficult to do better than have some of your original ideas stare back at you from an in-flight magazine!

Although now I had sufficient orders to keep the artists busy most of the time, I really needed more.

It was obviously a road to disaster to cheapen things by flooding the London market and upsetting the dealers who were enjoying a profitable exclusivity although the first few crude attempts at copying were beginning to appear.

To relieve the situation, it was the American market, chosen selectively, which was to be my chosen course of action. No more than one dealer in any of the big towns on the East coast would be sufficient to generate all the business needed to absorb my surplus.

Walking along Fifth Avenue for the first time is an experience no one forgets – but I had the added excitement of seeing one of my carvings in the window of Bergdorf Goodmans, surrounded by various pieces of painted furniture, aged over three thousand miles away by gypo Dave in rural England. I was suddenly aware that half way across the world I had started a new decorative vogue altogether. The carving was one of our *'distressed seamen'* – a bearded Jack Tar with a wooden leg, holding out in front, a collection box, which I had suggested the signwriters letter, *'Please give a Penny. Home for Distressed Seamen'* ... I went in. *'Wasn't it just too wonderful, all these old things coming in from England!'* – the shop assistant enthused, as I pretended to be a possible buyer. *'This figure Sir? Yes, just $4,500.'* I think the last one I had sold to Burge in Sloane Street had been priced at £285. The price tags on the furniture told the same story. I was on to a good thing if I could export directly.

I had imagined that in New York I was going to find bulk importers, like one-armed Knapp. No such luck. The warehouses and showrooms I found in Lower Manhattan were stocked with the traditional residue of sales-rooms: sets of chairs, ormolu lamps and the odd Boule table – boring. The only decorative items on offer were low-grade Italian. None of the proprietors of these depressing stores were interested in what I could supply and actually seemed quite unaware of what was going on in England and the new direction the antiques market was taking. Just where, I wondered, had all the hundreds if not thousands of smaller, lettered, trade and painted pub signs gone which my artists were turning out on a weekly basis? Just who was buying them?

Next day I took a train from Grand Central up to Boston. The old waterfront had been magnificently transformed. Reconstituted architectural embellishments were everywhere, worked into interesting shop fronts, new restaurants, pavement cafes and bars with mahogany and brass fronts. Here was a potential market.

Indeed, as I wandered the length of the old quays, spellbound, I saw many of my own creations: some of my clipper half-hulls and in a bar, one of my father's tugs! There was a stern-board I had sold to Burge and in a restaurant men's room, just inside the door, there was a Crapper's sign, *'comfort assured'* and I even knew which of my signwriters had done it.

In the city I came across antique shops which clearly had connections in the London trade and I made some useful contacts.

However, I had come to see one dealer in particular, Thomas Coughlin. From the shipping labels I had seen at the Indian's emporium next door to 'Trad', I gathered his business was in Boston. I had seen his stickers on everything from divers' helmets to telescopes, which the Indian was having made up in the Farringdon Road, to my own half-models and nautical signs.

Finding my man was not difficult. He was well-known. He was in Kingston, some miles outside the city. I set out for Kingston next morning.

His business, Thomas Coughlin Imports Inc., was housed in several large 19th century buildings that had originally been Kingston's largest lumber mill.

I knew at once things were going to turn out well. He seemed very interested that I had come to the US myself – not many English dealers did in those days. Those who did were respected. He was friendly and direct, a little older than me, perhaps in his early forties. Before the morning was out, I felt I knew him pretty well.

He ordered 48 halfmodels, 20 assorted nautical signs, 6 seamen's boxes – he already had one there that he particularly liked. He asked me if it was one of mine, which of course it was. He went over to it and opened up the lid, which had once been painted white but now was yellowed with age and bore some writing. *'I like this bit'* he said, reading out what was written in a careful script across it: *"I Josiah Copthorn First Mate of the whale-ship Hatteras do this day the 29th October 1873, commit my soul to the good Lord in the hopes I may survive. My ship has foundered, carrying with her all the crew and I am left alone in a small boat half stoven in after a great storm off the Marquesas Islands. May it please God to take care of my good wife Molly to whom I will all my worldly goods trusting she may be kept safe – signed Josiah Copthorn." Any touch like that is a real good seller,'* he said. I knew that already, needless to say, and it always gave me immense enjoyment dreaming up such epitaphs and scribbling them down at odd moments in the office. One last thing he mentioned. On a trip to London he had seen an outsize sextant in Sloane Street. He regretted not buying it, because he was sure he had seen the very same one displayed in the Smithsonian a few months before. Could it have been something I had made? Since the first I had had made by Francis Boxhall at Lynsore Bottom, David Richards had certainly made more than three or four for me over the past year and one of these I had, in fact, sold to Burge, in Sloane Street.

I never found out the answer. Several trips later I visited the Smithsonian and asked at the enquiry desk if they had an example of an early instrument maker's sign in the shape of an outsize sextant. They could have done at some time, they thought, but the displays changed from time to time. So I never got to know. I like to think even the Smithsonian Institute had been fooled by my old hand-cut nails, rusted brackets and special finishes!

*********

The stage was now set for John Goldsmith's arrival.

We were to work together in my studio office, across the big red lacquer desk I'd originally made for the 'Naïve Gallery'.

John seemed to enjoy hugely the apparent madness of it all, the diverse characters with their particular foibles and my own driving force and the creativity which enabled some new sign to be dreamt up one day, to appear as a finished article looking a hundred years old just a few days later. For him it must have all come as something of a very wide eye-opener to be pitched into the often grubby world of dealers, but he revelled in the bizarre challenges and he was certainly going to encounter more than a few.

His initiation came on his first trip to London when delivering various items including two butcher's signs to Eddy at 'Trad'. It was Eddy's habit to have a good look over everything when it had been unloaded onto the pavement, while he asked Pat, his female helper in the shop, to check off all the items which had been listed on my scribbled invoice. Once done, Eddy would retire to the glass booth office at the back, and have a few words with Pat before pulling out his cheque book. John later told me exactly what had happened. Eddy, being unaware that he was standing close outside the office, apparently with a sly smile, turned to Pat and was distinctly heard to say, *'James has missed off the two butcher's signs Pat, – let's not mention it!'* Coming out of the office she brushed past John and confirmed in a whisper: *'Two butchers not on it,'* as she handed him the cheque. John sensibly paused as he turned towards the door then checked, as if remembering, by which time Eddy had begun rearranging the stock in the shop, and said, *'Sorry Lord Bangor but I forgot to put down the two butchers … sorry about that!'* Eddy, pretending innocence, went back to the office, looked at the scribbled invoice and then somewhat grumpily came back and gave John another cheque. No wonder everyone in Portobello Road liked Pat – she at least was genuine.

Common sense told John that the way I was running the business was chaotic and he was clearly surprised that it all hung together the way it did. He saw to it that proper order sheets, laying out the progress of each and every sign or carving we had on order were made out with the customer's name and promised delivery date. He was tactful in dealing with the sensitivities of the touchy artists, but best of all he had seen through the all too brash and amusingly plausible Gypo Dave and had guessed at some of his funny goings on, which were very soon to be revealed.

One day, John told me he had some amusing and interesting news, which might prove very useful.

The local representative of the Pyrene Fire Extinguisher Company had chanced upon the office in the field and had decided to try his luck. While he was trying to persuade John to buy one of his company's products, he'd noticed one of my special half-hulls, hanging on the wall. He had said how interesting those old days must have been and how lucky John was to own something like that. Just what was the business being carried on here? So John explained that similar half-models were just one of the many lines which craftsmen were making for us. This appeared to interest the salesman more than selling an extinguisher and he went on to say he had done calligraphy at college and if we were going to make more of this type of thing in the near future, perhaps he could have a try at doing the markings and the lettering. He lived nearby, in Faversham.

The half-hulls were rolling out in a steady stream, but John had been quick to realise that there was more often than not a bottleneck between the making and finishing stages, as none of the signwriters liked working in the small detail on the hulls and boards because they could earn far more working on the larger lettering of the standard signs. Hulls were highly profitable and no matter how many times I gently pressed the signwriters, there was a delay at this stage. The arrival of Ken Filmer, ex-postman, soon to be ex-Pyrene Company salesman could be heaven-sent if, in fact, he was able to do them.

Before he handed in his notice to the Pyrene Company, every evening, sitting in his armchair with a half-hull and its backboard positioned, with pen and fine-lettering brush he worked away painstakingly until the result was perfect. He thrived on working in small detail and with the assurance that I would be able to keep him going for the foreseeable future, he proceeded with his notice and joined us. The demand for the half-hulls did not diminish and from then on sales increased. And over thirty years later, his fingers gnarled with arthritis, unassuming, benign and affable Ken put the name on the last of my imagined clippers, quite unaware of just how many he had done. It was over forty thousand.

John was adamant that I should get rid of 'the gypo', as we called Dave Smith. I really hadn't the heart to do it on the strength of the few very dubious things I knew he had been up to such as the odd item 'lost', which I was pretty sure had been simply stolen. I thought, so OK he doesn't sometimes roll up for a day or more after he's made some delivery, but he always manages to catch up in the 'pot department' as he called it. He was quite a character, sometimes blaming his 'awful little wife, that stupid Betty,' whenever he was late or something had gone wrong. We all knew he knocked her about and on one of his late appearances, he had said it was because he had had to go to the Police after one particularly nasty incident. Looking back, it must be said his charm was only skin-deep at best and really he was a fairly despicable character.

His end however was getting nearer. The first incident occurred after I had asked him to make a delivery to a dealer near Brighton – stupidly I was still relying on him and his old van for collections and deliveries and, of course, this was a mistake. John had seen that only too clearly. Instead of getting back that day, I didn't see him until well into the following afternoon when he came somewhat sheepishly to the office with the dealer's cheque and a small wad of cash. A lot of dealers didn't like invoices, whenever possible paying in notes, and this of course I understood. The odd thing was the amount of cash and cheque didn't tally with the overall amount I knew the deal was worth. *'Ah, well yes,'* he said, reddening slightly. The explanation came out. Going over the level crossing at Effingham Junction, he'd skidded on the rails and three of the signs had got broken and he had taken it upon himself to reduce the prices on them.

I was fairly certain that in fact he had come to some agreement with the dealer, who if I did ring him, would corroborate his story. On the other hand, if I had let him know he had been rumbled it wasn't beyond him to go whining to the *'employment'* about how I wasn't giving him his stamp and so on and this would certainly have produced a small can of worms. So I let it lie and kept him on.

The end came not long after. The delivery this time was to Mark Maley at Ayala Designs up in Suffolk, for the new English pub they were opening in Abu Dhabi. John took a call from a dealer in Ipswich. I dealt with no one there. The man was obviously aware of Ayala, had been there and knew the kind of business they were involved in and had seen our signs, but not knowing where they came from until a rather run-down van arrived with a tall, unusually well-dressed man who wanted to sell a few of the things inside. It all seemed very suspicious – the unlikely man, the improbably low price for the signs, the smell of drink. So he had spoken to Ayala who had put him on to us.

So now I knew for certain.

I had never sacked anyone. Thinking it would make my task easier I first approached Irish Johnny, who I was quite sure must have known exactly what his friend Dave was up to. Johnny knew the game was up but he also wanted to keep his own job in the *'pot'* department. So, professing total innocence when I told him what his friend had tried to do, with almost religious fervour, our wartime deserter went on to spill the beans, missing not one detail. He knew Dave had been taking things out of the Rameses stockpile in the stable loft. Some he was just selling – that's why he was late back so often after deliveries – other things he was getting copied. He'd apparently bought his own Polaroid camera and he now had a woman and a couple of art students copying some of our painted furniture, somewhere in the area. For some time I had been concerned about the copying that was going on – there had always been a lot of photos kicking about – and I had asked a solicitor friend if I could do anything about it, but he said it was virtually impossible to protect artwork by any form of patent.

Dave came to the office. I could tell from his look he knew it was the end. I threatened him with legal action if he did anything to harm the business, backing that bluff with the added threat that I would go to the police about the thefts. I told him to get out and keep away and he knew I meant it.

The saga of Gypo Dave does not stop there.

Although I never set eyes on him again, others did. Apparently he prospered mildly, was seen in pubs nattily dressed, often in summer sporting a Panama hat. He still saw Irish Johnny and went out drinking with him and one thing Johnny did tell us was that Dave had nearly murdered *'his stupid little wife'* one night and the police had come and she had finally left him for good. Dave had moved out of their council flat and she had got a job as a live-in maid to a retired small-time manufacturer from the Midlands who had bought a seaside villa near Broadstairs. Three years later, he died, leaving her his entire estate of over £3 million! She was often seen driving a drop-head Mercedes in Canterbury. When news of her good fortune filtered back to Dave it apparently so enraged the man that he broke down and cried, seething with hate and envy. Soon after that he left the area, to avoid becoming a laughing stock.

\*\*\*\*\*\*\*\*\*\*

Around this time, I spent a very pleasant fifteen minutes in a London buying agency chatting to an American called Cyrus Harvey, whose brainchild was Crabtree & Evelyn. This now famous company had begun as a cottage industry, deep in the Connecticut countryside, with genteel ladies making the highest quality jams and chutneys for the export market. Cy and I got on well and as soon as Crabtree & Evelyn began opening shops here in the U.K. and expanding into the worldwide business it is today, he asked me to make all the exterior hanging signs for every shop, together with many of the interior fittings and special displays – even at one stage asking me if I could go over and fit out the first of his *'English style'* shops in Manhattan. Unfortunately the American labour laws and the stance of the unions made it impossible on such an extensive rebuild, but 'James Croft Decorations', as we had now become, did make and ship out a complete small shop for insertion into an existing premises in Philadelphia. His final compliment was a contract to fit out his flagship London premises at the bottom of Church Street, Kensington. Sadly after that his worldwide operation became too slick to warrant the somewhat time-consuming *'old English'* expertise which my limited workforce could provide and his company's image subtly changed and lost a small part of the character we had first given it.

Apart from the ever-present smell of varnish there was a smell of success in the air. Demand for everything we were making was increasing. New types of restaurants were opening weekly. Eddy and Marjory of 'Trad' had bought a house a few miles inland from St. Tropez on the strength of the continual flow of business and the Madrasi Indian next door was now making frequent trips to Florida, where, he said, he had opened a large shop on Highway One. Farbey never failed to keep in touch, sometimes ringing from his house in Malaga: *'Need a pair of nice carved Griffens, Cock... doing a villa for some Arab near Puerto Banus.'*

With John comfortably sharing the helm, I decided the time had come to take a break and drive down with Mamie through Spain and on to Morocco.

On the way to Southampton, we passed the signpost for Winchester. Somewhere, in the outskirts, my brother lived. As I had never been to see him there, it gave me a strange feeling. He would have been embarrassed if I had just rolled up. We hadn't much in common after all – he with his orderly life and his even more orderly Norwegian wife – probably referring to *'That brother Jimmy of yours... what on earth is he up to now?'* The Gant's progeny – my sister, brother and I – lived very separate lives and it was only once in the last two years that my sister – now married and living near Avignon - had been in touch to ask if her husband, the spoilt child of elderly parents, could buy a substantial amount of the things I was turning out. He was thinking of starting up some kind of business in San Tropez, selling my things. It turned into the inevitable failure in due course and left me with the unenviable task of having to repossess his stock and lend him money that I knew would never be repaid.

On the way back from Morocco, we took the Cadiz road, before dipping down towards the southernmost tip of Spain and the small fishing port of Tarifa, a small Moorish town, built inside once fortified walls. In the little plaza by the harbour we ate our tapas to the sound of the year's first swooping swallows and fell in love with it all.

There was no sign of any kind of tourist development. Apparently this was primarily due to the fact that this part of the coast suffered from almost constant winds coming up from the Sahara, hot and dry and abnormally strong, during many months of the year. Mamie suggested we take a potholed road leading up towards the hills in order to explore a little before we left. After a mile or so, the road began to rise and became a track and then, as it flattened, we found ourselves in an enchanted valley. Each side was covered with swathe upon swathe of multicoloured flowers. Here and there small primitive buildings made of boulders and thatched with palm, dotted the landscape. Most appeared either partially or totally collapsed, with the remains of their walls spilling down the hillsides with remnants of what once must have been animal enclosures or perhaps a crude garden with two or three old orange trees. Everywhere the wild herbs were growing in profusion and the air was filled with their scent. It was unbelievably beautiful and calm.

From an old woman wearing black, carrying a loaf and prodding an uncooperative donkey along the track, we managed somehow, in pidgin Spanish, to ascertain that a few of these old dwellings were in fact still occupied, presumably by peasant farmers because she pointed to cattle on the far side of the valley and then to one of the gullies where oleanders grew in abundance, meaning there was water. There was no sign of power cables or telephone lines: nothing but the boulder-strewn slopes and a single eucalyptus tree standing among the cork trees and the only sound was of cattle bells on the opposite slope and the squeak of bee-eaters as they flew overhead. Behind was a vista of tranquillity with the Straits shimmering under a cloudless sky.

We talked about the experience excitedly as we bumped back to the main road and I promised Mamie that should it ever be possible I would buy one of those deserted houses, rebuild it and from time to time escape to enjoy a dream-life in the hills behind Tarifa, in the valley called Puertollano. Which is in fact what I eventually did – but not before a rather serious business setback which, at one stage, looked as if it might be the end of my cottage industry.

This reversal of fortune was unintentionally wished upon me by my friend and principal client in Paris, Georges Woolf. Georges was a man of culture, whose 'Brocante Store' in the Rue Jacob specialised in decorative items and small pieces of furniture in the English taste – very much in vogue in the Paris of the 1970s.

Georges was the very antithesis of the short pot-bellied man in a fedora hat I met at Canterbury station. He had rung me a few days after my return from Spain, saying he had been to 'Brocante Store' in Paris, where a Mr. Woolf had given him my phone number in response to his query as to where he might be able to buy similar items that he had seen in the shop as he wanted to decorate a barge he'd bought on the Thames outside London. In itself a harmless enough enquiry and Georges, thinking he would be doing me a favour, had given him my phone number. Little did he know where the introduction was to lead – not only for me, but also for two of my principal clients in London, Christopher Wray and C. P. Burge of Sloane Street.

He introduced himself as Gene Zimmerman, international lawyer, representing the Town and City Property Company, listed on the London Stock Exchange – one of the high flyers of the property boom. He had seen my things in New York, then in Paris and had sniffed out the possibility of harnessing this new line of decorative signs and antiques to his own advantage somehow, knowing that the American market was hungry for anything from dear old England.

Lawyers have a way with words. He spoke with such assurance, barely pausing, as he laid out his ideas with mesmerising certainty as to how this highly desirable new line of mine was going to hit it *'real big time,'* if it could be marketed properly in the U.S.

As I drove along, from an expensive-looking briefcase he took a large manilla envelope, on which he had jotted down the basis of an agreement to set up a company with exclusive rights to sell my products and the guarantee of setting up franchises in at least three major cities – Chicago, Philadelphia and Toronto. Nothing would interfere with any of my present customers and I could look to a hugely increased income. All I had to do was to initial the outlined proposal, and the whole thing would be up and running in no time. He would be the majority shareholder but my share would of course be substantial and we could sort that out later. He looked over at me for an answer as I pulled up in the lane – and I signed.

God alone knows how I could have been so gullible as to allow him to worm his way into my life. I should have known better!

Before I took him to catch the London train, he had seen my new works, looked through the photographs and said that the first very substantial order would follow as soon as he was back in the States. At the time he was making transatlantic flights twice a week, staying at the 'Inn on the Park' while he waited for the houseboat he had bought at Chiswick to be fitted out.

Within days I had a letter from Toronto where Zimmerman was based. Inside was a very large order together with an open ticket to Chicago. Could I go there and meet the first franchise investor? His name was Birnbaum. Zimmerman couldn't come himself, but would keep in touch. The implication was of urgency and it came as more of an order than a suggestion. The company, he ended up by saying, was going to be called 'Jas Neville Ltd' – the first and last of my Christian names – it sounded very English, he said. There was a second franchise all ready to go in Philadelphia, with a man called Bauer who manufactured parachute harness.

Two days later, I left John to run the business, kissed my lovely Mamie goodbye and flew BOAC to Chicago, O'Hare.

Mel Birnbaum met me at the airport, paunchy, affable, delightfully effusive in his typically American welcome. He took me straight to his temporary office which overlooked the Wrigley building. Zimmerman had told Mel that he was introducing him to a sharp young Englishman with many imaginative and artistic ideas and how he was sure he was going to be able to do business – 'real substantial business' with him. He had obviously prepared the ground well. Mel, poor sucker, had been persuaded to give up his vice presidency of the Colgate-Palmolive Company to enjoy the more cultural delights of dealing in the world of real old English decor. He was clearly under the spell of the fedora-sporting Zimmerman.

Although he himself was diminutive, Zimmerman's ego was enormous, as was his enthusiasm, so not only was Birnbaum hooked, but it was falling to me to be the front guy in Zimmerman's manipulative scheme to make some easy money on the side and this newcomer was being swept along on the crest of his persuasive promises.

The first thing that happened, most likely on Zimmerman's suggestion, was that Mel and I made a seemingly endless tour of Chicago's Furniture Mart – a huge trade centre for all American furniture and decor manufacturers. There were nine floors in all, each the size of Selfridges. We took in every style of furniture and decor, from the imported Italianate look, to New England traditional, Shaker rustic – on and on – all the time Mel asking interminable questions. I sensed he was floundering. He was a nice man and I hated to think how much Zimmerman had taken off him for the franchise. It was a world away from washing powders and deodorants. He seemed to have no feel for it at all, but I could hardly tell him it was all a waste of time.

Zimmerman came through on the phone from London. He had arranged for me to meet the parachute-harness manufacturer the next afternoon in Philadelphia. This was typical Zimmerman pressure. He gave me the address of a suite of offices in Peach Street, saying there were several possible flights that would get me there well before teatime. What he didn't tell me was that he'd set Robin Burge up as the dealer who would be supplying all, or at least most of the furniture, for this new franchise, if it came off.

I only saw Mel one more time. One large first order did come through, followed by three more, each one diminishing in volume, but he was punctilious in paying and I really hoped he'd make it. I never knew where he had opened. Perhaps he had even taken a stand in the furniture mart. His goods went to his shipping agent's address and I knew no more than that. Zimmerman never said a thing. By the end of the year I did hear that the scheme had failed and he had moved up to his wife's home town near Stamford, Connecticut, where she had opened a small gift shop. Some time later, when I was once again in New York, he must have heard from Zimmerman that I was staying at the Waldorf and he came to see me. It was sad; that clean, erstwhile executive so keen and so gullible had been shabbied by the failure. He showed no rancour and was as pleasant as ever and I watched with real regret as he drove away down Park Avenue in an old Volvo, back into his world of broken dreams.

My involvement with the parachute-harness man was even briefer. I think he had anyway smelled a rat. Unknown to me, Zimmerman had coerced Robin Burge into going to Philadelphia ahead of me acting as his London furniture purveyor in order to impress Bauer – he was to follow on by going down to Chicago further to bewilder poor Mel Birnbaum. In fact, American furniture is in general not only of better quality but far cheaper than most of the traditional lines imported from England. It was just the cachet of being English and that brass-bound *'military'* look which Americans associated with the Old Country that made it a good selling line at the time.

Robin's shop in Sloane Street, C.P. Burge Ltd., was well-known throughout the trade, and its turnover must have been prodigious, because just from my own small set-up it absorbed a van full of widely varied signs, artefacts and painted furniture virtually every week. But it was in trouble. I wondered why at times Robin seemed over friendly, delaying payments just a shade, hinting at closer ties. He had fallen into the trap of over-selling – promising deliveries of items ordered and paid for – which could not be met, taking money up-front. The creditors and dissatisfied clients began pressing and the end was nigh.

The surprise of seeing Robin Burge standing outside the address in Peach Street struck me like a scene from a weird dream. He was equally astounded to see me. I could tell neither of us really believed in what we were doing there. We were pawns in Zimmerman's machinations, on a futile mission.

I disliked Bauer and although I did get an initial order myself, that was all, and then the association fizzled out, much as I thought it would. Burge, also, did get one large furniture order from the Philadelphia adventure. Robin and I laughed when we were next on the phone talking of the episode. His order had included a number of my decorated chests and seamen's boxes and so it hadn't been a total waste of time. After this Robin faded from the picture but, bound by my agreement, my own involvement with Zimmerman lasted some months longer. At this point I think he realised that the franchise idea was not going to be the success he had originally planned.

The Yom Kippur War was about to start. Zimmerman opened in Toronto and again he had me over to be his English *'front man'*, expenses paid. But by now, however, things were turning a little sour and he owed me a considerable amount of money. Quite apart from that I was discovering that the agreement I had signed was constraining dealings not only with some of my existing American clients, but also the percentage of output I could sell to my established clients in London. He had been very clever in the wording.

In a nutshell, Zimmerman controlled us. He ordered yet more. John was suspicious of what the outcome might be. My small company's existence was threatened by a mounting overdraft and it was going to get worse unless Zimmerman paid up in full. In desperation, hoping we might be able to break the agreement that had been foisted onto me, John urged me to take legal advice. Together we went to my solicitor and showed him my copy of the Jas. Neville agreement. Zimmerman had made it virtually watertight. The position appeared to be dire. We were advised to seek Counsel's opinion. John accompanied me and we saw a leading QC specialising in the commercial field. We were advised that indeed Zimmerman was in a controlling position and could sue us should we not adhere to the original agreement. There was, however, a possible way out. The agreement stated that Zimmerman had the exclusive right to buy all goods 'for the American market'. The QC suggested that we list all our current stock, declare it to be for the American market and send him the bill. Brilliant. But before trying this, we had to get the money already owed. We thought of threatening Zimmerman that unless he paid up by noon on a certain date, we would consider the agreement null and void. I knew it would be a huge blow to the man's ego if he lost his exclusive rights. However, I am not good at confrontations and against John's advice, decided to wait a little longer.

Zimmerman came over just once more, just before the collapse of the property market, swanning down to see me, still with the wretched fedora, this time driving a vintage Bentley. By now I hated him, but was still afraid that a confrontation might precipitate an even worse position. With the market not looking so good, I was unable to bring myself to break free.

The weeks went by and war raged in the Middle East. The property market nose-dived and trade in general collapsed to an alarming level and for the first time ever, stock was building up unsold. Things were bad.

John said he would go and confront Zimmerman in New York or Toronto, wherever he was, with the hope that our threat would make him pay up in full. I had my doubts. John rang to discover he was in New York on company business and left the next day. He rang me very late to say he had seen Zimmerman and as forcefully as he could, had issued the threat. Although there was no offer of an immediate cheque, he said he was certain Zimmerman was desperate to continue in business with us, principally for reasons of ego, and therefore he had given the date as the following Friday, twelve o'clock our time, when the National Westminster Bank was to be in receipt of a draft for the full amount owed.

Friday arrived. I rang the bank at eleven. Nothing. John looked gloomy. I again rang the foreign department at noon and to my heartfelt relief heard that the draft had reached the account.

We waited for a few weeks then wrote to Zimmerman along the lines suggested by our QC. Zimmerman must have realised that he was up against a better legal brain. We never heard from him again.

With the Middle East War over and my daily preoccupation with the Zimmerman problem gone, it was possible to take stock of the coming year. Although times were difficult, there was money in the bank and I decided to make an exploratory visit to Tarifa, hoping I might be able to buy one of the empty little peasant hill farmhouses which Mamie and I had seen in that enchanted valley overlooking the Straits.

My four-day visit to Andalucia brought an undreamt of success. After problems establishing exactly who had owned the tumbledown house and surrounding hillside, by the spring of the New Year, Mamie and I became owners of what had once been a Spanish peasant's family home – two rooms, a thatched roof, on its hillside of land covered with low herb bushes and with a stream running down through a rocky gully lined with oleander and pomegranate trees. A grove of cork trees formed the higher boundary behind the house where there was a spring and that was it. No access, no running water, but all the tranquillity in the world. Several ancient peach trees grew close to the house and by the remains of its stone cattle enclosure, four or five stunted orange trees struggled to survive. It was like paradise; a world away from the lifestyle I had encountered, when on the way back I took the opportunity to look up Farbey in his villa near Marbella, uninvited.

He and some ex-pats, including an over-tanned Norwegian couple, who were dripping in gold jewellery, were sitting at a huge marble table near the pool, drinking. He seemed pleased to see me, his useful old protégé, but I felt distinctly out of place.

*'A good buy, don't you think, Cock,'* he said slapping the table top, which I noticed had a coat-of-arms on it, together with some inscription in Spanish. It must have been all of 8 foot long and have weighed at least a ton: God knows how he'd got it there.

*'Found it in Granada. Came from some grandee's tomb. Looks good on that base, no?'* He said looking down at the two ionic capitol tops, one of which supported each end. You had to hand it to him – such imaginative taste! *'Those came from the gallery I used to have a stake in in Mount Street – remember that?'*

*'Fantastic',* I said. He hadn't changed. Very soon all I wanted to do was to get away and leave behind all the ensuing throwaway talk of how many hectares so and so had bought; about the arrival of the Arabs on the Costa; how large someone's new pool was going to be and how there had been a few lucky buys of Roman pillars up in Seville and the discovery of some new source for the enormous earthenware oil jars which had become *de rigeur*, in order to impress anyone looking round your villa's garden.

I'd noticed that Farbey had this large carved stag, which was bleaching out in the sun on his patio, and I realised it was one he had asked me to make ages ago. At the time I had thought it was for his property hire company, but he'd brought it out to Spain and it certainly did look impressive in its new surroundings. I had got the idea for the first one I'd had one of my carvers make, from a sign over the entrance to a smart pub called the 'White Hart' I'd seen once on my way back from Haywards Heath. Once it had been carved, I had put real antlers on it and had a collar carved in the shape of Fleur-de-Lys round its neck, for a finishing touch.

By now I had made five altogether and three of these I had sold to one of the Pimlico dealers, Robin Gage, an old Etonian.

One day, unexpectedly, Robin Gage rang me to ask if I had seen a copy of *Country Life* lately. Not exactly! *'Well have a look,'* he said.

*'Malletts are advertising one of your stags for £5,000!'* I hurried to the Smiths in Canterbury and there it was – under the Royal Crest, *'Malletts, By Appointment Antique Dealers to the Late Queen Mary'*, were offering a *'rare 16th century'* carved wood stag, bearing a fleur-de-lys collar.

At the time, these stags were listed in my trade photographs, as No. 73 – price £285!

Gage was piqued, somewhat understandably, seeing the price and knowing it was one that I had originally sold him. He had been outdone by even smoother dealers!

It so happened that he knew the principal buyer at Malletts – another old Etonian – and feeling stung, he admitted to me later that to get his own back, he had rung the man at Malletts and said he really ought to be utterly ashamed to be selling something described as 16th century, when he must have known it had no real age at all and had come from a firm called 'James Croft Decorations', down in Kent. A few days later I got a call from a man called Maitland, who Robin had spoken to at Malletts. He asked me if I would be kind enough to go to London and inspect the stag to see if in fact it was the one I had made. This of course I did, much to Maitland's embarrassment, telling him I had made several and that this one was neither worse nor better than the others. It was plain to see that Maitland did not like this situation one bit, but just before I left, he asked me what a pair to it would cost, if they were to ask me to make one facing the opposite way: £285, I told him! A pair of anything is of course far more valuable than a single. In this case, a pair of 16th century stags at Malletts, would have fetched something in the region of £20,000. I think perhaps Maitland was wise not to ask me for another, bearing in mind what was to come. But more of that later.

Meanwhile, as to Farbey, who had played a central part in my life throughout a very interesting period of my dealer's education, I rarely heard from him after this. Word, filtering down from his erstwhile contacts in London, had it that he was living permanently in Spain, into property in a big way – so it was said – backed by an ageing movie star, who when he died soon after was most unsurprisingly, found to have had very few dollars left in his bank account. My last contact was, when years later, just before going to see a specialist about a wonky hip, the phone rang and a voice said in his inimitably urbane voice, *'Hello Cock. I'm in London,'* and I knew instantly just who it was.

Curious as to why he should have bothered to ring after all this time, I went round to the address he had given me, just off the Brompton Road. It was his pied-à-terre. One spectacular room, complete with zebra-skin rugs and the odd Roman marble bust on a plinth for good measure. The same old operator.

*'Got anyone still working for you James? I want something rather special.'* Just bear in mind that by this stage the man must have been almost eighty. Yet still up to his old tricks.

*'What I want's a crate, Cock.'* This sounded more than a little odd: a crate. He could get a crate made anywhere. *'Bit of a special crate: got to have been "made in the forties". Old looking wood, a bit of faded lettering stencilled on, everything just right, old rusted nails, no fresh-looking saw cuts – got to be perfect: nobody better for the job than you, Cock!'*

I was bewildered. What follows is the story he told.

One day someone had rung at his villa, saying he had heard that he – Rubin Farbey – was an authority on Roman and classical 18th century marble figures. The caller said he'd got a bust he wanted to sell and he would like Farbey to have a look at it, to which Farbey agreed. This took him to an unprepossessing house inland from Puerto Banus, where the man explained he had once been a bank manager in Cairo, during the last years of King Farouk's reign. Nasser came along and the bank was closed down. The bust he had been given had come from one of Farouk's palaces. It clearly hadn't, or if it had, Farouk had no taste; it was a late 19th century copy. *'Not worth tuppence, Cock!'*

Along with the head, being a reliable bank manager, some things had been entrusted to him by the palace, for 'safe keeping' until the bank re-opened. So far, so good! Then, into the realms of fantasy. As Farbey said he was leaving the house, he passed the open doors of the retired bank manager's garage, and inside there was a crate and on it were stencilled letters reading, 'Bank of Lebanon & Sidon. Property of H.M. King Farouk'... still in safe-keeping! And that was the crate I was being asked if I would make. At this point Farbey shows me a photograph of an octagonal table top. *'Lapis, Cock. The only other thing of any size made of that, is in the Wallace Collection, and that, about a quarter of the size.'*

At this juncture, I am beginning to put two and two together. Farbey is telling the story to convince himself that this *is* what happened, but in reality I guessed, he had had the table top made himself! He *had*! He went on to explain that, at great expense, he'd tucked away an incredibly skilled stonemason who he could trust, in a warehouse out on the Essex marshes, who had been working on making it for almost a year; making it from pieces of lapis he had somehow fixed to be brought back to England, some years previously, quite legally, by hippy back-packers who his wife had befriended over time, knowing it was a good investment, with the guarantee that he would give them a much better price than might be expected if they had tried to flog it on the open market. With some pride, Farbey told me the idea had come to him when some well-connected young wastrel, heavily into the drug scene, had arrived to see his wife, telling her he had been given the bit of blue stone, by some of the Muhadajeen with whom he used to hang out in the caves up in the Bora Bora mountains, in the days before the Russians invaded. Thereafter, friends and friends of friends, on the hippy trail, brought back a steady supply, for which Rubin gave them 'top dollar.'

The deceit goes on... Pleasure lighting up his toad-like face, he explained to me that a photograph, showing the table top, still wrapped inside the crate marked 'Property of H.M. King Farouk', would indisputably authenticate his find, that afternoon on the Costa del Sol.

*'It's worth a million Cock – mind you, it's already cost me nearly one hundred and thirty; my chap's been at it for over a year now. I've only got to get a base for it. I know someone who's got a fantastic Venetian marble lion, going for a couple of grand, which would be superb for the job. That table, Cock, will be worth a bomb: I am going to ask a million for it.'*

I can just hear him say it, as if it was only yesterday; the Farbey of the Rameses days, at his best!

*'There are only two people who are collectors of the rarest lapis items – one's the Sultan of Brunei, and the other is Versace, and he's not short of a few bob.'* There was simply *no one*, at least no one I had ever come across, who could have conceived such a scam as this and I think I did one of the more sensible things in my life, by declining to become involved, leaving the crate for someone else to make.

I don't know how the saga ended. I went into hospital and after that I didn't hear from him again. But a year or so later when I bumped into a Fine Art dealer I had known in the seventies and who I knew had been something of a friend of Farbey's, I couldn't stop myself from casually asking him if he'd seen Rubin recently. He said he hadn't, but wait, yes, he had *heard* something about one of Versace's hangers-on, who was meant to be something of art expert, going to see him about some deal and a terrific bust-up had ensued, involving a few big names in the art world. Word gets around, and it's my guess that Farbey never made the killing he had hoped for, but knowing him, it didn't end up in a second-hand shop in Battersea.

I felt I had to tell that tale of the last of Farbey – he was, and remains, an unforgettable character of the heady sixties – but in the telling it did rather make me digress from initially reminiscing about seeing the carved wooden stag that afternoon, at his villa in Spain, where my thoughts were more concentrated on that humble peasant's dwelling in the hills behind Tarifa, the gnarled old orange trees, struggling for life and the oleanders and the noise of bee-eaters squeaking as they flew over the cork trees.

When finally the *'notario'* in Algerciras sent the deeds of this idyllic retreat I gave them to Mamie as her birthday present and by the year's end, the house had been rebuilt, had a lavatory with a septic tank and what passed for the smallest of kitchens, converted from what had probably once been an animal shelter beside the rough peasant patio. Our water came from the spring whose source was hidden amongst the rocks some little way up the hillside behind the house, together with a bathroom with a tap and hot water thanks to a tiny Calor heater I had taken down by car and a bath you could lie in after dark, watching the lights of Tangier across the Straits. In bed, with the doors open to the hillside, you could smell the waft of herbs and listen to the soft distant throb of diesel coming from the fishing boats as far away as Cape Trafalgar.

**********

These were wonderful days, but John was keen to get back to writing and asked me if he could introduce a replacement now that the time had come for him to move on.

She turned out to be currently working as a P.A. at one of the City's leading merchant banks, who was keen to quit town-life and live in the country near her fiancé on the Romney Mashes, half an hour's drive away from my office in the field. Her name was Felicity.

For a while John stayed on while she found her feet. It must have come as something of a culture shock after city boardrooms. She was ferociously efficient and very quickly had a grasp of things, although many of the workers, that strange batch of self-made artists, did not take kindly to the new authority. They were a touchy lot, added to which there were now 26 of them.

Times were improving. The business outlook seemed good. No other company covered the wide field of decorative artefacts and signs that we did. Special work for hotel clients was taken for granted. John and I had dreamt up the most diverse assortment of signs, from early coaching to rural artisan, to trade and tavern and to the military and nautical, in all their branches, lettered and pictorial, some with relief, some without. We were making a host of small sundry items apart from the standard chests and boxes. Numbered photographs now ran into the hundreds and for one reason or another so many had washed out into the trade that the inevitable poor copies began to appear in the cheap and cheerful antique shops. But in general we held the monopoly and the client base was firm, well-established and on the increase. Our signs appeared frequently on television sets, and in London you could walk into a good number of hotels and see our things in the foyers, dining-rooms and coffee shops. Yet another of my stags appeared in the food column of the *Sunday Times*, sitting on a plinth to the side of one of the Savoy's prestigious restaurants. The efforts of my carvers and artists had begun to bear substantial fruit and it bore witness to the possibilities the business was now offering to the catering trade, as well as others. I had undertaken the complete fitting out of each of the new chain of 'Oodles' eating houses that was springing up in the West End and our close association with Crabtree & Evelyn meant my small company was accepted as probably the best in the specialist decor field.

Although the disappearance of C. P. Burge of Sloane Street was a substantial loss in turnover terms at the time, supplying the antique trade went from strength to strength as the public began to become more aware of amusing and interesting themes for decoration. 'Dodo' in Westbourne Grove, which had been one of the first shops to establish the new trend, had become a manufacturing business based near Tunbridge Wells. In the Portobello Road, 'Trad', with Eddy and Marjorie Bangor, thriving, with Farbey's prop hire company buying many of their really unusual things. (Often supplied by 'James Croft Decorations' of course!) Nautical signs and the kind of brass and copper things which I had specialised in when I had my old dog and the Bedford van, were sold in quantity by the Indian's emporium next door, mostly reproduction now, while direct exporting to the continent and the U.S. increased month on month. By now the supply of old chest of drawers and boxes had begun to dwindle, but any I did find were now fetching an even better price, once the artists had decorated them with their usual touch of authenticity, military or nautical.

New clients from the most unlikely areas of commerce were beginning to make contact: men's clothing manufacturers asking us to make signs and requesting ideas for masculine-oriented decor for their outlets; companies such as 'Façonnable', in France and Italy (something like our 'Gap'), the Hardware Clothing Company, based in the U.S., while the Spanish market opened up with orders coming from 'El Corte Ingles', Spain's best-known retail group with stores in every major Spanish city. And to crown it all, came an order from an American clothing firm called 'Gant!'

I had not seen or heard from my father for years. But one day Mamie took a phone call from a woman by the name of Mary. She said she was married to *'Jimmy's' father*. She didn't refer to him as Gant or Arthur, just *'Jimmy's father.'* Could the two of them come over?

They arrived in a very clean little Riley 1100, the Mary woman driving, slowly creeping up the drive. The cottage had been enlarged and two horses grazed in the field where I had my office. I had made a largish gravel area edged with low walls of brick and flint. To one side I had also built an aviary. Inside was our pet rook, cawing at the arrival of the new visitors.

I recognised Mary as Mrs. Tinsley, who had lived near the Admiral's house in Folkestone. She said something along the lines of how it had been such a long time since she'd seen Jimmy, while my father, obviously ill at ease, looked around. I thought I detected some slight smile of admiration. This time, one of the last times I saw him, he did not huff and puff and say anything about pissing before my water came. He knew I had succeeded where he had failed and not for the first time I felt sorry for him – this time for having been 'bought' by Mrs. Tinsley.

There were no repeat visits, though Mamie and I did go once to have rather an awkward and vapid hour in Mrs. Tinsley's small conservatory with its crimplene cushions, down near Hythe. After my father died, I had a call from Mary. *Would I look in and collect the things he had left. They were in a wooden box that had the Admiral's name on a brass plate on its lid just inside the door in case she was out and missed me. And – Oh yes, there was a wine bill of your father's in an envelope on top of the box. And a pair of bellows, he knew you'd like to have, were too big for the box, and these would be beside it.'* The bellows didn't work anyway and the only thing of real interest in the box was a cutting from *The Times*, dated August 1921, showing how he had passed in top from Woolwich to Sandhurst R.M.A. for officers, to be commissioned in the cavalry and foot-guards and his official chauffeur's badge issued by the Los Angeles Transport Department, No 96714.

I have often wondered since if Mary had bought any other paper than the *Sunday Times* because on 11th December 1977, not long after that last and only visit she and my father made to the cottage, one of the national Sunday papers splashed headlines with news of an outrageous event involving no one less than little Jimmy, her stepson.

This somewhat bizarre story began one Sunday morning when I was in the fruit cage by my tennis court, pruning raspberries. I saw a car I didn't know coming up the drive. I had a feeling it was somehow odd and walked across. A not very well-dressed man got out holding a file of papers. He introduced himself as Clive Cooke, a freelance journalist and opening the file, he asked: *Do you know about this?'* – showing me a copy of the *Country Life* advertisement for the 17th century stag, sitting proudly under the royal warrant of Mallet & Co.

I just laughed. *'Not that thing again!'* I remember saying. *'What's happened now?. That was years ago for God's sake. I've had several more made since then,'* And I went on to explain just what my business did. He was suitably intrigued.

It turned out he had made a scoop, or so he thought, which the *News of the World* had agreed to buy once the last few details had been strung together and I was one of those last details and that was why he had come down to see me. He wanted me to go and positively identify the stag once again. It was now in Harrods' Antique Department, priced at £9,800!

Just how he had picked up on the story of that wretched stag, I didn't know, but I did find out later from someone who had known Burge in the Sloane Street days. Apparently being reduced to living in a rented council house not far from Esher, Burge had met Cooke the journalist, in a pub, and in the course of conversation told him something about the dubious activities of dealers, amongst whom was my old Pimlico friend Robin Gage. The story of the Malletts stag came up, when it had first surfaced at £5,000. Clive Cooke had sniffed a story and given Burge £100 for the information.

The journalist went to work, tracing the stag's journey, first from Pimlico, where I had sold it, then on to a chateau near Le Breuil sur Merie, where a woman by the name of Madame Lecerf – one presumes a dealer – eventually sold it on to a visiting buyer from Malletts. His name was Maitland and the price he paid was £2,500. Things then became even more interesting when he discovered it was now for sale in Harrods' Antique department for £9,800. Cooke was now certain he was on to something really tasty and he was sure the paper would be delighted with an exposé of the art-world and its inhabitants, especially now that the name of the Honourable Peter Dixon had crept into the picture – he was a Malletts director who, unable to sell the stag, had passed it on to Harrods on a sale or return basis.

Lawyers acting for the *News of the World* made one last stipulation so the story could be run with impunity and if necessary, the dealers involved could be accused of making false statements as to the carving's provenance, age and value. This stipulation was that

I should personally make one last identification of the stag, without arousing any suspicion, to confirm that it was the same one that I had been asked to look at in Malletts in 1974.

Now for some pure farce, involving subterfuge and legal manoeuvrings and a box of cigars!

It just so happened at this time I was playing number two string for a Canterbury Squash Club and had been befriended by a young solicitor called Joe who was maniacally keen to learn the more subtle arts of the game. After an early evening game on the Monday following the journalist's visit, Jo and I were enjoying a drink in the club bar afterwards and I, with much excitement and amusement, recounted the story of the stag and how I had been asked to go and identify it in Harrods' Antique Department the following day without anyone noticing. Joe looked worried. Serious reputations were at stake. The exalted name of Malletts would be on the line – not to mention Harrods under the stewardship of Sir Hugh Fraser and the Fraser Group of Companies which included the *News of the World*. I was going to have to be very careful. I could be sued. The onus of the proof would be on me. Joe said that might raise serious difficulties; it could well be disastrous. And what might the impending article say about my company?

Suddenly I realised that, apart from being some kind of dubious compliment, a total exposure of what we did would destroy the shadowy mystique surrounding our products and at the same time wipe out any ideas of exclusivity my clients were enjoying. If it were to be known just how easily all the signs, carvings and paintings could be obtained simply by getting on to 'James Croft Decorations', it would be disastrous. Up to that moment, I had regarded the whole thing as a joke that might just result in selling a few more stags at a very good price. Even everyone in the works that morning had been highly excited at the thought of such publicity, and publicity, I had forgotten, was something I had always tried to avoid. It was the turn of my young opponent to take me under *his* wing and the legal protection of Messrs. Gander & Cropper of 2 Castle Street, Canterbury.

The first thing he said was to make sure that nothing detrimental to my own business was going to be published, should the story go to press. The newspaper's editor would have to submit a copy of the intended article for approval before publication. Jo said we held the trump card, as without our co-operation in finally identifying the stag in Harrods, there could be no story.

Joe had a verbal agreement from the paper's lawyers the following morning. In the event of a successful outcome, our co-operation was going to cost the paper Joe's legal expenses, my travel costs, together with one box of my favourite cigars.

Joe was going to accompany me to Harrods that afternoon. We would go into the Antique Department separately and while he diverted the attention of the salesman, I would surreptitiously go about my identification and if it was possible, Joe was to take a flash photo of a nearby piece of furniture, on the pretext of showing his wife, which hopefully would show me close to the stag and prove I had been there.

The scene was set. It was all too easy. Only one smarmy salesman was visible and we could see the reclining stag, not particularly prominently displayed, set on some kind of plinth, half obscured by a sofa. While Joe steered the salesman towards a set of Hepplewhite dining chairs (probably no more than *'in the style of...'*), I sauntered casually towards the stag – took a quick look round, bent to re-tie a lace and with a nail file, quickly gouged a small section of the emulsion paint from behind the animal's rump. Standing up I saw a flash and heard Joe say something about showing his wife the design and I knew he had been able to synchronise his part of the act. I eased towards the department exit, where a few moments later I was joined by Joe, by now barely able to contain his laughter.

So that was it. Of course, as soon as I saw it, I knew the stag was mine, the one from Malletts. The chip of paint was just in case, but it was never needed.

So now, with all the protestations of innocence of those involved in the nefarious journeyings of the stag ringing in his ears, Cooke finally had his story knitted together for a splash exclusive. More shit was bound to hit the fan – people love it when big institutions are found to be behaving in an unscrupulous fashion. This was something the *News of the World* was going to like. Sunday sales would be up by at least 200,000! And they did like it!

By Friday Jo3, had seen a copy of the intended article. It sketched the journey of the stag from Pimlico to France and back again to London, with all the wriggling explanations of the dealers who had handled it and now, to their horror, had finally discovered they had been duped. How was Malletts to know that I had not made a mistake when they had first asked me to go and look at it in 1974? It was quite clear that they had been exposed as one of the guilty parties, out to make a killing. The article contained nothing more than a bland reference to 'James Croft Decorations' who had initially *'acquired'* it in the first place, together with some carefully chosen and appropriate photographs.

It was customary for Sir Hugh Fraser, famous Laird, entrepreneur and newspaper owner, to sit in on the week's final editorial meeting, prior to the Saturday print run of *News of the World*. The Editor, who had been working with Cooke once he had agreed to buy the story, had obviously been too engrossed in the usual kind of *News of the World* stories to realise that there was any conflict of interest between this exposé and the wider world of the House of Fraser. Sir Hugh on the other hand, immediately understood that any shit hitting his flagship's fan, was going to be shit hitting the entire Fraser Group. Any hint of funny goings-on in the fine arts and antiques department at Harrods would, without doubt, have reflected very badly on the reputation of the great Knightsbridge store.

The story was rejected.

It must have been heartbreaking for poor Clive Cooke, after months of assiduously sleuthing through the scam, with such success. Cooke, however, was a freelance. The story still belonged to him and he had a few friends in Fleet Street. It wasn't going to end there. He rang me later that day and told me he had strightaway approached the Mirror Group who'd agreed to buy the story and run it in their Sunday edition. Knowing just how concerned Joe would be that the original agreement he had made with the *News of the World* would not apply to the Mirror Group, I rang him – luckily he was in – and told him of the change. Much to my relief, he rang me back a little later to say I had no need to worry; he had come to the same agreement with the Mirror Group.

The headline splashed across the front of the *Sunday Mirror* read: 'HARRODS HOODWINKED' alongside a picture of the Malletts stag. I wonder how many tens of thousands read the story.

Everyone at the works of course had their copy. I kept several for the records. There I am pensive at my desk, *'designing'*, Havana in hand and Frank the carver, referred to as the *'maker of the stag'*, with his carving chisels chipping at a coat-of-arms – and Madame Lecerf, looking furtive in her château – no more than a passing mention that the stag had been acquired from 'James Croft Decorations Ltd' in 1973 and after which it had disappeared into the antique trade. No mention of what the company did, which was what I wanted, and it was not long before the event faded into the past.

Just one more article did appear. In one of the broadsheets, the middle of the following week, it was said that a carved wooden stag, owned by Malletts of Bond Street, which had been on sale at Harrods, had been sent to Cambridge for carbon-dating. Subsequently when it was found to be modern, on the instructions of the owners, it was broken up.

It's a story I have told many times. It says a lot about the world of fine art – nothing changes. Featuring in the headlines of a national newspaper was certainly some kind of accolade, even if dubious and I have always been proud of that distinction, it must be said!

Finally, perhaps sadly, I had cast off the mantle of the scavenging little boy and had become a businessman, almost grown up and half respectable. Even so for years I suffered from recurring nightmares of still being in the Navy, struggling for my resignation to be accepted. In the dream it was never accepted and sometimes I woke, sweating, as the wind moved in the high beeches outside the bedroom window.

But by now, the disreputable midshipman, failed poet and scratcher of Benson and Hedges tins, was happy. He had, after all, *swallowed the anchor*. He went on dreaming up new ideas for his bizarre bunch of self-made artists to turn into reality. At home, on the valley's edge, there was still the small flint office building, in the field below the house, where so much nonsense had been conceived and more than a few Havanas smoked, and the smell of freshly-mown grass hanging over lawns which reached down to where once a row of tin hoppers' huts had stood.

One thing is certain: at any time, day or night, somewhere in the world, people are eating and drinking in surroundings which are decorated with signs and artefacts which I dreamt up and produced during the seventies and eighties, and became the benchmark for later copiers, who have made their imitations into the cheap currency they are now. In their time, mine were the best and today, I am told, are distinctly collectable. And somewhere, in all probability, a proud house-owner, recently moved in on some classy Neo-Georgian estate, and pleased to be thought of as a connoisseur of antiques, or equally, someone in some pleasant 18th century house in the country, discreetly furnished, might be showing his dinner guests over his new home before sitting down to dinner. Briefly inspecting the upstairs rooms, to impress his guests he might well pause a shade longer, looking into his son's newly-decorated room. Facing the door, the first thing his guest would see would be an old instrument dealer's sign with a nicely curved top; on it a small gilded sextant, star-globe and telescope all in relief. On either side of this, a half clipper ship whose name would have been somehow familiar to me, had I seen them. The name at the top of the sign reads *'Lars Thorensen'* and it looks as if it has come from an old dockside chandlers in the days when I knew it had not been unusual for Scandinavian seafarers to settle in northern ports. *'We decided on a nautical theme as the boy's thinking of going for the Navy,' says the host. 'My wife chose the colours. I think it comes off rather well, don't you?' 'Very nice,'* the guest replies, *'And weren't you lucky to find a 19th century painted sea chest like that. Pretty difficult to get hold of such things nowadays… those signs too. I bet the marvellous stuff could tell a tale or two! Look, it's even got the fellow's name on the side – Lieutenant Babb RN – wonder who he was and where he came from'* … *'Yes,'* comes the host's reply, *'I thought the same thing myself. The Christie's catalogue didn't say – just "origin unknown".'*